W9-BBD-174

MODERN ART DESSERTS

MODERN ART DESSERTS

Recipes for Cakes, Cookies, Confections, and Frozen Treats Based on Iconic Works of Art

CAITLIN FREEMAN

Photography by Clay McLachlan

Contributions from Tara Duggan | *Curator's notes by Janet Bishop*

Foreword by Rose Levy Beranbaum

TEN SPEED PRESS
Berkeley

Copyright © 2013 by Caitlin Freeman
Photographs copyright © 2013 by Clay McLachlan
Foreword © 2013 by Rose Levy Beranbaum

All rights reserved.
Published in the United States by Ten Speed Press, an imprint of the Crown Publishing Group, a division of Random House LLC, New York, a Penguin Random House Company.
www.crownpublishing.com
www.tenspeed.com

Ten Speed Press and the Ten Speed Press colophon are registered trademarks of Random House LLC.

Rose's Downy Yellow Butter Cake and Rose's White Velvet Cake reprinted with permission from *The Cake Bible* by Rose Levy Beranbaum.

Pages 7, 16, 18, 19, 35, 80, 82, 84, 186: Photos and illustrations by Caitlin Williams Freeman

Page 17: Photos by Charles Villyard

Page 33: Artwork © Wayne Thiebaud/Licensed by VAGA, New York, NY; photo by Don Myer/Lee Fatherree

Page 55: Artwork © Wayne Thiebaud/Licensed by VAGA, New York, NY; photo by Don Ross

Page 63: Artwork © Robert Ryman / Artists Rights Society (ARS), New York

Page 69: Artwork © Estate of Roy Lichtenstein; photo by Ben Blackwell

Page 79: Artwork © 2012 Mondrian/Holtzman Trust c/o HCR International USA; photo by Ben Blackwell

Page 93: Artwork © The Richard Diebenkorn Foundation; photo by Richard Grant

Page 99: Artwork © Rineke Dijkstra

Page 103: Artwork © 2013 Banco de Mexico Diego Rivera & Frida Kahlo Museums Trust, Mexico, D.F. / Artists Rights Society (ARS), New York; photo by Ben Blackwell

Page 107: Artwork © 2013 Barnett Newman Foundation / Artists Right Society (ARS), New York; photo by Ian Reeves

Page 111: Artwork © Andrew Kudless; photo by Don Ross

Page 117: Artwork © 2013 The Andy Warhol Foundation for the Visual Arts / Artists Rights Society (ARS), New York; photo by Ben Blackwell

Page 123: Artwork © Rosana Castrillo Diaz; photo by Ian Reeves

Page 127: Artwork © The Richard Avedon Foundation

Page 135: Artwork © Luc Tuymans; Courtesy David Zwirner, New York / London and Zeno X Gallery, Antwerp

Page 141: Artwork © 2013 Succession H. Matisse / Artists Rights Society (ARS), New York; photo © 2013 Archives H. Matisse

Page 147: Artwork © Ellsworth Kelly; photo by Ian Reeves

Page 151: Artwork © John Zurier; photo by Ben Blackwell

Page 155: Artwork © 2013 Tony Cragg / Artists Rights Society (ARS), New York; photo by Don Ross

Page 159: Artwork © Alejandro Cartagena; photo by Don Ross

Page 163: Artwork © Artists Rights Society (ARS), New York / VG Bild-Kunst Bonn, Germany; photo by Ben Blackwell

Page 171: Artwork © Estate of Tobias Wong; photo by Don Ross

Page 177: Artwork © 2013 Cindy Sherman

Page 181: Artwork © Ruth Laskey, courtesy Ratio 3, San Francisco

Page 185: Artwork © Jeff Koons; photo by Ben Blackwell

Page 191: Artwork © The Estate of R. Buckminster Fuller, All Rights Reserved

Page 195: Photo by Captain Charlie Jennings

Page 197: Artwork Courtesy George and Betty Woodman

Page 201: Artwork © Mark Bradford; photo by Bruce M. White, 2010

Library of Congress Cataloging-in-Publication Data

Freeman, Caitlin.
  Modern art desserts: recipes for cakes, cookies, confections, and frozen treats based on iconic works of art / Caitlin Freeman with Tara Duggan; foreword by Rose Levy Beranbaum; photography by Clay McLachlan; curator's notes by Janet Bishop. -- First Edition.
        pages cm
  Includes index.

  Summary: "Taking its cues from works by Andy Warhol, Frida Kahlo, and Matisse, this collection of uniquely delicious dessert recipes (and step-by-step assembly guides) gives readers all they need to make their own edible masterpieces"-- Provided by publisher.

  1. Sugar art. 2. Desserts. 3. Art, Modern. I. Title.

TX799.F73 2013

641.86--dc23

                                        2012047905

ISBN 978-1-60774-390-3
eISBN 978-1-60774-391-0

Printed in China

Design by Betsy Stromberg

Food and prop styling by Caitlin Freeman, Clay McLachlan, Leah Rosenberg, and Tess Wilson

10 9 8 7 6 5 4 3

First Edition

CONTENTS

FOREWORD BY ROSE LEVY BERANBAUM . . . 1 | INTRODUCTION . . . 5

EQUIPMENT . . . 21 | INGREDIENTS . . . 27

A TRIO OF THIEBAUD CAKES
33

THIEBAUD CHOCOLATE CAKE
55

RYMAN CAKE
63

LICHTENSTEIN CAKE
69

MONDRIAN CAKE
79

DIEBENKORN TRIFLE
93

DIJKSTRA ICEBOX CAKE
99

KAHLO WEDDING COOKIES
103

**BUILD YOUR
OWN NEWMAN**
107

**KUDLESS
S'MORES**
111

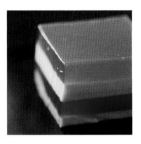

WARHOL GELÉE
117

**CASTRILLO DÍAZ
PANNA COTTA**
123

AVEDON PARFAIT
127

**TUYMANS
PARFAIT**
135

MATISSE PARFAIT
141

**KELLY
FUDGE POP**
147

ZURIER ICE POP
151

**CRAGG ICE
CREAM CONE**
155

**CARTAGENA ICE
CREAM AND
SORBET TRIO**
159

**FRITSCH ICE
CREAM
SANDWICH**
163

**WONG
ICE CREAM
SANDWICH**
171

**SHERMAN ICE
CREAM FLOAT**
177

**LASKEY
LEMON SODA**
WITH BAY ICE CUBES
181

**KOONS WHITE
HOT CHOCOLATE**
WITH LILLET
MARSHMALLOWS
185

**FULLER
HOT CHOCOLATE**
WITH
MARSHMALLOW
AND SEA SALT
191

**WOODMAN
CHEESE AND
CRACKERS**
197

**BRADFORD
CHEESE PLATE**
201

RESOURCES . . . 205 | ACKNOWLEDGMENTS . . . 209 | INDEX . . . 212

EAT YOUR ART OUT!

FOREWORD BY ROSE LEVY BERANBAUM

I first met Caitlin in 2004 when I visited her Miette Bakery production in Oakland. The purpose of the trip was to interview top bakeries for an article for *Food Arts Magazine* called "High Tide in the Bay Area Bakeries." The concept was that, although San Francisco had led the way in artisanal bread baking, it had lagged behind in the area of pastry. Michael Batterberry, visionary publisher of *Food Arts*, perceived this as changing and assigned the article.

Meeting Caitlin turned out to be the highlight of the interviews. I had been given a set of questions to ask each baker. When I asked Caitlin where she and her partner, Meg, had gotten their training, to my astonishment Caitlin's answer was that she had started with *The Cake Bible* (my book). Was it any wonder that she captured my attention? But beyond the compliment, and in addition to her solid organizational and technical skills, I was struck at once by Caitlin's extraordinary creativity. The signature Miette cake, which she named the Tomboy, consists simply of three unadorned dark chocolate layers, filled and topped with a contrasting white buttercream, and decorated with just one small pink sugar rose in the center. Caitlin most generously gave me permission to include the recipe in my book *Rose's Heavenly Cakes* and even sent me some of the pink sugar roses for photography. The art director loved the cake so much that she used the photo to span the end pages, and by enlarging it created an impressionistic dreamy appearance, contrasting spectacularly with the all-dark chocolate cake I had designed for the cover.

Over the years, as I watched Caitlin's work evolve, I saw that generosity, creative genius, and integrity were the hallmarks of her personality and character, permeating everything she touched. With every project or visit, Caitlin continued to gain my respect, and ultimately a deep friendship evolved. It may sound like a small thing, but any baker will realize how much it meant to me that when I traveled to San Francisco to make my friend chef Daniel Patterson's wedding cake, Caitlin loaned me a turntable from her bakery, and not just any turntable but the one that turned the most smoothly. She also drove all over the Bay Area amassing the equipment and special ingredients I deemed essential for my production.

The launch of my most recent book, *Rose's Heavenly Cakes*, coincided with the opening of James Freeman's (Caitlin's husband) Blue Bottle roastery in Oakland. Caitlin came up with the inspiration to have a book party at the new roastery and invite bakers from the Bay Area to make their versions of recipes from the book. Caitlin and her baking partner, Leah, made artistic renderings of the Diebenkorn using my génoise, mini Mondrians using my white velvet cake, and a Josef Albers cake using layers of my carrot cake, quail egg cake, and red velvet cake, each covered with rolled fondant from *The Cake Bible*. People came from all over the Bay Area to taste the cakes, enjoy a special coffee drink created for the occasion, meet the bakers, and the author who never stopped meeting, greeting, signing books, and talking for a solid three hours.

I first met James Freeman at the Old Oakland Farmers' Market when Caitlin and he had just started dating. I remember thinking that he had the same reverence for the quality of his coffee as Caitlin and I had for our baking. Given the grace, harmony, and focus of her life choices, is it any wonder that Blue Bottle coffee happens to be the best coffee I have ever tasted? Happily, Blue Bottle coffee and Caitlin's wonderful pastries are now available in New York City as well as the Bay Area.

When Caitlin started to create recipes for SFMOMA inspired by designs from paintings she loved, I knew this would be the perfect expression of her talents as artist and baker. Three of Caitlin's edible art desserts, featured in this book, that I find the most enchanting are the white velvet cake and chocolate ganache, consisting of cake squares and rectangles of different sizes and colors held together by thin lines of ganache—a perfect replica of Piet Mondrian's *Composition (No. III) Blanc-Jaune / Composition with Red, Yellow, and Blue*; the pistachio and honey parfait with cardamom/white chocolate—a stunningly simple cube constructed from thin white chocolate squares, charmingly decorated with line drawings of bees, and containing a deliciously ethereal filling, inspired by Richard Avedon's *Ronald Fisher, beekeeper, Davis, California, May 9, 1981*; and the adorable salted chocolate and vanilla bean ice cream sandwich—shaped to emulate the poodles in Katharina Fritsch's *Kind mit Pudeln* (Child with Poodles).

I'm so proud and honored that Caitlin chose to use two of my cakes as the base for some of her creations. She asked permission, saying: "They are perfect as they are— I'd rather credit you than adapt and change them." How like Caitlin not to change things just for the sake of "owning" them. To me that is the ultimate sign of creative integrity and shows such a strong sense of certainty and security in her vision. Beyond the visual beauty, and engagingly accurate renditions of the paintings that inspired them, Caitlin's desserts are also uncompromisingly delicious. This book is unlike any other and a perfect reflection of the soul of Caitlin Williams Freeman. It is with great pleasure that I welcome this dear friend and fellow baker to the world of cookbook writing.

INTRODUCTION

To find the Blue Bottle Café at the San Francisco Museum of Modern Art, you must first pay admission to the museum and then make your way up to the fifth floor. From the fifth floor galleries, a footbridge flanked by a shimmery and subtle *Untitled* mural by Rosana Castrillo Díaz on the right and a perfect view of the San Francisco city skyline on the left leads across to the Rooftop Garden. Ahead is a glass wall, beyond which you may see Louise Bourgeois's *The Nest*, five huge entwined spiders that often dominate the indoor pavilion, or a large Alexander Calder sculpture hanging from the ceiling. As you approach the glass wall, automatic doors open and the smell of baking cake and coffee greets you as you enter. Lovely baristas are making drinks on a custom hand-built espresso machine and two talented bakers are making cookies, cakes, ice cream, and other treats inspired by the art that surrounds you.

Early in the morning, before the museum starts filling with activity, the Blue Bottle bakers weave past the sculptures and into our tiny little kitchen. We put on chef coats and head to our workstation, which is filled with as many artist monographs as recipe books. We take sketch breaks on the benches of the Rooftop Garden and we troop through the museum, notebooks in hand, wearing our flour-dusted work uniforms and looking for inspiration.

Blue Bottle Coffee is the company that my husband, James Freeman, started in 2002. A former professional clarinet player, he started roasting coffee at home and then founded a small company to roast beans and sell coffee drinks at Bay Area farmers' markets. A few years and two cafés later, he was approached by the San Francisco Museum of Modern Art to operate a café inside their soon-to-open Rooftop Garden.

I had just sold my businesses, Miette Pâtisserie and Miette Confiserie, and had started a small pastry department within Blue Bottle, making cookies and cakes for the cafés. I was enjoying a semiretired work schedule, baking unfussy desserts, and letting someone else worry about accounting, human resources, and other messy parts of owning your own business. As a cog in the wheel, baking and delivering all of the pastries myself, I was looking forward to a few relaxing months while I sorted out my professional career—a professional career which, at that point, was totally up in the air.

FOLLOWING MY SWEET TOOTH: HOW I BECAME AN ANTI-DENTIST

As a latchkey kid growing up in the 1980s in Ojai, a tiny Southern California town, I didn't have any dreams of being a baker. There were no fancy cakes on display in bakery windows, no trips to France to set my young mind ablaze, no Food Network chefs to emulate. But I did have a sweet tooth. With a penchant for maple bar doughnuts, Duncan Hines frosting in a can, and Skittles, I saved my lunch money for after-school candy, begging the Twinkie from my best friend's lunch to tide me over until school was out. My plan to follow in my grandfather's footsteps and become a dentist may have been undone by my own sweet tooth. That, and I had an incredibly inspiring high school art teacher, Linda Taylor, in whose class I found a subject in which I excelled. When I unearthed my father's 1970s-era Pentax Spotmatic camera with an embroidered leather strap, I had found my medium. Taking black-and-white photos of my Doc Marten–encased feet and chronicling the lives of my classmates for the yearbook, I started to see the world through the viewfinder on a camera.

After high school, I found the perfect home in the art department at University of California, Santa Cruz, the college I chose with some lingering idea of becoming a dentist when I grew up. Santa Cruz felt positively urban compared to Ojai, and there were so many cool and inspiring people that I wanted to be like. They were artists and punk rockers, and they were organizing their own art shows in coffeehouses and rock shows in stinky basements. Anything seemed possible, and finding the expression of my true being felt incredibly important. I took self-portraits and gauzy photos of the quiet neighborhoods around me. I majored in photography, even though I had no intention of being a professional photographer, and I spent a lot of time in self-reflection to learn what truly made me the happiest. (Bless my father for funding this time of my life!) It was during a school trip to SFMOMA, standing in front of the painting *Display Cakes* by Wayne Thiebaud, that I first felt the warm happiness I was searching for. We were at the museum to look at photography, but I strayed into the painting galleries and stumbled upon *Display Cakes*. Once I discovered it, I found myself sneaking off for illicit visits while my classmates ogled the old Walker Evans photos. Wanting more of that feeling, I applied for a job at Santa Cruz's fanciest bakery, Kelly's French Pastry, requesting the 5:30 a.m. counter shift to accommodate my school schedule. Nothing was available at their Santa Cruz shop, but I was offered a spot at their café twenty

minutes south in a small town called Aptos. My pastry desperation was intense and I had a car, so I took it. I would wake at 4:30 a.m., work until noon, take classes until 5 p.m., and then spend the evening in the photo lab or at a concert in San Francisco. It turns out that this kind of hectic schedule was good training for starting a bakery. More on that later.

After graduation, I made the natural migration north to San Francisco. It was 1997 and the dot-com boom was ramping up, so I bounced my way between various Internet jobs (anyone could get a job paying way more than we ever thought we'd make), trying once again to find something that would make me happy. Instead, I found carpal tunnel syndrome, obnoxious boy-men playing shootout games at work all day, and the procrastination technique called Napster. Three years passed, and I hadn't taken a photograph since college when my boyfriend's mother asked us to take her to the Wayne Thiebaud retrospective at the Legion of Honor. Not having thought about his paintings in years, I was excited to see the artwork that had so inspired me in college. I vividly remember turning the corner into the exhibition, Thiebaud's painting of gumballs in a machine to the left and his most famous confectionary painting *Cakes* to the right, and being overcome with the same warm happiness as when I first happened upon *Display Cakes* at SFMOMA. I walked through the galleries, taking it all in and, as I stood in front of *Cakes*, I declared that *that* was what I would do with my life.

I wasn't exactly sure what that meant, but I had the idea to make beautiful cakes and then photograph them, channeling my love for sweets into art. The problem was that I didn't have any experience baking, and I certainly didn't know how to frost a cake. I started researching cooking schools in San Francisco, thinking that would be a good first step, but I quickly learned that even part-time programs were expensive! After an interview at San Francisco's most illustrious cooking school, I was sure of a few things: a) the administrators thought that my plan to learn how to make cakes for a photography project was crazy, b) there was no way I would ever be able to pay off those loans, especially if I did what was logical and used the degree to become an underpaid pastry chef (there is no other type), and c) it was ridiculous to spend money on a trade school when I already had an expensive college degree that I wasn't using. I decided to forgo cooking school and find somewhere that would take me on as an intern. I was willing to wake at 2 a.m. and work for free before heading out to an office job, and I couldn't imagine why anyone wouldn't jump at the chance to have an eager, smart girl in their kitchens. Every letter I sent went ignored, and when the hippie co-op bakery in my neighborhood blew off my request for an informational interview, I knew I was sunk.

Frustrated and unsure of what to do next, I headed off to San Diego for a Thanksgiving holiday (my last, as it would turn out; winter holidays just don't exist to retail bakers) to assess my career path, where I decided that a better plan for my life would be to become a high school art teacher. I already had a head start with my art degree, and I would have summers off. I also really wanted to inspire others the way Ms. Taylor had inspired me. Coincidentally, I watched the movie *The City of Lost Children* that weekend and, captivated by the main character, I jotted down her name, Miette, in my notebook.

The following week at my dreary desk job, I made my usual trek down to the Tuesday farmers' market, which, at that time, was set up in Justin Hermann Plaza, just across from the Ferry Building in San Francisco. While pecking around, I stumbled upon a woman whom I had never seen before. She had a card table covered with a green plaid tablecloth and tiny cakes perched on vintage cake stands. Those were the cakes I wanted to photograph. Those were the cakes I needed to learn how to make. I picked up her pink and white card with a sketch of a cake and looked at the business name: Miette. Stunned, all I could do was stammer the words "You have my dream job." Mind you, I was wearing a vintage dress, cat-themed mary jane shoes, and a ridiculous black winter hat topped with cat ears. I was glassy eyed and awestruck. It was 2001, and fancy little cake shops just didn't exist—we were still a few years from the pink, brown, and polka-dotted cupcake shop explosion.

I had made a pretty terrible first impression, and the woman behind the card table, the person who would eventually become my business partner, later confirmed that, along with the starry-eyed expression on my face, I was also wearing the clothing of a maniac. I'm glad I didn't give her my name at that moment—because it would pop up in her email inbox later that day with an offer of free help. And, with that, my future career in education tumbled away.

LEARNING AS I GO:
MY EDUCATION IN BUSINESS, CONSTRUCTION, AND PASTRY

With severance pay, no kitchen experience, and more gumption than I would ever have, Meg Ray started Miette in 2001 after being laid off from her Silicon Valley job. With only two part-time helpers and two weekly farmers' markets to bake for, she wasn't experienced enough to know to blow me off like the rest of the bakeries I had hounded. I arrived at the Miette kitchen a few Fridays later, wearing jeans and Converse sneakers, and helped out however I could. With my feet still aching, I returned the next week. And the week after. Persistence paid off, and eventually I bought a decent pair of kitchen clogs and graduated from dishwasher and floor sweeper to gumpaste flower production and light cake decorating. I also started working the Miette booth at the Saturday farmers' market in Berkeley, where I would don lovely vintage dresses and feel the glamorous (albeit sleep-deprived) side of the baking business. That farmers' market is where I met the man who would become my husband, and where I realized that baking was what really I loved, not just what I wanted to photograph. A few half-hearted photographs taken with my grandfather's WW2-era, mildew-encrusted Voigtländer camera were the only evidence that remained of my original plan.

Miette flourished, and in 2003 we were asked to open a shop in the recently renovated Ferry Building. Meg asked Liz Dunn and me, her two faithful helpers, to become partners in the business, and we officially jumped on board. I was finally able to quit my day job and devote myself entirely to baking. Opening the shop required an incredible amount of work. Fueled by a $10,000 loan from my father, a good helping of sleep deprivation, and a whole lot of cake, we sanded, painted, tiled, and baked like crazy. On October 9, 2003, we opened the doors of our tiny slip of a shop in the Ferry Building. Liz left shortly after the shop opened; Meg and I continued on for four more years, eventually building a gorgeous candy shop, Miette Confiserie, that became my whole world. On October 29, 2008, almost seven years after first laying eyes on those little cakes and, coincidentally, on the day James and I were married, I sold my shares of the business with both a heavy heart and plenty of heartburn. I was officially married and unemployed.

Exhausted and unsure of what I would do next, I took a few months off to settle into our new house and my life as a married woman. A little depressed that I had chosen such a low-paying and physically demanding profession, I started to wonder why I hadn't applied my manic determination to becoming a doctor or a lawyer. Becoming a baker was all I hoped for in my midtwenties, but it now seemed like the most ridiculous aspiration. As hard as it was, Miette had been my everything—it changed my life, introduced me to James, and felt like the very expression of my being. Every cake that I designed, recipe that I developed, and piece of candy that I sold embodied all that was important to me. Having given everything to a business that was no longer mine, I felt depleted and unsure that I had anything left for this profession.

But, after a few lovely months of reflecting, I had to get back to work. With the sale of my Miette shares also went the wholesale pastries Blue Bottle had been buying for its cafés, so James asked me to start a little baking program within the company. Rustic, simple bites that paired well with coffee felt like an easy next project. The pastries I baked weren't fancy or particularly beautiful, but they were just perfect for Blue Bottle. It was comforting to have a goal (tastes good with coffee) to work toward, and it was exciting to know that I could find creativity in an interesting and external way, that baking didn't have to be so personal. I was happy working a few days a week, puttering around our little rental kitchen, baking cookies and cakes and delivering them to our two retail locations.

And then SFMOMA called.

The San Francisco Museum of Modern Art is a big deal in our city. It's a huge honor that the museum wanted to include a Blue Bottle Café as part of their new expansion, and although it was going to be a pretty difficult café to access, James didn't hesitate to sign on to the project. I was thrilled to be invited to put on a hardhat and tour the under-construction Rooftop Garden just three short weeks before it was scheduled to open. I hadn't been thinking about my role in the café, but once I was standing in the space, I had a flash of inspiration—I was standing inside the building that had inspired me to be a baker! I could make Thiebaud cakes right inside the museum! Nearly exploding with excitement, but trying to appear focused and interested in the foreman's tour of the space, I tugged on James's sleeve, whispered my idea into his ear, and got a somewhat distracted nod of approval. That was all I needed. I had three weeks to plan a menu and have Thiebaud cakes ready for opening day.

Leaving the museum that day, I headed straight to the Ferry Building to see the one person in this world that I wanted to work with on this project with me: Leah Rosenberg. I had hired Leah to work at Miette—adorable, hard working, and sweet, she was a great presence behind the counter. But what really made her the perfect girl for the job was her obsession with cakes. As a graduate student working on her thesis project at the California College of the Arts, she was becoming known for her striped paintings and the identically striped cakes that she baked and served at her art openings. Simultaneously obsessed with art and cake, I knew she would be thrilled to hear about my plan. I explained as much as could be breathlessly babbled across the Miette pastry counter, and though I couldn't hire her right away, I persuaded her to spend some time with me working on the first round of concepts before the café opened.

During those next few weeks I spent countless hours at SFMOMA planning other art-inspired desserts to make in addition to the Thiebaud cakes, often hauling friends with me to help brainstorm. On my first sketching trip, I brought along my best friend, Vanessa Gates Mowell. She was the one who encouraged me to take that first art class in high school and she was my classmate in the art department at UC Santa Cruz. Later, she managed the Miette shop, and then became the retail manager for all of Blue Bottle's West Coast shops. She knows me, she knows what I like, and she's helped me execute plenty of my hair-brained schemes.

I came up with a lot of great ideas in those few weeks before we opened, but the most important cake to take shape was the Mondrian Cake (page 79) that Leah and I created a few days before the café opened. The Mondrian Cake is the perfect example of how Leah and I collaborate: she brings her art knowledge and a brain unencumbered by all of the roadblocks that would limit our creativity, and I bring practical and technical knowledge, and the ability to visualize how we can bring the sketches to life in the kitchen. This is still, more or less, how Leah and I work on all new desserts.

I limped through the first four months after the opening, making as many Mondrian Cakes, Thiebaud Cakes, and Fritsch Ice Cream Sandwiches as I could manage. Once we were pretty certain that customers would actually come find us, and that they would, in fact, buy desserts based on the artwork at the museum, I offered Leah the position of assistant pastry chef at our café. She arrived to work much in the

same fashion that I arrived to work at Miette—never having worked in a kitchen before, unsure of what to wear, and without the basic commercial baking skills that one would expect of a professional. I could show her how to crack an egg, advise her on the best kitchen clogs, and teach her how to bake, but what Leah brings with her is a deep understanding of modern art, her curiosity about new art and pastry techniques, and her indelible organizational skills—all of which have kept our little pastry department current, growing, and changing since she came on board.

With the exception of the Trio of Thiebaud Cakes and the Mondrian Cake, which are, more or less, faithful representations of the originals, the desserts we make at SFMOMA are only conceptually *inspired* by the art. The artwork serves as a jumping point from which I chart my own path, combining my interpretation of the piece and my point of view as a pastry chef. Leah brings a conceptual mind, as someone who knows art and has a distinct point of view in her interpretation of it. While I am in awe of the technical prowess of some of my pastry heroes, Leah's skills are so much more valuable in our SFMOMA kitchen than being able to execute an eighteen-tiered confectionary masterpiece. In looking for collaborators, I seek people whose taste I find immaculate, who understand beauty and know how to capture inspiration—people whose creativity and artistry extends beyond the edible.

Tess Wilson is a willowy stunner who understands beauty down to her bones. She was a regular customer at the Miette Confiserie while I was in charge, and I had a vision one evening (while in the bathtub, of all places) that Tess *had* to work for me at the candy shop. I didn't have her contact information, so I had to wait until the next time she stopped by. When she finally came in for her salted black licorice fix, I bounded up to her and blurted out, "Oh my gosh, I've been thinking about you, but I didn't know how to get in touch with you. You see, we need someone to work here, and I was in the bathtub the other night and all of a sudden it popped into my head that you're the perfect person. Do you want a job?" Much to my surprise, she didn't slap me in the face for sounding like such a creep—and even more surprisingly, she said yes! She became the personification of a Miette candy girl and brought an incredible level of beauty and sophistication to that shop. She carried on as the manager of the shop after I left, but it wasn't long before I was nudging her to come join Leah and me at the museum. Another untrained baker, and a vegan at that, I knew Tess's precision and keen sense of beauty was exactly what we needed. The other details could be worked out.

FINDING INSPIRATION: HOW WE TURN ART INTO DESSERT

On Thursday mornings, Leah, Tess, and I sit at one of the tables in the Rooftop Garden, a crock of hand salve between us (baking is murder on the hands), and we talk about art and pastry. Leah comes equipped with museum checklists, spreadsheets full of descriptions and thumbnail images of each of the artworks in the upcoming shows. Leah is the self-appointed note taker and day-to-day liaison with the museum, so she knows when shows are opening and what previews are happening when, and she keeps all of us on track. Tess and I flip through the checklists, trying to make out any details from the tiny images, and talk about pieces that we connect with. Leah has usually already found any reference to food in the artwork, and we start to talk about how we might incorporate them into desserts. We go on tangents, we come up with ridiculous ideas, we get stumped, and then I'm usually the one to suggest that we step back from the details and focus on the images that resonate with us as a group.

The process of coming up with a new dessert involves a number of factors, but, first and foremost, we're looking for inspiration to come from the artwork itself or for artwork that elicits a strong response, good or bad. In the fall of 2010, SFMOMA presented a photo exhibition entitled *Exposed: Voyeurism, Surveillance, and the Camera Since 1870*. It was a provocative exhibition that explored photography's role in invasive looking, from paparazzi and surveillance photographs to sexually explicit imagery. Photographs are generally the hardest medium to work with, but we were really stumped by how to interpret the act of watching, of being watched, and masking one's identity. We had the kitschy idea of putting together a chocolate spy kit including a chocolate camera, a chocolate moustache, and a prop mirror. But a joke bag seemed too corny for an exhibition with such a dark and challenging theme, so we scrapped it. With no inspiration coming from the checklists, we waited until the show opened to see the actual images and how they were presented in the galleries. My first pass was a skim through the entire exhibition: I glanced at the collection to see, from an overview level, if there were any images that stuck with me. It was a challenging group of photographs, and the one that stayed with me for the next few days was of a man in a three-piece suit, cropped at the chest and thighs, with his genitals exposed through the unzipped pants. One of Robert Mapplethorpe's most well-known photos, *Man in Polyester Suit,* is certainly not an image most people would associate with dessert, but each time I went back through the galleries, this shocking photo (to my dainty constitution, at least) was the one that I couldn't forget.

Remembering some failed experiments with a white chocolate–covered banana (see Koons White Hot Chocolate, page 185), I thought that a dark chocolate–covered frozen banana would be a subversive and appropriate homage to *Man in Polyester Suit.* But I knew that it might cause some ripples, so I checked with folks at the museum to (hopefully) get their blessing on my new dessert. Of course, the reactions were mixed depending who I spoke with; the tug of tit-tering publicity was exciting to some, but the onslaught of potential complaints about little kids interacting with an edible phallus was a deal breaker to others. I should have probably scrapped the idea after hearing a single no, but I couldn't shake the fact that a penis was on the wall of the museum and I wasn't allowed to make a silly chocolate covered banana. The injustice! I revisited the exhibition to get an idea of how the museum approached the sensitive material, and found a warning sign posted outside the gallery alerting visitors to the explicit content beyond. Perfect—I just needed a warning sign for my banana! I designed a white acrylic display box with a peep hole (at adult height), through which you could see the chocolate covered banana. Emblazoned with the admonition, "Warning: This dessert may not be appropriate for all viewers," the privacy box encouraged curiosity and brought attention to the fact that the dessert was not for all audiences. But because we had made such a big deal about it, the reaction was almost always, "But, it's just a banana." Not a single complaint was registered.

In some cases, we have what we think is a great idea, only to be thwarted by the dessert not living up to our expectations. In the spring 2012 exhibition *Photography*

in Mexico, I fell in love with a small black-and-white photo called *Convento* by Pedro Meyer. Taken in 1969, the photo shows a young girl, about 9 years old, sitting in a wooden chair with her hands clasped together. I assumed from the title that the girl was in a convent, so I researched "convent desserts" online, thinking I might be able to unearth a delicious treat made by Mexican nuns. I was thrilled to find a blog post describing the *bienmesabe,* a rice, coconut, and almond pudding onto which the shape of the Virgin Mary is stenciled in cinnamon. Bingo! I raced home to make my own Virgin Mary stencil and whip up a batch of rice pudding with coconut. Not to pat myself on the back, but the cinnamon stencil was incredible. Unfortunately, the rice pudding was not. We tested batch after batch of it, but nothing turned out refined or delicious enough to hold up to the other desserts we serve at the café. There was also the fear that, as with the *Exposed* exhibition, we might get caught up in controversy, this time over religious iconography. Defeated and tired of eating rice pudding, we decided to look for another piece to use as inspiration. As it so often happens, we had devoted weeks to wrestling with a failed idea and, once we stepped back to take a look at the exhibition with fresh eyes and find a new focus, an exciting and delicious dessert came about within days (in this case, the Cartagena Ice Cream and Sorbet Trio, page 159).

Occasionally, we execute a dessert that perfectly captures an artwork, only to have the rug pulled out from under us by none other than the artist himself. For SFMOMA's seventy-fifth anniversary, a series of shows were planned to exhibit some of the most prized pieces in the museum's collection. One of the most terrific rooms assembled for the *Focus on Artists* show was the gallery of Richard Serra sculptures. My favorite of them all was gravity-defying piece called *Right Angle Plus One,* which consisted of three enormous square steel pieces held upright by a steel beam that spanned the top edges. It seemed like the perfect format for a cookie plate, so we made a graham cracker, a ginger snap, and a chocolate sablé (a French butter cookie) in identical square shapes, and then rolled a citrus tuile into the shape of a beam. The cookies were presented flat atop a cocktail napkin with an illustrated guide showing how to assemble them to re-create the Serra sculpture. The cookie plate was a phenomenal success and many Serra-like cookie sculptures

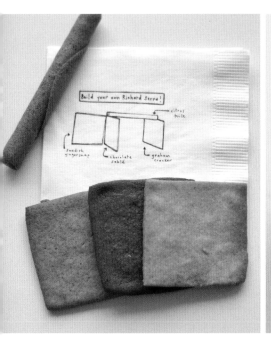
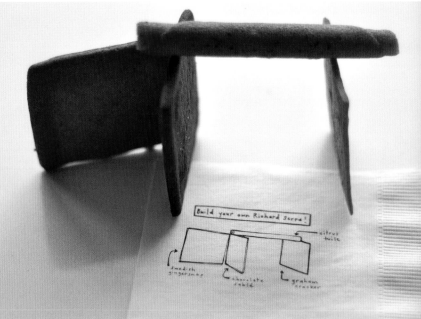

were built then nibbled away. But, ten months after we began making the cookie plate, we received an email from the painting and sculpture department saying that Serra had caught wind of our dessert and insisted that we immediately stop production. We respectfully stopped making the cookies, understanding that it was important for SFMOMA to maintain good artist relations—especially with Serra since a retrospective of his drawings was planned for the following year. We had a secret hope that once the artist himself was at the museum for the big opening we would be able to charm him into being excited about having his work as the inspiration for a dessert. When his retrospective finally opened, curator Gary Garrels brought Serra up to the coffee bar for a meeting. Jumping at the opportunity to sweep him off his feet, Leah (who is, let me remind you, the sweetest person on earth) started chatting with him about our desserts as he waited for his coffee. She didn't exactly get the no she was fearing, but when he walked away from her, mid-sentence, it was pretty clear that we would not be resurrecting the cookie plate for his show.

One of the positive lessons we learned from the Serra episode was that a cookie plate is a really great addition to our lineup of desserts. As much as we want to let

the art dictate the desserts, we do need to curate a well-rounded menu. Our location on the top floor of the museum means that guests sometimes arrive tired, a little cranky, overstimulated, and undercaffeinated. A collection of quirky desserts inspired by art is sometimes the highlight of a guest's day, but it can also be alienating and frustrating for someone who is already alienated and frustrated by modern art. For those cases, a cookie plate is great: a few bites of delicious cookies will satisfy anyone, regardless of whether they are willing to turn them into an edible sculpture or run around the Rooftop Garden in a game of art scavenger hunt, as we propose with our most recent cookie plate. At the café, we only make desserts based on art that can be seen within the walls of the museum, and it is our greatest hope that guests will connect with one of our pastries, prompting a trip back through the galleries. Or, better yet, that our pastry will be so clever and clear that it would be impossible not to know what it's based on.

In the pages of this book, I'm thrilled to be able to present the desserts side by side with the art that has inspired each. It's a luxury that we've only ever been able

to experience in the few times when we have created a dessert based on a sculpture in the Rooftop Garden. When creating our desserts, Leah, Tess, and I rely on art books, our college educations, and the Internet to inform us about the artwork. For this book, Janet Bishop, curator of painting and sculpture at SFMOMA, has written illuminating descriptions of each artwork, providing insightful information and fun behind-the-curtains art world details that will help bridge the gap between the original pieces and the desserts that they've inspired.

In June 2013, SFMOMA will close for two and a half years, during which time a massive expansion project will more than double the size of the museum and provide San Francisco with a truly extraordinary venue for seeing modern art. And, with the temporary closure, our café in the Rooftop Garden will also be on hiatus. It will mark four years since my construction-site epiphany and the start of my grand adventure in art and cake that has been the most fun four years of my life.

EQUIPMENT

I hate clutter, and I'm especially annoyed by specialty equipment that hogs space and rarely gets used. But I am attached to some specialized pieces of equipment that elevate precision in baking, reduce failed attempts, and, gloriously, eliminate some unnecessary objects in the kitchen.

That said, all of the recipes in this book can be made with a pretty basic set of kitchen tools. I've simplified all of the recipes and artwork assemblies so that they only use equipment that a moderately well-stocked kitchen would have. If your intention is to go above and beyond and make the artwork-inspired desserts just as we do at SFMOMA, there will very likely be pieces of specialty equipment, tools, and display details that you will need to purchase (I've included information on specialty items in Resources, page 205). Keep in mind that those purchases may only ever be used to make that one specific dessert. But, oh, what a stupendous dessert it will be! The following list includes basic tools that will streamline your time in the kitchen and make baking more fun.

BAKING PANS AND BAKING SHEETS

With the exception of the Mondrian Cake, which uses a 16 by 4 by 4-inch loaf pan (also known a Pullman loaf pan), the recipes in this book that require baking pans call for standard sizes. Rimmed baking sheets should measure 13 by 18 inches. If a recipe offers the option of using a nonstandard pan, it will send you to Resources on page 205 for purchasing information.

CAKE TURNTABLE

I am devoted to my cake turntable, but I understand that this tool isn't in most home kitchens. (It should be, though, since there are inexpensive models out there!) If you're not yet ready to commit to a cake turntable, you can use a lazy Susan instead. Or, try your hand at the old-school French method: hold the cake in your nondominant hand and spread the frosting using the other.

DIGITAL KITCHEN SCALE

Although the rules of publishing dictate that the recipes in this book are written in volumetric measurements (cups, teaspoons, and tablespoons), I've also included weight measurements in ounces and grams. Small quantities can be measured accurately in teaspoons and tablespoons, but for any quantity greater than 3 tablespoons, measuring by weight is far more accurate than measuring by volume. Accuracy doesn't have to be expensive—a really nice digital gram scale can be purchased for about $20, less than half the price of an instant ice-pop maker. (An instant ice-pop maker? Really? I can guarantee that the time you save weighing ingredients will outweigh the time you save freezing ice-pops!) With a digital scale, all you need is a bowl or two to measure ingredients—you won't need to dirty multiple dry measuring cups plus your liquid measuring cup.

ANATOMY OF A RECIPE

In this book, every ingredient measurement larger than 3 tablespoons has three measurements: one by volume (cups) and two by weight (ounces and grams). Fluid ounce volumetric measurements are not included.

So, for an ingredient listing like this
    1 cup (8.6 oz / 240 g) water
the volume is measured in a liquid measuring cup, and the weight is measured as 8.6 ounces on a pound scale, or 240 grams on a gram scale.

In this example
    1 cup (4.9 oz / 140 g) all-purpose flour
the flour is measured in a dry measuring cup, and the weight is measured as 4.9 ounces on a pound scale, or 140 grams on a gram scale.

IMMERSION BLENDER

Originally marketed as a smoothie maker, an immersion blender is one of those tools I was skeptical about purchasing. I didn't buy one until I had jaw surgery and was forced to eat pureed soup for eight weeks. And while, yes, it's brilliant for making soups, sauces, and salsas, in the pastry kitchen we rely on the immersion blender for creating perfectly smooth fillings. Almost effortless, super-shiny ganache and smooth, silken lemon curd earns the immersion blender a top spot in my kitchen.

MICROPLANE

A Microplane grater is a woodworking tool that has been co-opted by the culinary industry and turned into an indispensable kitchen tool. Inexpensive and easy to find, a Microplane makes zesting citrus a snap by shaving off only the fragrant and oil-rich skin and leaving the bitter pith on the fruit. My home Microplane also moonlights as an excellent cheese grater, and as a tool for making chocolate confetti for ice cream sundaes.

MICROWAVE OVEN

The microwave oven is a handy little secret of pastry chefs. From quickly warming cream for making ganache to easily tempering chocolate, there are many places throughout this book where I suggest the use of a microwave. My home is one of the ten percent of American homes without a microwave oven, so when baking in my own kitchen, I have a few low-tech alternatives to the counter-hogging beast. For example, my gas oven has a pilot light that keeps the temperature around 100°F, which is great for bringing chilled buttercream to a usable temperature or for quickly getting cold butter to room temperature.

OFFSET SPATULA

An offset spatula is a stainless steel metal blade with an angled handle that is perfect for frosting cakes, smoothing cake batter and layers of cream or ice cream, removing cakes from their pans, and transferring cookies from the baking sheet to the cooling rack. I use a small $4^1/_4$-inch offset spatula for almost everything in my pastry kitchen, but a medium $7^5/_8$-inch offset spatula is handy for frosting the sides of taller cakes. An offset spatula is a relatively small investment that will make your life in the pastry kitchen much easier.

PIPING BAG, TIPS, AND COUPLER

A recipe calling for a piping bag may seem intimidating and, frankly, even I get a little stressed out looking at a wall of pastry tips. Decorating a cake with elaborate borders and making lifelike flowers with buttercream is a skill that I hope to someday master, but in this book, the most complicated piped decorations I will ask you to make are the little red dots on the Thiebaud Chocolate Cake (page 55). A piping bag is often used to create elaborate embellishments, but it can also be a handy tool for neatly filling small cups with lemon mousse for the Diebenkorn Trifle (page 93) and for making a simple circle of whipped cream for the Dijkstra Icebox Cake (page 99). A reusable 14-inch bag, a coupler, and small selection of piping tips requires only a small investment, and then you will be equipped to start practicing fancy borders for a grand wedding cake.

STAND MIXER

I received my pink KitchenAid stand mixer on my twenty-fourth birthday, a generous gift from my father when I first became obsessed with cakes. It's big and cumbersome, and the kind of object I would normally hate having in my kitchen. But, oh, the cakes and buttercreams that come out of that machine are lovely! I have written these recipes with the assumption that you will be using a stand mixer whenever a mixer is needed, but most have been tested with a hand mixer and, in some cases, with just a wooden spoon and a bowl. In all cases, the results were quite good. If you aren't using a stand mixer, let your intuition and experience with your own equipment guide you.

THERMOCOUPLE

A thermocouple is a temperature sensor that is typically used in the science industry and for testing the temperature of ovens and air conditioning. They're sold in hardware stores and are fairly inexpensive, absolutely accurate, and very easy to use and clean (see Resources, page 205). I use mine for verifying my oven temperature and for taking temperature readings on sugar syrups and other temperature-sensitive recipes.

BAKING TIMES

From brand to brand and model to model, ovens are so different that it would be impossible to give perfectly accurate baking times that would work in every home kitchen. Thanks to my group of recipe testers, the recipes in this book were made in a variety of ovens: my old Wedgewood oven at home, new ovens with spot-on calibration, and, of course, our commercial convection oven in the SFMOMA kitchen. As expected, the baking time varied a bit for each recipe, so using the visual (and sometimes auditory) cues to assess the doneness baked goods is the most fail-safe way to go.

INGREDIENTS

The temperature of ingredients is often an important factor to making a successful dessert. For any ingredients where temperature is a great consideration, I have specified so in the recipe. To help you shop and prep for recipes, here is some information about often-used and important ingredients.

BUTTER

All of the recipes in this book call for unsalted butter. Buying unsalted butter gives you the power to control the amount of salt in a pastry rather than relying on non-standardized amounts in various brands of salted butter. In any recipe where butter is creamed with sugar, it is of the utmost importance that the butter is at room temperature. To quickly get cold butter to room temperature, cut it into small pieces and let it stand in a warm spot in the kitchen for about ten minutes.

CHOCOLATE

When choosing chocolate to use in recipes in this book, opt for high-quality chocolate, one that you would love to eat on its own. For bittersweet chocolate, look for types with cacao solids of at least 60 percent. For milk chocolate, I choose a higher-end brand, such as Valrhona or TCHO, because I find they are slightly less cloyingly sweet and have a more rich chocolate flavor. Although boutique chocolatiers, who have focused primarily on dark chocolate, have begun to delve into the world of milk chocolate (much to my delight), white chocolate is still a bit of the black sheep in the chocolate factory. White chocolate is inherently sweet and can contain a ghastly amount of vanilla, but the El Rey and Valrhona brand white chocolates have a great texture and pair well with the citrus and cardamom I love to add to white chocolate.

COCOA

Cocoa powder can be found in many forms in grocery stores or specialty foods shops. For most of the recipes in this book, I call for natural (not Dutch processed) unsweetened cocoa powder; the most commonly available brands are Hershey's, Scharffen Berger, and Dagoba. To make the Chocolate Sablé Dough black in color for desserts such as the Dijkstra Icebox Cake (page 99) and Wong Ice Cream Sandwich (page 171), I replace half of the natural cocoa powder with black cocoa powder, a highly alkalized Dutch-processed cocoa powder with a deep black color (see Resources, page 205, for ordering information). Black cocoa powder will also give the cookies the distinct taste of Oreos.

EGGS

Not all eggs are created equal, which is why the United States Department of Agriculture (USDA) has set standards for the sizing and grading of chicken eggs. All of the recipes in this book were developed and tested using large, grade AA eggs. On average, a large egg has an out-of-shell weight of 50 grams (1.8 ounces), with the white weighing about 30 grams (1.1 ounces) and the yolk 19 grams (0.65 ounces). But if you're like me and you often buy eggs from a local farmer, there's no telling how far an egg might stray from the USDA standards, so for the most accurate measurements, especially when using the whites and yolks separately, a digital scale is a must. You'll be surprised to see how much variation exists from one egg to the next.

To get cold eggs to room temperature quickly, place the whole eggs in their shells in a small bowl, cover with lukewarm water (between 90°F and 100°F), and let stand for about 10 minutes.

INGREDIENTS

FLOUR

In most of my recipes, I use all-purpose flour, a wheat flour with medium-gluten content that is the most widely available. The two cake recipes developed by Rose Levy Beranbaum call for cake flour, which is a lower gluten flour that yields an exceedingly tender cake with a perfect downy texture. If you don't have cake flour on hand, you can substitute ³/4 cup (3.7 oz / 105 g) all-purpose flour plus 2 teaspoons of cornstarch for each 1 cup (4.6 oz / 130 g) of cake flour.

MEASURING FLOUR

Of all of the ingredients used routinely in baking, flour is the trickiest to measure accurately by volume, yet an accurate measurement is often critical for success. This is why I strongly recommend weighing ingredients. For all-purpose flour, for example, I use the equivalent of 5 ounces (140 grams) per cup. This weight is based on the dip-and-sweep method of measuring dry ingredients. To measure your flour, dip the dry measuring cup directly into the container, scoop up the flour, and then sweep off the excess with a knife or other straight edge. The dip-and-sweep method fills the cup with almost 0.7 ounces (20 grams) more flour than spooning the flour into the cup. Whole wheat flour and pastry flour behave similarly, though the weights of both are slightly different than all-purpose.

FOOD COLORING

I have a really uneasy relationship with food coloring, and with the exception of candy, I actively avoid eating artificially colored food (because candy just doesn't count). And yet, on the cover of this very book is a photo of a cake with three big, bright artificially colored swatches.

In my baking, I always to try to avoid using food coloring—sometimes going through elaborate measures (see Romancing the Red Velvet, page 75)—and usually find a way by using colorful fruits, nut pastes, or spices. So when developing the Mondrian Cake, I was certain that there had to be a way around artificial coloring. I tried every natural food coloring and plant-based alternative to standard food dyes that I could find, but it turned out that there is nothing in nature that replicates primary colors of Mondrian's paintings in the same way that artificial food coloring does. The Mondrian Cake just wouldn't be a Mondrian Cake without the vivid colors that science has provided us with, so eventually I gave in.

There are only a few recipes in this book that employ artificial coloring to enhance color, but using it is entirely optional. At the SFMOMA café, we use Ameri-Color brand food coloring (see Resources, page 205), a soft gel paste that adds concentrated color without much adding liquid.

Since there are many types of food coloring available, each with a concentration different from the next, I advise you to follow this guide for how much to use: add food coloring until you reach the hue you find most appealing, as the color will not change during baking.

GELATIN

Gelatin is used to turn a liquid into a gel, and it's an ingredient that I use quite often. From preserving the featherlight texture of a mousse to creating the most American of all desserts, Jell-O, gelatin is easy to use and has many applications. It is available in two forms: powder and sheets (or leaves). While powdered gelatin is more widely available, I much prefer to use sheets in our work kitchens and at home, as I find it simple to use, easier to measure, and it eliminates the headache of undissolved gelatin granules. See Resources (page 205) for more information.

SALT

I like my sweets on the salty side, often with large grains mixed in or sprinkled on top for an unexpected hit of salt. In these recipes, I usually call for one of two different types of salt: kosher salt, which has a medium-size grain and is good for seasoning foods without calling attention to itself, or large, flaky-grained Maldon sea salt for when I want to add a distinct saltiness. Because there are many varieties of salt to choose from and you may not always have the type a recipe calls for, here's a quick and easy conversion that will allow you to substitute one type for another: 1 teaspoon large-flake sea salt (such as Maldon sea salt) = $1/2$ teaspoon kosher salt or other medium-grain salt = $1/4$ teaspoon table salt.

Wayne Thiebaud
Display Cakes
1963
oil on canvas
28 in. x 38 in.
SFMOMA, Mrs. Manfred Bransten Special Fund purchase, 73.42

Art © Wayne Thiebaud/Licensed by VAGA, New York, NY

Long one of California's most highly regarded painters and beloved teachers, Wayne Thiebaud (born 1920) started his career in cartooning and commercial art. By the early 1960s, still lifes, especially of sweets, became a favorite subject of his art and have remained so ever since, taking a prominent place within an extraordinary body of realist pictures that also includes streetscapes, landscapes, and figures.

In *Display Cakes*, Thiebaud presents a trio of different cakes ready to be sliced into or purchased whole. Each drum-like form is echoed by its shadow, adding rhythm and complexity to the frontal composition. The cakes themselves were painted with a palette knife, rather than a brush, lending them a particularly edible quality. And in classic Thiebaud style, each form is articulated by glowing colorful edges.

A TRIO OF THIEBAUD CAKES

When I was a college student, *Display Cakes* hung on the second floor of SFMOMA, near Robert Bechtle's *Alameda Gran Torino*. But, ironically, when I arrived at SFMOMA as the in-house pastry chef, the painting had been rotated out of the galleries and sent to storage. Working from memory and programmed to frost for perfection, my early Thiebaud cakes had a sweet, albeit robotic, charm to them, not the swooping delectability that I remembered in Thiebaud's rendering. One morning, I was chatting with SFMOMA imaging coordinator Susan Backman about my struggles with the frosting, lamenting that I could no longer stand in front the painting and study it. "That's not a problem," she said. "I can have someone pull it from storage for you to see. Give me about an hour."

Butterflies in my stomach, I finally descended to the basement of the museum and was led to an area thrillingly called the Vault. *Display Cakes* had already been removed from its rack and placed on a table in the middle of the room. Walking toward the painting, I was struck by how odd it was to see it laying horizontally rather than hanging vertically on the wall. Standing above the painting, I tried to be clinical about my work—I needed to understand the paint application and internalize the forms and brushstrokes so that I could mimic the effect with frosting. But I totally lost my cool. Alone in a room with the painting that had directed the path of my life, I began to cry my eyes out. Afraid I would be caught sobbing like a baby, or worse, that tears would fall onto the painting, I wiped my cheeks with the sleeve of my chef's coat and scurried back to my kitchen to channel his brushstrokes into frosting. It took me a few months to loosen up, but eventually I re-trained myself to harness the power of my offset spatula and the speed of my cake turntable to create the depth and motion of the *Display Cakes*.

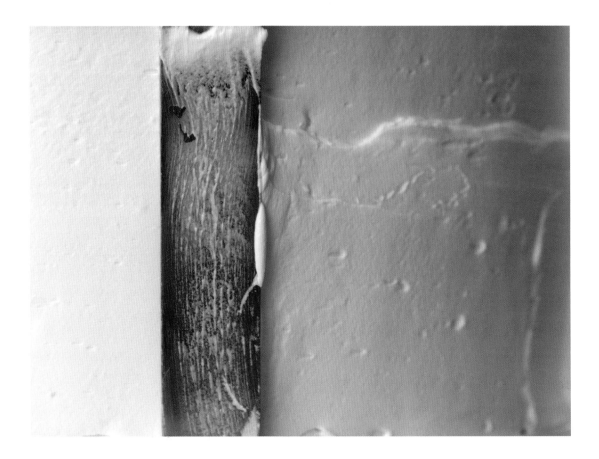

On May 6, 2009, SFMOMA hosted a press preview for the soon-to-open Rooftop Garden. It was the debut of the Blue Bottle Café, and the day that I unveiled my art-inspired desserts. The *New York Times* heard rumor of my plan and sent a photographer to capture my recreation of *Display Cakes* for *T Magazine*. I worked through two sleepless nights and, on the day of the press preview, I raced to the SFMOMA with a car full of Thiebaud and Mondrian cakes. Thinking about sleep, the *Times*, and how late I was, my attention strayed from the stoplight ahead. With a yellow light in front of me and a split second to decide, I instinctively hit the brakes.

I hadn't had time to buy boxes to transport the desserts, so the Thiebaud cakes that had been floating around on a sheet pan in the back of my car were now stuck together. Furious that I stopped at a stupid yellow light in the middle of nowhere with no one around, I arrived at the museum on the verge of tears. In the cafe's tiny kitchen, I managed to patch the Thiebaud cakes together, finding unmarred sides for the front and hiding the less-than-pretty parts in the back. As I set the cakes on their stands in the Rooftop Garden, it began to rain, so James, my husband, and my assistant Mod stood over them with umbrellas as the photographer captured the perfect image of my very first Thiebaud cakes at home at the SFMOMA.

THIEBAUD WHITE CAKE

MAKES ONE 8-INCH CAKE, SERVING 8 TO 10
HANDS-ON TIME: 1 HOUR
FROM START TO FINISH: 1 DAY

The white cake is the most unadorned cake in the trio of *Display Cakes*, and one of the simplest cakes Thiebaud ever painted. When deciding on a flavor, I wanted the cake to pair well with the other two in the painting, and I also wanted it to be different from Thiebaud's similar-looking *Chocolate Cake* (page 55). Of the cakes in the painting, I adore the white cake most of all, so I thought, why not take flavor inspiration from my all-time favorite dessert: strawberry shortcake? Perhaps it's not the most avant-garde of combinations, but layering a yellow cake with strawberries and frosting it with vanilla buttercream couldn't be more perfect.

The practice of moistening cake layers with simple syrup is typically used with sponge cakes, with cakes soaked with alcohol (like rum cake), and to extend shelf life. Although Rose's Downy Yellow Butter Cake is perfectly moist without syruping, I like to give each layer a nice brushing before assembly for a bump of extra flavor.

DO AHEAD: This cake has many different components that require preparation before the cake can be assembled. The cake needs to be baked and thoroughly chilled before assembly, so consider making it the day before. It will keep for up to 5 days in the refrigerator or for up to 2 months in the freezer. The berries and syrup need to macerate for 1 to 2 hours before using, so consider preparing them while the cake is baking. They can be kept for up to 1 week in the refrigerator, or for up to 4 months in the freezer. The buttercream is easiest to use when it's freshly made, but it can also be made ahead and easily rewarmed before frosting the cake. It will keep for up to 1 week in the refrigerator or for up to 4 months in the freezer. The simple syrup can be made shortly before assembling the cake but, if made ahead of time, will keep for up to 3 weeks in the refrigerator. To store leftover cake, press plastic wrap against the cut sides; the leftover cake will keep for up to 3 days at room temperature or for up to 1 week in the refrigerator. If refrigerated, bring to room temperature before serving.

Rose's Downy Yellow Butter Cake (page 39)

Macerated Strawberries with Syrup (page 41)

Vanilla Buttercream (page 42)

Simple Syrup (page 44)

To assemble the white cake, place the cooled cake on a flat, stable work surface. Using a long, serrated knife, slice off the rounded top of the cake so that it is perfectly level. An even, flat top is key to the look of this dessert.

Using the serrated knife, split the cake horizontally into 2 even layers. Split each half in half again so that you have a total of 4 layers. Place the bottom layer on an 8-inch cardboard cake round or directly on the serving platter and set on top of a cake turntable, if you have one. Generously brush the surface of the cake with simple syrup.

Prepare the buttercream by warming and whipping it to achieve a mayonnaise-like consistency (see Working with Buttercream, page 43). Measure out $1/2$ cup (2.6 oz / 73 g) of buttercream and, using an offset spatula, spread it evenly on the bottom cake layer, being careful not to let it blop over the sides. As you spread the buttercream, let a small wall (about $1/4$ inch high) form around the outer edge, creating a well for the macerated strawberries.

Evenly distribute $1/2$ cup (2.5 oz / 70 g) of the strawberries in the well. Set another cake layer on top and brush with simple syrup; spread with buttercream, creating a well; and fill with berries just as you did with the first layer. Repeat with the third layer. Top with the final cake layer.

If necessary, warm the buttercream once again. Measure out 1 cup (5.2 oz / 146 g) of the buttercream and use the offset spatula to apply it as a crumb coat, a thin coating covering all surfaces of the cake; a crumb coat will seal the exterior of the cake to help prevent crumbs from marring the final frosting. (It's important to measure out buttercream specifically for the crumb coat so that the unused buttercream remains crumbfree.) Refrigerate the cake for 10 to 15 minutes to set the crumb coat.

Reserve about $^1/_2$ cup (2.6 oz / 73 g) of buttercream for the top of the cake. Using an offset spatula, apply a thick layer of the remaining buttercream to the sides of the chilled crumb-coated cake. At this point, it's not important that the cake look pretty—it's most important that the buttercream be evenly distributed around the sides. With the cake sitting squarely in the middle of the turntable and with the offset spatula held vertically against the frosting, begin spinning the turntable. Keep the cake moving steadily in one direction and apply light pressure with the spatula; the buttercream will begin to even out. I like to imagine the spatula as the needle that stays steady while the record (or cake) spins round and round on the turntable. My goal is to make the sides perfect before adding any Thiebaud personality. Make sure to watch the vertical line of the cake; I find it helpful to look at the right side of the cake at eye level while spinning the turntable. You can add more buttercream to any spots that seem thin and whittle down any thick spots with the spatula.

Once the sides are perfectly vertical and smooth, create as much or as little texture as you want in the buttercream. I constantly refer back to *Display Cakes* as I try to capture the casual, slightly imperfect look of Thiebaud's cakes onto my neatly frosted sides. It's not easy! While spinning the cake on the turntable, I often hold my offset spatula vertically and gently wobble it back and forth, or I take a quick swipe at the cake with the spatula blade as the turntable spins.

When the sides are to your liking, you'll find a ring of buttercream standing up above the surface of the cake. Lightly "grab" the excess buttercream in one area with the offset spatula and pull it toward the center of the cake, spreading it toward the center. Repeat until you have a nice, clean edge all around.

If necessary, warm the reserved buttercream, and then mound it up on top of the cake in the center. Using a small offset spatula, start from the center and begin smoothing out the buttercream, inching it closer and closer to the edge of the cake. I work fairly slowly when doing this in order to get a nice, voluminous lip of buttercream where the sides and the top of the cake meet, re-creating the ring that appears around the top edge of Thiebaud's white cake.

The cake is best served immediately.

Rose's Downy Yellow Butter Cake

HANDS-ON TIME: 15 MINUTES
FROM START TO FINISH: 1 1/4 HOURS

Baking is a science. It's about ratios and chemical reactions and, over the years, I have learned where variations can be made and how best to modify a recipe to achieve my ideal. But I've also learned that sometimes a recipe is just too good to modify. There is a lot to be said for exercising restraint and knowing when a recipe wouldn't be improved with your fingerprints all over it. Rose Levy Beranbaum's Downy Butter Yellow Cake and White Velvet Cake (page 88) are two such recipes. They are the foundations for the two most iconic works of art in this book, and I am happy to admit that I couldn't have invented a better recipe to use in these desserts.

Wayne Thiebaud's painted cakes are classic, nostalgic, and all-American. They're not challenging in flavor—they're just simple cakes, like the type your mother might've made for your birthday. Rose's Downy Yellow Butter cake is the perfect recipe with which to create cakes commemorating Wayne Thiebaud.

NOTE: This cake uses egg yolks only, which is convenient because my favorite frostings are made with egg whites. Save whites that are untainted by bits of yolk in a clean airtight container to use in a frosting; they will keep for up to 4 days in the refrigerator.

DO AHEAD: Wrapped tightly in plastic wrap, the cake will keep for up to 5 days in the refrigerator or up to 2 months in the freezer.

5 large egg yolks (3.25 oz / 95 g), at room temperature

3/4 cup (6.4 oz / 180 g) whole milk, at room temperature

1 3/4 teaspoons vanilla extract

2 cups (9.3 oz / 260 g) cake flour (see note, page 28)

1 1/4 cups (8.8 oz / 250 g) sugar

1 tablespoon baking powder

1/2 teaspoon kosher salt

10 tablespoons (5 oz / 140 g) unsalted butter, cut into pieces and at room temperature

Preheat the oven to 350°F. Butter and flour the sides of an 8 by 3-inch round cake pan and line the bottom with a parchment paper round that has been cut to fit.

In a medium bowl, whisk together the egg yolks, 1/2 cup (4.3 oz / 121 g) of the milk, and the vanilla.

Sift the flour, sugar, baking powder, and salt into the bowl of a stand mixer fitted with the paddle attachment, and mix on low speed for 30 seconds. Add the remaining $^1/_4$ cup (2.1 oz / 60 g) of milk and mix on low speed until moistened, about 15 seconds. Add the butter and beat on medium speed for $1^1/_2$ minutes or until smooth and aerated. Scrape down the sides of the bowl with a rubber spatula. Add the egg mixture in 3 batches, mixing on medium speed for 20 seconds and then scraping down the bowl after each addition.

Transfer the batter to the prepared pan and smooth the surface with an offset spatula. Bake, rotating the pan midway through baking, until the cake springs back when gently pressed in the center, 55 to 60 minutes. You can also test for doneness by listening to the cake: Remove the pan from the oven, set it on a wire rack, lower your ear to the cake, and listen. If you hear the cake snap, crackle, and pop, it needs a few more minutes in the oven. If it's quiet, it's done.

Let the cake cool on a wire rack for 30 minutes, and then run an offset spatula around the inside of the pan. Invert the cake onto the wire rack, lift off the pan, and remove the parchment. When the cake is cool enough to handle, after about 20 minutes, reinvert it so the top is facing up. Let cool completely, wrap tightly in plastic wrap, and refrigerate for at least 3 hours before assembling.

VARIATIONS

If you're going above and beyond with the Thiebaud Pink Cake (page 45), butter and flour the sides of two 6 by 3-inch round cake pans and line the bottoms with parchment paper rounds that have been cut to fit. Divide the batter evenly between the prepared pans. Decrease the baking time to 45 to 50 minutes.

If you're going above and beyond with the Ryman Cake (page 63), butter and flour the sides of two 8-inch square cake pans with 2-inch sides and line the bottoms with parchment paper squares that have been cut to fit. Divide the batter evenly between the prepared pans. Decrease the baking time to 30 to 35 minutes.

Macerated Strawberries with Syrup

MAKES 1 1/2 CUPS (7.5 OZ / 210 G) FRUIT AND 1 CUP (8.4 OZ / 240 G) SYRUP
HANDS-ON TIME: 15 MINUTES
FROM START TO FINISH: 2 1/4 HOURS

Macerating strawberries with sugar and lemon juice lightly softens the fruit and brings out its flavorful, ruby-red juice. It's a very simple way to extend the life of fresh strawberries without cooking them. I use both the berries and their syrupy juice in recipes throughout this book, but always separately.

DO AHEAD: Stored in an airtight container, the berries and syrup can be kept for up to 1 week in the refrigerator, or for up to 4 months in the freezer. Strain the juice from the strawberries before using.

2 pounds (908 g) fresh strawberries
1/2 cup (3.5 oz / 100 g) sugar
1/4 cup (2.1 oz / 60 g) fresh lemon juice

Wash, dry, and hull the strawberries. Cut the berries in half or quarter them if they are especially big.

In a large bowl, combine the berries, sugar, and lemon juice and toss with your hands until the berries are evenly coated with sugar. Cover the bowl with plastic wrap and let stand at room temperature until the strawberries soften and have released about 1 cup (8.4 oz / 240 g) of liquid, 1 to 2 hours.

Vanilla Buttercream

MAKES ENOUGH FOR ONE 8-INCH CAKE
HANDS-ON TIME: 45 MINUTES
FROM START TO FINISH: 45 MINUTES

Almost nothing makes me happier than buttercream at the perfect temperature, a small offset spatula, and a beautiful cake waiting to be frosted. There are different types of buttercreams, but I prefer the Italian-meringue version, perhaps because its consistency is very similar to thick oil paint, Thiebaud's medium in *Display Cakes*. If you're making one of the variations, ensure that whatever you're adding is at room temperature and incorporate it slowly.

NOTE: This recipe requires an accurate thermometer for taking the temperature of the sugar syrup. Instant-read thermometers are notoriously inaccurate (which is why I love my thermocouple; see page 25), so if you own an instant-read thermometer, it's good practice to check its calibration before beginning. Simply bring a small pot of water to a boil and verify that the thermometer registers 212°F (at sea level) when inserted into the water. To easily clean a pan or measuring cup that's sticky with the remnants of sugar syrup, fill it with warm water and let it stand until the sugar dissolves, about 30 minutes.

DO AHEAD: Stored in an airtight container, buttercream will keep for up to 1 week in the refrigerator or for up to 4 months in the freezer. See Working with Buttercream, opposite, to return the frosting to the proper consistency before use.

1^1/$_3$ cups (9.5 oz / 266 g) sugar

^{1}/$_3$ cup (2.9 oz / 80 g) water

7 large egg whites (7.4 oz / 210 g), at room temperature

^{1}/$_2$ teaspoon cream of tartar

2 cups (16 oz / 454 g) unsalted butter, cut into 1 tablespoon pieces, at room temperature

2 tablespoons vanilla extract

The sugar syrup and egg whites will need to be ready at roughly the same time, so preparing them will require some coordination. In a small saucepan over medium-low heat, bring the sugar and water to a simmer, swirling occasionally, and cook until the sugar dissolves. Continue simmering, without stirring, until the syrup reaches 248°F on a digital thermometer, about 5 minutes.

Meanwhile, in the bowl of a stand mixer fitted with the whisk attachment, whip the egg whites and cream of tartar on medium speed until the whites hold soft peaks, 8 to 10 minutes.

Immediately transfer the sugar syrup to a heatproof liquid measuring cup. With the mixer running on medium-high speed, add the hot sugar syrup to the whites in a thin, steady stream; aim to pour it into the small space between the mixer bowl and the whisk. Continue to whip the mixture until thick and shiny and the outside of the bowl feels cool to the touch, about 10 minutes.

Decrease the speed to medium and, with the mixer running, add the butter one piece at a time. The mixture won't resemble perfect buttercream until the last of the butter has been added. If it's looking deflated, wet, or broken during mixing, make sure the butter is at room temperature and slow down the additions, adding the next piece only after the last one has been fully incorporated. Add the vanilla and beat on medium speed until well combined, about 1 minute, until the texture is similar to mayonnaise.

VARIATIONS

For the Thiebaud Pink Cake (page 45) substitute Strawberry Concentrate (page 46) for the vanilla extract, adding it slowly with the mixer running.

WORKING WITH BUTTERCREAM

In order to make the most beautifully decorated cake, your buttercream must be perfectly smooth and spreadable. Whether you're using a just-made batch or one that has been made ahead and refrigerated, to get it to the optimal consistency for decorating, it's necessary to warm and rewhip it. Here's how.

Place about 2 cups (10.4 oz / 292 g) of buttercream in a microwavable container. (If you do not have a microwave, see page 23 for one approach to rewarming buttercream.) Heat it for no more than 5 seconds at a time at full power until it begins to look slightly glossy but not at all melted; it should still be solid, with a sheen from a softened exterior—not unlike ice cream on a cone as it begins melting and dripping onto your hand. (It's very easy to overheat and melt buttercream, so it's better to warm only a couple cups at a time and to use short bursts in the microwave.) Beat the warmed buttercream in the bowl of a stand mixer fitted with the paddle attachment until it resembles mayonnaise, about 30 seconds. Repeat as needed.

Simple Syrup

MAKES ¾ CUP (6.4 OZ / 180 G)
HANDS-ON TIME: 5 MINUTES
FROM START TO FINISH: 10 MINUTES

I use simple syrup for keeping cake layers extra moist. Plain simple syrup works perfectly well on its own, but when I have used vanilla bean pods on hand, I like to steep them into the syrup (feel free to keep them stored in the syrup indefinitely). It's an unnecessary step, for sure, but I always welcome a little extra pop of vanilla flavor in my cakes.

DO AHEAD: Stored in an airtight container, simple syrup will keep for up to 3 weeks in the refrigerator.

---

¹/₂ cup (4.3 oz / 120 g) water
¹/₂ cup (3.5 oz / 100 g) sugar

Combine the water and sugar in a small saucepan. Bring to a boil over medium heat and cook until the sugar dissolves, stirring occasionally. Remove from the heat and let cool before using.

VARIATION: SIMPLE SYRUP WITH RASPBERRY EAU-DE-VIE

If you're making the Diebenkorn Trifle (page 93), you can make simple syrup with raspberry eau-de-vie instead of plain simple syrup. Replace ¹/₄ cup (2.1 oz / 60 g) of the water with an equal amount of raspberry eau-de-vie.

THIEBAUD PINK CAKE

MAKES ONE 8-INCH CAKE, SERVING 8 TO 10
HANDS-ON TIME: 1 HOUR
FROM START TO FINISH: 1 DAY

The most dainty and cute of the three, this little pink cake was the one that propelled me into a life in cake making and was the original inspiration for the cakes I made at Miette. For the SFMOMA, I make the Thiebaud Pink Cake pink by cooking down strawberry syrup and adding it to the buttercream, and I top the frosted cake with either a red buttercream dot or a big, ripe raspberry if they're in season. I use lemon curd in the filling because, being the giant kid that I am, I love the combination of strawberry and lemon in a dessert—to me, it always tastes like Froot Loops.

DO AHEAD: This cake has many different components that require preparation before the cake can be assembled. The cake needs to be baked and thoroughly chilled before assembly, so consider making it the day before. It will keep for up to 5 days in the refrigerator or for up 2 months in the freezer. The lemon curd takes 3 to 4 hours to set, so consider preparing it while the cake is baking. It can be kept for up to 1 week in the refrigerator or for 4 months in the freezer. The strawberry concentrate can be made ahead and stored for up to 1 week in an airtight container in the refrigerator or 4 months in the freezer, but should be at room temperature before using. The buttercream is easiest to use when it's freshly made, but it can also be made ahead and easily rewarmed before frosting the cake (see Working with Buttercream, page 43). It will keep for up to 1 week in the refrigerator or for up to 4 months in the freezer. The simple syrup can be made shortly before assembling the cake but, if made ahead of time, will keep for up to 3 weeks in the refrigerator. To store leftover cake, press plastic wrap against the cut sides and refrigerate for up to 1 week. Bring to room temperature before serving.

ABOVE AND BEYOND: In the painting *Display Cakes*, the pink cake is the smallest of the three. But since 6-inch cake pans aren't common in home kitchens, I've made this cake the same size as the other two. To make a more faithful replica of the painting, bake the cake batter in two 6 by 2-inch cake pans; see Variations in Rose's Downy Yellow Butter Cake (page 39) for details. Split each baked cake into 2 even layers so that you have a total of 4 layers. Build the cake on a 6-inch cardboard cake round or directly on a serving platter, using slightly less simple syrup, buttercream, and lemon curd on each layer.

STRAWBERRY CONCENTRATE

$^1/_2$ pound (227 g) fresh strawberries

$^1/_2$ cup (4.3 oz / 120 g) water

$^1/_4$ cup (1.8 oz / 50 g) sugar

—

Rose's Downy Yellow Butter Cake (page 39)

—

$^3/_4$ cup (6.4 oz / 180 g) Lemon Curd (page 49)

Vanilla Buttercream (page 42; see Variations)

Simple Syrup (page 44)

1 fresh raspberry

To make the strawberry concentrate, wash, dry, and hull the strawberries. Cut the berries in half or quarter them if they are especially big.

Combine the strawberries, water, and sugar in a medium nonreactive saucepan and bring the mixture to a simmer over medium-low heat, stirring to help the sugar dissolve. Turn down the heat to the low, cover, and simmer until the berries are soft, 8 to 10 minutes. Remove from the heat and let the berries rest, covered, for 5 minutes.

Transfer the berry mixture to a fine-mesh sieve set over a medium nonreactive saucepan. Once all of the juice has drained, set the berries aside to use in another project. Bring the juice to a simmer over medium-low heat until it has reduced down to $^1/_4$ cup (2.1 oz / 60 g), about 10 minutes, and set aside to cool.

To assemble the pink cake, place the cooled cake on a flat, stable work surface. Using a long, serrated knife, slice off the rounded top of the cake so that it is perfectly level. An even, flat top is key to the look of this dessert.

Using the serrated knife, split the cake horizontally into 2 even layers. Split each half in half again so that you have a total of 4 layers. Place the bottom layer on an 8-inch cardboard cake round or directly on the serving platter and set on top of a cake turntable, if you have one. Generously brush the surface of the cake with simple syrup.

Prepare the buttercream by warming and whipping it to achieve a mayonnaise-like consistency (see Working with Buttercream, page 43). Measure out $^1/_2$ cup (2.6 oz / 73 g) of buttercream and, using an offset spatula, spread it evenly on the bottom cake layer, being careful not to let it blop over the sides. As you spread the buttercream, let a small wall (about $^1/_4$ inch high) form around the outer edge, creating a well for the lemon curd.

Evenly distribute $^1/_4$ cup (2.1 oz / 60 g) of the lemon curd in the well. Set another cake layer on top and brush with simple syrup; spread with buttercream, creating a well, and fill with lemon curd just as you did with the first layer. Repeat with the third layer. Top with the final cake layer.

If necessary, warm the buttercream once again. Measure out 1 cup (5.2 oz / 146 g) of buttercream and use the offset spatula to apply it as a crumb coat, a thin coating covering all surfaces of the cake; a crumb coat will seal the exterior of the cake to help prevent crumbs from marring the final frosting. (It's important to measure out buttercream specifically for the crumb coat so that the unused buttercream remains crumb free.) Refrigerate the cake for 10 to 15 minutes to set the crumb coat.

Reserve about $^1/_2$ cup (2.6 oz / 73 g) of buttercream for the top of the cake. Using an offset spatula, apply a thick layer of the remaining buttercream to the sides of the chilled crumb-coated cake. At this point, it's not important that the cake look pretty—it's most important that the buttercream be evenly distributed around the sides. With the cake sitting

squarely in the middle of the turntable and with the offset spatula held vertically against the frosting, begin spinning the turntable. Keep the cake moving steadily in one direction and apply light pressure with the spatula; the buttercream will begin to even out. I like to imagine the spatula as the needle that stays steady while the record (or cake) spins round and round on the turntable. My goal is to make the sides perfect before adding any Thiebaud personality. Make sure to watch the vertical line of the cake; I find it helpful to look at the right side of the cake at eye level while spinning the turntable. You can add more buttercream to any spots that seem thin and whittle down any thick spots with the spatula.

Once the sides are perfectly vertical and smooth, create as much or as little texture as you want in the buttercream. I constantly refer back to *Display Cakes* as I try to capture the casual, slightly imperfect look of Thiebaud's cakes onto my neatly frosted sides. It's not easy! While spinning the cake on the turntable, I often hold my offset spatula vertically and gently wobble it back and forth, or I take a quick swipe at the cake with the spatula blade as the turntable spins.

When the sides are to your liking, you'll find a ring of buttercream standing up above the surface of the cake. Lightly "grab" the excess buttercream in one area with the offset spatula and pull it toward the center of the cake, spreading it toward the center. Repeat until you have a nice, clean edge all around.

If necessary, warm the reserved buttercream, and then mound it up on top of the cake in the center. Using a small offset spatula, start from the center and begin smoothing out the buttercream, inching it closer and closer to the edge of the cake. I work fairly slowly when doing this in order to get a nice, voluminous lip of buttercream where the sides and the top of the cake meet, re-creating the ring that appears around the top edge of Thiebaud's pink cake.

Place the raspberry in the center of the cake.

The cake is best served immediately.

Lemon Curd

MAKES 3³/₄ CUPS (32 OZ / 900 G)
HANDS-ON TIME: 1 HOUR
FROM START TO FINISH: 5 HOURS

The name "curd" belies the silken beauty that is this tangy lemon custard. Some lemon curd recipes do live up to this chalky and lumpy sounding moniker, but this is not one of those recipes. There's no need for cornstarch or any other thickening agent—perfect lemon curd requires only four ingredients, some heat, and a little time.

The magic of this recipe is that it's incredibly easy, requiring very little hands-on time, and the beautiful results keep for up to four months, which is why I suggest making such a large batch. As long as you're devoting an hour to lemon curd, you may as well make enough to give as gifts or to freeze and enjoy for yourself for the next few months.

NOTE: This recipe can easily be halved or quartered. Refer to the *Modern Art Desserts* recipe that you're making for the quantity of lemon curd that you'll need.

DO AHEAD: Stored in an airtight container, the lemon curd can be held for up to 1 week in the refrigerator or for 4 months in the freezer.

12 large egg yolks (8.1 oz / 228 g)

2 cups (14.3 oz / 400 g) sugar

1 cup (8.6 oz / 240 g) fresh lemon juice

Grated zest of 4 lemons

1 cup (8 oz / 227 g) unsalted butter, cut into 1 tablespoon pieces, at room temperature

In a saucepan over medium heat, bring 2 to 3 inches of water to a simmer.

In a heatproof medium bowl, whisk together the egg yolks and sugar until thoroughly combined. Whisk in the lemon juice and zest and set the bowl on the saucepan, making sure the bottom does not touch the simmering water. Cook, whisking occasionally, until the mixture is thick enough to coat the back of a spoon and the temperature registers 180°F on a digital thermometer, 20 to 30 minutes.

Strain the curd through a fine-mesh sieve set over a clean medium bowl. Add the butter a few pieces at a time, stirring with a rubber spatula. When all the butter has been incorporated, blend with an immersion blender until the curd is completely smooth, about 30 seconds.

Strain the curd once again, this time into a storage container. Press plastic wrap onto the surface and refrigerate until chilled and set, 3 to 4 hours.

THIEBAUD YELLOW CAKE

This cake vexed me for years. I still can't quite understand what it is that Thiebaud painted to the left of the white cake in *Display Cakes*. At first, I thought it might be a Boston cream pie, but the yellow in the top layer seems much too bright to be pastry cream. The most delicious solution I could concoct is a pool of lemon curd floating in a buttery cake filled with soft piles of whipped cream. It's a little challenging to hollow out the top cake layer to make a shallow well for the lemon curd, but it's definitely worth the effort. A hybrid of a lemon cake and a lemon tart, this dessert may not be exactly what Thiebaud had in mind, but it looks beautiful and tastes absolutely delicious.

The finished cake needs at least 3 hours for the lemon curd to set before serving. If cut before the lemon curd has fully set, the cake will be a delicious mess.

DO AHEAD: This cake has many different components that require preparation before the cake can be assembled. The cake needs to be baked and thoroughly chilled before assembly, so consider making it the day before. It will keep for up to 5 days in the refrigerator or for up to 2 months in the freezer. The lemon curd takes 3 to 4 hours to set, so consider preparing while the cake is baking. It can be kept for up to 1 week in the refrigerator or for 4 months in the freezer. The simple syrup can be made shortly before assembling the cake but, if made ahead of time, will keep for up to 3 weeks in the refrigerator. To store leftover cake, press plastic wrap against the cut sides and store for up to 1 week in the refrigerator.

1^1/$_2$ cups (12.4 oz / 348 g) cold heavy cream
^{1}/$_4$ cup (1 oz / 28 g) confectioners' sugar
Rose's Downy Yellow Butter Cake (page 39)

1 cup (8.6 oz / 240 g) Lemon Curd
(page 49), at room temperature
Simple Syrup (page 44)

In the bowl of a stand mixer fitted with the whisk attachment, whip the cream and confectioners' sugar on medium speed until the cream holds medium-soft peaks, about 2 minutes. Alternatively, whip the cream and confectioners' sugar in a large bowl with a hand mixer or whisk. If you're not ready to use the whipped cream right away, cover with plastic wrap and refrigerate for up to 1 hour.

Place the cake on a flat, stable work surface; I like to use my cake turntable for the most control. Using a long, serrated knife slice off the rounded top of the cake so that it is perfectly level. An even, flat top will make it easier to create a well for the lemon curd. Using the serrated knife, split the cake horizontally into 2 even layers, each about 1^1/$_2$-inches thick.

Set aside the bottom layer and set the top layer on the cake turntable. Using a paring knife, score the cake around its circumference about ^{1}/$_8$-inch in from the edge, cutting down about ^{1}/$_4$-inch deep. With the knife held horizontally and using the turntable to help keep the movement steady, begin shaving away thin sheets from the center of the cake until you have a ^{1}/$_4$-inch-deep well. Work from the center out until you reach the scored line just inside the edge; the wall of the well should be about ^{1}/$_8$-inch thick. Carefully set the top cake layer aside.

Place the bottom cake layer on an 8-inch cardboard cake round or directly on the serving platter and set on top of the turntable. Generously brush the surface of the cake with simple syrup. Mound the whipped cream in the center and, using a small offset spatula, begin smoothing out the cream, starting from the center and inching it closer and closer to the edge, stopping about $1/4$-inch inside the edge. I like to do this slowly, coaxing the whipped cream outward in order to get a nice, billowy edge that will peek out from between the layers. Very carefully retrieve the top layer and place it atop the whipped cream. Gently press down on it to push the whipped cream to the edge of the cake.

Fill the well with the lemon curd and carefully transfer the cake to the refrigerator. Refrigerate until the curd is completely set, at least 3 hours. Serve chilled.

The cake is best served as soon as the lemon curd has set.

Wayne Thiebaud
Chocolate Cake, from the portfolio *Seven Still Lifes and a Rabbit*
1971
lithograph on Arches paper
30 in. x 22^{1}/$_{4}$ in.
SFMOMA, William L. Gerstle Collection, William L. Gerstle Fund purchase, 72.15.7

———

Thiebaud has made prints throughout his career, and has described his work with etchings, lithographs, silkscreens, and other graphic techniques as an extension of "the continuing thrill" of learning about how paintings and drawings can be made. Part of the learning specific to prints is the process of pulling and proofing each image in collaboration with printers at fine arts presses.

In 1971, Thiebaud made *Seven Still Lifes and a Rabbit* (and another portfolio called *Seven Still Lifes and a Silver Landscape*) at Parasol Press in New York. In *Chocolate Cake*, a single-color lithograph printed in chocolatey brown ink, the artist takes a slice out of one of his signature cylindrical desserts and draws it as well, thereby incorporating varying geometries and textures (the inside of the cake) to the composition.

Art © Wayne Thiebaud/Licensed by VAGA, New York, NY

THIEBAUD CHOCOLATE CAKE

MAKES ONE 8-INCH CAKE, SERVING 8 TO 10
HANDS-ON TIME: 1 HOUR
FROM START TO FINISH: 1 DAY

When I had the chance to visit the SFMOMA archives to see *Display Cakes*, I realized there may be more Thiebaud pieces hiding down there than just the one that I was in love with. I asked to see a list of the entire Thiebaud collection and was presented with an inventory of beautiful images that spanned his career, from cityscapes and portraits to gauzy aquatints and meandering aqueducts. I was particularly interested in his 1971 portfolio *Seven Still Lifes and a Rabbit*, a series of eight prints that included a charming lithograph of a chocolate cake with a slice removed. At our café, we take liberties with the insides of the *Display Cakes* because they're not visible in the painting, but with the *Chocolate Cake* lithograph we could finally replicate a Thiebaud dessert down to the very last crumb.

DO AHEAD: This cake has many different components that require preparation before the cake can be assembled. The cake needs to be baked and thoroughly chilled before assembly, so consider making it the day before. It will keep for up to 5 days in the refrigerator or for up 2 months in the freezer. The buttercream and chocolate-coffee ganache are easiest to use when they're freshly made, but they can also be made ahead and easily rewarmed before frosting the cake. Stored in an airtight container, the ganache will keep for up to 1 week in the refrigerator. See Working with Chocolate Ganache, page 91, for reheating instructions. The buttercream will keep for up to 1 week in the refrigerator or for up to 4 months in the freezer. The simple syrup can be made shortly before assembling the cake but, if made ahead of time, will keep for up to 3 weeks in the refrigerator. To store leftover cake, press plastic wrap against the cut sides; the leftover cake will keep for up to 3 days at room temperature or for up to 1 week in the refrigerator. If refrigerated, bring to room temperature before serving.

ABOVE AND BEYOND: The closest match I could find to the plate in the lithograph—one with a completely flat surface and a nice defined edge—is a salad plate made by Heath Ceramics (see Resources, page 205).

Old-Fashioned Chocolate Cake (page 60)

Vanilla Buttercream (page 42)

CHOCOLATE-COFFEE GANACHE

4 ounces (112 g) high-quality bittersweet chocolate (62% to 70% cacao), finely chopped

2 tablespoons espresso or strong, freshly brewed black coffee

1/4 cup plus 2 tablespoons (3 oz / 87 g) heavy cream

—

Simple Syrup (page 44)

Red food coloring (see page 30)

To assemble the cake, place the cooled cake on a flat, stable work surface. Using a long, serrated knife, slice off the rounded top of the cake so that it is perfectly level. An even, flat top is key to the look of this dessert.

Using the serrated knife, split the cake horizontally into 3 even layers. Place the bottom layer on an 8-inch cardboard cake round or directly on the serving platter and set on top of a cake turntable, if you have one. Generously brush the surface of the cake with simple syrup.

Prepare the buttercream by warming and whipping it to achieve a mayonnaise-like consistency (see Working with Buttercream, page 43). Reserve about $^{1}/_{4}$ cup (1.3 oz / 37 g) for the piped decoration. Measure out about $^{1}/_{2}$ cup (2.6 oz / 73 g) of buttercream (enough to create a $^{1}/_{4}$-inch layer) and, using a small offset spatula, spread it evenly on the bottom cake layer, being careful not to let it blop over the sides. As you spread the buttercream, let a small wall (about $^{1}/_{4}$ inch high) form around the outer edge, creating a well for the chocolate ganache.

Meanwhile, to make the ganache, put the chocolate and coffee in a medium heat-proof bowl.

In a small, heavy-bottomed saucepan over medium-low heat, warm the cream, stirring occasionally, until it registers 180°F to 190°F on a digital thermometer and bubbles start to form around the edges. (Alternatively, put the cream into a microwavable liquid measuring cup or bowl and microwave at full power for about 60 seconds.)

Pour the hot cream over the chocolate and, using rubber spatula, stir until the chocolate is mostly melted. Blend with an immersion blender or transfer to a food processor and process until the chocolate is completely melted and the mixture is smooth and shiny. (Alternatively, set the bowl over a saucepan of just simmered water and whisk until the chocolate is melted and the mixture is smooth.) Pour a generous layer of ganache, about $^{1}/_{4}$ cup (2.3 oz / 63 g), into the well, smoothing, as needed, with an offset spatula.

Set another cake layer on top and brush with simple syrup; spread with buttercream, creating a well; and fill with ganache just as you did with the first layer. Top with the final cake layer.

If necessary, warm the remaining buttercream once again. Measure out 1 cup (5.2 oz / 146 g) of buttercream and use the offset spatula to apply it as a crumb coat, a thin coating covering all surfaces of the cake; a crumb coat will seal the exterior of the cake to help prevent crumbs from marring the final frosting. (It's important to measure out buttercream specifically for the crumb coat so that the unused buttercream remains crumb free.) Refrigerate the cake for 10 to 15 minutes to set the crumb coat.

Reserve about $^{1}/_{2}$ cup (2.6 oz / 73 g) of buttercream for the top of the cake. Using an offset spatula, apply a thick layer of the remaining buttercream to the sides of the chilled crumb-coated cake. At this point, it's not important that the cake look pretty—it's most important that the buttercream be evenly distributed around the sides. With the cake sitting squarely in the middle of the turntable and with the offset spatula held vertically against the frosting, begin spinning the turntable. Keep the cake moving steadily in one direction and apply light pressure with the spatula; the buttercream will begin to even out. I like to imagine the spatula as the needle that stays steady while the record (or cake) spins round and round on the turntable. My goal is to make the sides perfect before adding any Thiebaud personality. Make sure to watch the vertical line of the cake; I find it helpful to look at the right side of the cake at eye level while spinning the turntable. You can add more buttercream to any spots that seem thin and whittle down any thick spots with the spatula.

Once the sides are perfectly vertical and smooth, create as much or as little texture as you want in the buttercream. I constantly refer back to Thiebaud's artworks as I try to capture the casual, slightly imperfect look of his cakes onto my neatly frosted sides. It's not easy! While spinning the cake on the turntable, I often hold my offset spatula vertically and gently wobble it back and forth, or I take a quick swipe at the cake with the spatula blade as the turntable spins.

When the sides are to your liking, you'll find a ring of buttercream standing up above the surface of the cake. Lightly "grab" the excess buttercream in one area with the offset spatula and pull it toward the center of the cake, spreading it toward the center. Repeat until you have a nice, clean edge all around.

If necessary, warm the reserved buttercream, and then mound it up on top of the cake in the center. Using a small offset spatula, start from the center and begin smoothing out the buttercream, inching it closer and closer to the edge of the cake. I work fairly slowly when doing this in order to get a nice, voluminous lip of buttercream where the sides and the top of the cake meet, re-creating the ring that appears around the top edge of Thiebaud's *Chocolate Cake*.

If necessary, warm the buttercream reserved for the decorative dots. Add enough red food coloring to tint the buttercream a vivid red and mix thoroughly. Fit a piping bag with a coupler and a plain $1/4$-inch tip. Fill the bag with the red buttercream. Pipe 10 small evenly spaced dots around the perimeter of the cake, about $3/4$ inch from the edge.

The cake is best served immediately.

Old-Fashioned Chocolate Cake

MAKES ONE 8-INCH CAKE, SERVING 8 TO 10
HANDS-ON TIME: 15 MINUTES
FROM START TO FINISH: 1 1/4 HOURS

This cake came from my good friend Nicole Krasinski, pastry chef/owner of the incredible San Francisco restaurant State Bird Provisions. Known for deeply layered flavor combinations and diverse textural elements in her desserts, Nicole is a very talented pastry chef with whom I would never associate a straight-up chocolate cake. She refers to this cake as "the old fashioned," but she has paired it with some pretty avant-garde ingredients. Nicole helped me tremendously by taking on a few baking shifts when the SFMOMA café first opened. During this time working together, I learned that one of our greatest differences is our stance on vanilla. Nicole absolutely refuses to use it, and I like to sneak a little extra in everything I make, especially chocolate desserts. When she made this cake for me as an idea for Thiebaud's *Chocolate Cake*, I knew it was almost perfect. I just needed to add a little bit of vanilla!

DO AHEAD: Wrapped tightly in plastic wrap, the cake will keep for up to 5 days in the refrigerator or up to 2 months in the freezer.

$1^1/2$ cups (7.4 oz / 210 g) all-purpose flour

1 teaspoon baking powder

$3/4$ teaspoon baking soda

2 large eggs (3.5 oz / 100 g), at room temperature

1 cup (8.6 oz / 242 g) buttermilk, at room temperature

1 teaspoon vanilla extract

11 tablespoons (5.5 oz / 156 g) unsalted butter, at room temperature

$1^1/2$ cups (10.6 oz / 300 g) sugar

$2/3$ cup (2.2 ounces / 62 grams) natural (not Dutch-processed) unsweetened cocoa powder

1 teaspoon kosher salt

Preheat the oven to 350°F. Butter the sides of an 8 by 3-inch round cake pan and dust with cocoa powder. Line the bottom of the pan with a parchment paper round that has been cut to fit.

Sift the flour, baking powder, and baking soda into a medium bowl. In a small bowl, lightly whisk the eggs to break them up. In a liquid measuring cup, combine the buttermilk and vanilla extract.

In the bowl of a stand mixer fitted with the paddle attachment, beat the butter on low speed until smooth, 1 to 2 minutes. Add the sugar, cocoa powder, and salt, and mix on low until well combined. Scrape down the bowl with a rubber spatula and beat on medium speed until the mixture is fluffy, 4 to 5 minutes.

Scrape down the bowl and add the flour mixture. Mix on low speed until just combined. With the mixer running on medium speed, add the eggs in a slow, steady stream and beat until well incorporated, about 30 seconds. Scrape down the bowl. With the mixer running on medium speed, add the buttermilk in a slow, steady stream. Scrape down the bowl and mix by hand until no lumps remain.

Transfer the batter to the prepared pan and smooth the surface with an offset spatula. Bake, rotating the pan midway through baking, until the cake springs back when gently pressed in the center, 60 to 65 minutes. You can also test for doneness by listening to the cake: Remove the pan from the oven, set it on a wire rack, lower your ear to the cake, and listen. If you hear the cake snap, crackle, and pop, it needs a few more minutes in the oven. If it's quiet, it's done.

Let the cake cool in the pan on a wire rack for 30 minutes. When the cake has cooled, run an offset spatula around the inside edge. Invert the cake onto the wire rack, lift off the pan, and remove the parchment. When the cake is cool enough to handle, after about 20 minutes, reinvert it so the top is facing up. Let cool completely, wrap tightly in plastic wrap, and refrigerate for at least 3 hours before cutting.

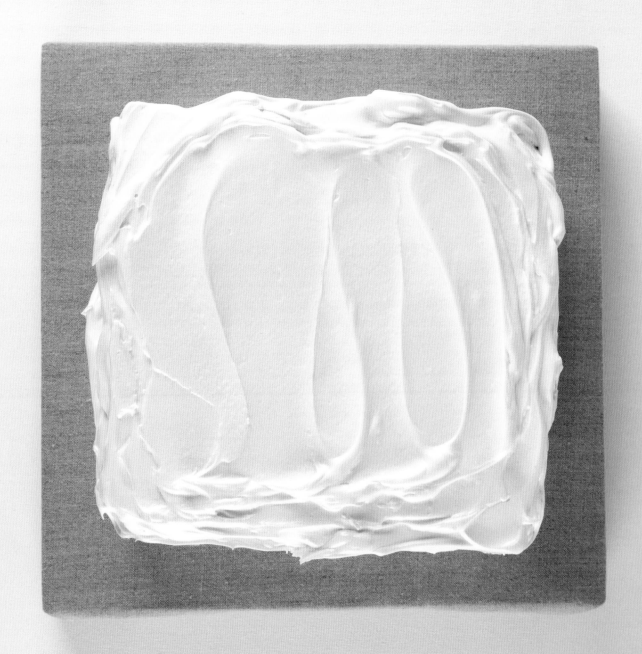

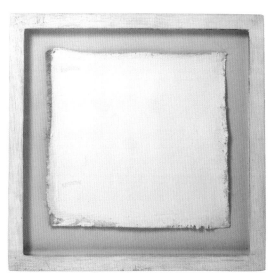

© Robert Ryman / Artists Rights Society (ARS), New York

Robert Ryman
An all white painting measuring 9¹/₂" x 10" and signed twice on the left side in white umber
1961
oil on linen canvas
13³/₄ in. x 13³/₄ in. x 1¹/₂ in.
SFMOMA, purchase through a gift of Mimi and Peter Haas, 99.362

——

Robert Ryman (born 1930) made his first abstract paintings in the mid-1950s while working as a security guard at The Museum of Modern Art in New York—a job that gave him ample opportunity to look at art. Since then, he has created works of astonishing beauty and range, nearly all within the self-imposed parameters of the square format and the color white.

In the early 1960s, Ryman produced a number of modest paintings on unstretched canvas. *An all white painting measuring 9¹/₂" x 10" and signed twice on the left side in white umber* describes itself with its title, thus calling attention to the individual elements that make up the whole. Ryman has commented on painting as having the capacity to convey "an experience of delight and well-being, and rightness. It's like listening to music. Like going to an opera and coming out of it feeling somehow fulfilled. . . ."

RYMAN CAKE

MAKES ONE 8-INCH CAKE, SERVING 8 TO 10
HANDS-ON TIME: 1 HOUR
FROM START TO FINISH: 1 DAY

In 2010, SFMOMA celebrated its seventy-fifth anniversary by filling the galleries with important artworks from its collection and throwing itself a birthday bash. Every party needs cake, so the museum asked six bakers to make art-inspired cakes. As one of the lucky chosen few, I decided to base my cake on a Robert Ryman piece. Like all monochromatic artworks, Ryman's paintings can be easily dismissed by modern art nonbelievers. But the guests coming to the party would surely get it, and they would hail me as a genius for taking a quiet, thoughtful piece and presenting it as a grand three-tiered birthday cake!

I built wooden supports and covered them in Belgian linen, reminiscent of the type Ryman used in his painting. I brushed a butter cake with strawberry syrup and stuffed it full of beautiful strawberries. I enveloped the cake in buoyant lemon verbena–flavored

Swiss meringue, taking special care with the way the meringue met the linen and mimicking the brushstrokes in the original. Leah and I confidently wheeled the cake downstairs to our table smack in the center of the room. Looking around, I witnessed masterpieces being erected: a human-size croquembouche; a "deconstructed cake" by celebrity pastry chef Elizabeth Falkner; stacked purple and black cakes with Richard Serra–esque curved chocolate pieces. My subtle homage to a minimalist master suddenly looked like the work of an amateur.

As guests filed in, they oohed and aahed over the impressive cakes. Each baker stood next to his or her creation and described it to admirers; Leah and I stood awkwardly next to our cake, clearing away the glasses people left on our table as they raced past it to the tower of cream puffs. After about an hour, we were relieved to get the go-ahead to chop up our cake—at last, making it go away. A crowd gathered around us as we served—partygoers had finally discovered our incredible piece of art, not because all of the thought and effort that went into it, but because it was absolutely delicious.

NOTE: To flavor the meringue, I use lemon verbena essential oil. Essential oils are highly concentrated distillations of herbs, flowers, or spices. As long they are steam-distilled and labeled food grade, they're safe to use in cooking. If you can't find lemon verbena essential oil in stores, it can be ordered online (see Resources, page 205), or you can substitute 1 teaspoon vanilla extract.

DO AHEAD: This cake has a few different components that require preparation before the cake can be assembled. The cake needs to be baked and thoroughly chilled before assembly, so consider making it the day before. It will keep for up to 5 days in the refrigerator or for up 2 months in the freezer. The berries and syrup need to macerate for 1 to 2 hours before using, so consider preparing while the cake is baking. They can be kept for up to 1 week in the refrigerator, or for up to 4 months in the freezer. The simple syrup can be made shortly before assembling the cake but, if made ahead of time, will keep for up to 3 weeks in the refrigerator. The Swiss meringue must be made just before use. To store leftover cake, press plastic wrap against the cut sides; the leftover cake will keep for up to 3 days at room temperature or for up to 1 week in the refrigerator. If refrigerated, bring to room temperature before serving.

ABOVE AND BEYOND: For the SFMOMA birthday bash, our Ryman cake was a grand three-tiered affair, each of the cakes atop its own custom-made, linen-covered cake stand. But since you probably don't need that much cake, and square cake pans aren't very common in home kitchens, I've modified this recipe as one 8-inch round cake. To replicate the top tier of our party cake, split the cake batter in two 8-inch square cake pans; see Variations in Rose's Downy Yellow Butter Cake (page 39) for details. Split each baked cake into 2 even layers so that you have a total of 4 layers.

This cake is delightful however you display it, but if you want to channel your inner Ryman, it's pretty easy to build your own linen-covered cake display. Have ready a staple gun, a 12-inch square wood art board, 1 square yard of unprimed Belgian linen (see Resources, page 205, for purchasing information for art board and linen). Cut the linen to a 20-inch square and lay the board face-down in the center of the linen. Pull one edge of the linen around the art board and staple it to the inside of the frame. Repeat with the opposite side, pulling the linen taut before stapling, and then repeat for the two remaining sides. At the corners, neatly fold the edges of the linen and staple to secure them. Assemble the cake directly on top of the board, and marvel at the lovely interaction you've created between the meringue and the linen.

Rose's Downy Yellow Butter Cake
(page 39; see Variations)

Macerated Strawberries with Syrup
(page 41)

LEMON VERBENA SWISS MERINGUE

8 large egg whites (8.8 oz / 240 g),
at room temperature

2 cups (14.3 oz / 400 g) sugar

2 teaspoons vanilla extract

2 drops lemon verbena essential oil
(see Note)

Strain the macerated strawberries, reserving the syrup.

Place the cake on a flat, stable work surface. Using a long, serrated knife, slice off the rounded top of the cake so that it is perfectly level. An even, flat top is key to the look of this dessert.

Using the serrated knife, split the cake horizontally into 2 even layers. Split each half in half again so that you have a total of 4 layers. Place the bottom layer on an 8-inch cardboard cake round or directly on the serving platter and set on top of a cake turntable, if you have one. Generously brush the surface of the cake with strawberry syrup. Top with about $3/4$ cup (3.8 oz / 105 g) of macerated strawberries, distributing the berries in an even layer over the cake.

Set another cake layer on top, brush with syrup, and top with about $^3/_4$ cup (3.8 oz / 105 g) of strawberries, enough for deliciously even coverage. Repeat with a third cake layer, syrup, and berries. Top with the final cake layer. Set the cake aside.

To make the lemon verbena Swiss meringue, bring 2 to 3 inches of water to a simmer in a saucepan.

In your mixer bowl or another clean, medium heatproof bowl, whisk together the egg whites, sugar, vanilla, and essential oil. Set the bowl on the saucepan, making sure the bottom does not touch the simmering water, and stir constantly until the sugar has dissolved and the mixture is slightly warm (about 110°F on a digital thermometer), 2 to 3 minutes.

Transfer to the bowl of a stand mixer fitted with the whisk attachment and whip on medium-high speed until the meringue holds soft peaks, about 10 minutes.

Using an offset spatula and working quickly (the meringue becomes more difficult to work with the cooler it gets), apply about 1 cup (2.3 oz / 65 g) of meringue in a thin layer to the sides and top of the cake; this is the crumb coat that will seal the exterior of the cake to help prevent crumbs from marring the final frosting. Once the crumb coat has been applied, spread the remaining meringue over the sides and top of the cake.

The cake is best served at room temperature.

RYMAN CAKE

Roy Lichtenstein
Rouen Cathedral Set V
 (detail)
1969
oil and Magna on canvas
63⁵/₈ in. x 141⁷/₈ in. x 1³/₄ in.
 overall
SFMOMA, Gift of Harry W.
 and Mary Margaret
 Anderson, 92.266.A-C

—

In the early 1890s, Claude Monet made some thirty pictures of a cathedral in Rouen, France. Monet used his lively palette and signature broken brushwork to capture the structure's Gothic façade as it appeared at different times of day and year, and under varying skies. When the American pop artist

Roy Lichtenstein (1923–97) saw reproductions of Monet's paintings in 1968, he became fascinated with the French master's serial approach and, mining art history to suit his purposes, began making his own "manufactured Monets." Lichtenstein's *Rouen Cathedral Set V*, from 1969, consists of three vertical panels: red and yellow on the left, red and blue in the middle, and the red and black panel (pictured here) on the right. Each panel is made up of thousands of dots, which recall the Benday printing technique used for the mass reproduction of images, painstakingly applied by hand.

LICHTENSTEIN CAKE

MAKES ONE 8-INCH CAKE, SERVING 8 TO 10
HANDS-ON TIME: 3 HOURS
FROM START TO FINISH: 1 DAY

Ever since my first dessert-sketching trip to SFMOMA, I had been mulling over how to decorate a cake with Lichtenstein-style Benday dots (the dot-based printing style widely used in comic books, which Lichtenstein appropriated in his paintings). I eventually devised a plan to use a polka-dot stencil from the cake supply store to create a bright-red dot pattern on a cake finished with white frosting. Continuing with a Pop-art color theme, I wanted the cake layers to be a primary color, but I couldn't think of any colorful cake possibilities other than red velvet cake. I've never been a big fan of red velvet cake, but it seemed fine for a first draft—it was really the stenciled print that I was after. I baked a red velvet cake, frosted it, let it firm up in the refrigerator for a few hours, and then used the stencil and an offset spatula to apply the dots. The results looked great. But my misgivings about red velvet cake kept me from serving it at the café, and I never made time to work out an alternative, so the Lichtenstein cake idea was put on my one-day-I'll-try-it-again list.

It turns out writing this book gave me the occasion to revisit the cake. Too proud to use a run-of-the-mill, food-coloring drenched red velvet cake, I set off on a journey to track down the cake's origins (see Romancing the Red Velvet, page 75) and re-create a historically correct version that I hoped wouldn't rely on artificial coloring for its vivid hue. Although I did create an excellent cake, I also learned that without the help of red food coloring, red velvet cake is a dull auburn color. I leave the decision to you: made with or without food coloring, the cake is delicious.

For beautiful, perfectly smooth cream cheese frosting, the key to success is in the details. Sifted confectioners' sugar, plus room-temperature butter and cream cheese will keep lumps at bay. I love to add a lemon zest to the frosting, but bits of zest may not be desirable—for example, if you'll be stenciling on dots. In all other cases, I add zest.

NOTE: If you're suspicious about using food coloring but don't want an auburn velvet cake in your Lichtenstein Cake, the Old-Fashioned Chocolate Cake on page 60 is a wonderfully delicious—and visually compelling—alternative to the Red Velvet Cake. For either cake, I like to leave the sides unfrosted, giving the finished cake the added graphic look of stripes on the side and dots on the top.

DO AHEAD: This cake has a few different components that require preparation before the cake can be assembled. The cake needs to be baked and thoroughly chilled before assembly, so consider making it the day before. It will keep for up to 5 days in the refrigerator or for up 2 months in the freezer. The cream cheese frosting is easiest to use when it's freshly made, but it can also be made ahead and easily rewarmed before frosting the cake. It will keep for up to 1 week in the refrigerator or for up to 4 months in the freezer. Before using, microwave the cold frosting at full power for 10 seconds at a time until it begins to look slightly glossy but not melted. Once softened, beat the frosting in a stand mixer with fitted the paddle attachment until it is supple and free of lumps. (If you do not have a microwave, see page 23 for one approach to rewarming frosting.) The simple syrup can be made shortly before assembling the cake but, if made ahead of time, will keep for up to 3 weeks in the refrigerator. To store leftover cake, press plastic wrap against the cut sides; the leftover cake will keep for up to 2 days at room temperature or for up to 4 days in the refrigerator. If refrigerated, bring to room temperature before serving.

ABOVE AND BEYOND: I like to bake this cake in a square cake pan, further emphasizing the graphic stripes of cake and frosting and really accentuating the dots on top. But since square cake pans aren't very common in home kitchens, I modified the recipe to use one 8-inch round cake pan.

To replicate the square cake just how I like to make it, divide the cake batter between two 8-inch square cake pans and bake for 30 to 35 minutes. Split each baked cake into 2 even layers so that you have a total of 4 layers. The cake is delicious without any special decorations, but Lichtenstein Benday dots (see page 73) are the added flair that makes this cake a Lichtenstein Cake.

RED VELVET CAKE

2 cups (9.9 oz / 280 g) all-purpose flour

1/2 cup (2.2 oz / 62 g) cornstarch

4 teaspoons natural (not Dutch-processed) unsweetened cocoa powder

1 teaspoon baking soda

1 cup (8.6 oz / 242 g) buttermilk, at room temperature

1 teaspoon vanilla extract

1 teaspoon apple cider vinegar

12 tablespoons (6 oz / 170 g) unsalted butter, at room temperature

2 cups (14.3 oz / 400 g) granulated sugar

1 teaspoon kosher salt

6 large egg yolks (3.9 oz / 114 g), at room temperature

Red food coloring (optional)

6 large egg whites (6.6 oz / 180 g), at room temperature

1 teaspoon cream of tartar

CREAM CHEESE FROSTING

2 cups (16 oz / 454 g) cream cheese, at room temperature

1 cup (8 oz / 227 g) unsalted butter, at room temperature

1 cup (4.1 oz / 115 g) confectioners' sugar, sifted

Grated zest of 1 lemon, if not finishing the cake with Lichtenstein dots

—

Simple Syrup (page 44)

Red food coloring, optional

Preheat the oven to 350°F. Butter and flour the sides of an 8 by 3-inch round cake pan and line the bottom with a parchment paper round that has been cut to fit.

Sift the flour, cornstarch, cocoa powder, and baking soda onto a large sheet of parchment paper no fewer than five times.

In a liquid measuring cup, combine the buttermilk, vanilla, and apple cider vinegar.

In the bowl of a stand mixer fitted with the paddle attachment, beat the butter on low speed until smooth, 1 to 2 minutes. Add the granulated sugar and salt and mix on low speed until well combined. Scrape down the bowl with a rubber spatula and beat on medium speed until the mixture is fluffy, 4 to 5 minutes.

With the mixer running on medium speed, add the egg yolks one at time, mixing until well incorporated after each addition, about 30 seconds. Scrape down the bowl, and then beat on medium speed for 30 seconds.

Scrape down the bowl. With the mixer running on low speed, alternate adding the flour mixture (in three batches) and the buttermilk mixture (in two batches), beginning and ending with the flour. Mix just until combined. This is the point at which to add the food coloring; add enough to tint the batter vivid red (the color won't change during baking). Mix on low speed for 20 seconds, scrape down the bowl, and then mix for 20 seconds longer to fully incorporate the coloring. Transfer the batter to a large bowl.

Working quickly, thoroughly wash and dry the mixer bowl. Add the egg whites and cream of tartar to the bowl and whip with the whisk attachment on medium speed until the whites hold soft peaks, 3 to 5 minutes.

Using a rubber spatula and working quickly, gently fold the egg whites into the cake batter. Stop as soon as you no longer see streaks of egg white.

Pour the batter into the prepared pan and smooth the surface with an offset spatula. Bake, rotating the pan midway through baking, until the cake springs back when gently pressed in the center, 60 to 65 minutes. You can also test for doneness by listening to the cake: Remove the pan from the oven, set it on a wire rack, lower your ear to the cake, and listen. If you hear the cake snap, crackle, and pop, it needs a few more minutes in the oven. If it's quiet, it's done.

Let the cake cool in the pan on a wire rack for 30 minutes, and then run an offset spatula around the inside edge. Invert each cake onto the wire rack, lift off the pan, and remove the parchment. When the cakes are cool enough to handle, after about 20 minutes, reinvert them so the tops are facing up. Let completely cool, wrap tightly in plastic wrap, and refrigerate for at least 3 hours before cutting.

To make the frosting, in the bowl of the stand mixer fitted with the paddle attachment, beat the cream cheese and butter on medium-low speed until smooth, 1 to 2 minutes. Add the sifted confectioners' sugar in 3 additions, mixing well after each. Scrape down the bowl with a rubber spatula and add the lemon zest. Beat on medium speed until thoroughly combined and the frosting is slightly fluffy, 2 to 3 minutes.

To assemble, place the cake on a flat, stable work surface. Using a long, serrated knife, slice off the rounded top of the cake so that it is perfectly level. An even, flat top is key to the look of this dessert.

Using the serrated knife, split the cake horizontally into 2 even layers. Split each half in half again so that you have a total of 4 layers. Place the bottom layer on an 8-inch cardboard

FROSTING WITH BENDAY DOTS

To create the dots, you will need the cake to have a perfectly even and level surface and a polka-dot stencil (see Resources, page 205). Refrigerate the frosted cake until the frosting is completely firm, about 3 hours. If necessary, warm the cream cheese frosting reserved for the decorative dots. Add enough red food coloring to tint the frosting a vivid red and mix thoroughly. Then, making sure the red-colored frosting is soft and spreadable, place the polka-dot stencil on the top of the cake and press lightly to flatten it onto the frosting. Gently hold the stencil in place and, using an offet spatula, swipe the red frosting over the stencil. Lift the stencil to reveal the pattern. Alternatively, you can fit a piping bag with an $1/8$-inch tip and apply the dots freehand, creating as even of a pattern as possible. Let the cake come to room temperature before serving.

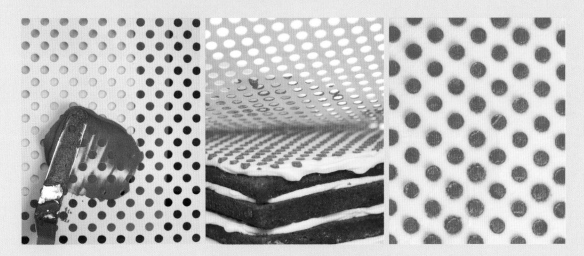

cake round or directly on the serving platter and set on top of a cake turntable, if you have one. Generously brush the surface of the cake with simple syrup.

If you're going above and beyond and will be decorating the cake with Lichtenstein Benday dots, reserve about $^1/_4$ cup (1.3 oz / 37 g) of the cream cheese frosting.

Measure out about 1 cup (5.2 oz / 148 g) of frosting and, using a small offset spatula, spread it evenly on the bottom cake layer, being careful not to let it blop over the sides. Set another cake layer on top, brush with simple syrup, and spread with 1 cup (5.2 oz / 148 g) of frosting. Repeat with a third cake layer, simple syrup, and frosting. Top with the final cake layer.

If necessary, warm and rewhip the frosting and mound 1 cup (5.2 oz / 148 g) on top of the cake in the center. Using a small offset spatula, start from the center and begin smoothing out the frosting, inching it closer and closer to the edge of the cake until the surface is completely covered. If you're going above and beyond and applying Lichtenstein Benday dots to the top of the cake (see Note), take extra care to make sure the surface of the cake is perfectly level.

The cake is best served at room temperature.

I have never understood red velvet cake.

I've seen so many divergent recipes and have heard enough urban legends to know not to trust any single description of what this cake is supposed to be. It's obvious where the "red" in the name comes from, but, to me, the "velvet" part is totally confounding because there is nothing about any of the red velvet cakes that I've eaten that warrants a comparison to velvet: they've all been either dry and spongy or oily and coarse-crumbed. The disparity in texture made me doubt that the cake has any credible history, and I suspected that "old family recipes" were just excuses to have fun eating a bright red cake. (Come on, just admit it!)

I've always politely brushed off requests to make red velvet cake and turned up my nose at the crimson cupcakes that line bakery shelves, but my quest to make a Lichtenstein Cake weakened my defenses, and I found myself in a red velvet pickle. So I decided to trace the cake's history and unravel its science. I wanted to take back the red velvet cake, to reveal its true nature and make it delicious again. I aimed to create an "authentic" red velvet cake, one that got its color from a natural chemical reaction and didn't need food coloring to be loved.

In my years as a baker, I've heard a number of claims as to the origins of the red velvet cake; the most widely circulated is that it was a cake made by the Waldorf Astoria hotel in New York. In the story, the recipe was requested by a guest and the Waldorf Astoria responded with the famous recipe along with a bill for $350. In retaliation, the jilted customer typed up the recipe and gave it to everyone she knew. I spoke with Dr. Jan Harold Brunvand, a retired professor of literature and folklore, who delved into this very subject in his book, *The Vanishing Hitchhiker*. In his research, Brunvand spent years collecting many variations on the Waldorf Astoria tale and ultimately debunked the myth, claiming it was as false as the similar tale about a Neiman Marcus cookie recipe.

With the most common origin tale busted, I moved on to the claims that the red velvet cake is a traditional Southern cake. In weeks of late-night Internet research, I discovered that many believe that the red velvet cake is a traditional Southern groom's cake with a special twist. Baked into the shape of an armadillo and covered in gray frosting, this "tradition" can be traced to the year 1989 and a romantic comedy called *Steel Magnolias*. Further down the Internet rabbit hole, I discovered the story of a baking supplies manufacturer from Austin, Texas, named Fred Adams, a man whose sales territory and a knack for clever marketing very well may have spread the red velvet cake like wildfire across the Southern states of America.

When Adams took over his family's baking-supply business in the 1920s, he devised a marketing campaign featuring an eye-catching red cake intended to help boost sales of flavored extracts and food colorings. With promotional posters of a glowing red cake and takeaway recipes for making it at home, Adams forged a marketing strategy that would soon be used by Nestlé with its Toll House Cookies. Whether red velvet cake existed before Adams co-opted the name or whether the cake was invented as a way to showcase red food coloring, butter-flavored extract, and vanilla extract is unknown, but there's no question that this was the marketing machine behind the bright red cake, catapulting it into popular culture.

Not satisfied that the Adams recipe would make a truly velveteen cake to live up to the name, I consulted Celia Sack, antiquarian cookbook expert and owner of Omnivore Books on Food, to learn more about velvet cake, which I assumed was the ancestor of red velvet cake. Celia pointed me to her section of old recipe books and pamphlets, where I found *Ballou's Monthly Magazine*, volume 33, published in 1871. Tucked between tips for using chloroform to remove paint and instructions for how to stop bleeding was the earliest recipe I found for velvet

cake. The cake called for both cream of tartar and baking soda, and was made with separated eggs. Versions of this cake began appearing in college and church pamphlets across the country, and around 1895, buttermilk began to replace water as the liquid. Fannie Farmer's 1896 recipe for velvet cake from *The Boston Cooking-School Cook Book* retained the spirit of the earlier velvet cake recipes, but employed more precision and more modern methodology than any of the others. But still, despite all my research, a non-dyed red velvet cake remained elusive, so I chose Farmer's velvet cake as the standard on which to base my own recipe for red velvet cake.

In his 1972 book *American Cookery*, James Beard suggests that artificial coloring is merely a way to enhance the color that results from the chemical reaction between the alkaline cocoa powder and acidic buttermilk in red velvet cake (but he still calls food coloring in his recipe). I thought a scientific approach might help me in my quest, so to figure out how to harness this chemical reaction and create the reddest possible cake, I spoke with Harold McGee, the king of food science and author of *On Food and Cooking*. He gave me a lesson on anthocyanins, red-purple pigments found in raw cacao beans and many other foods, and then suggested that to maximize the redness in the cake, I use "lightly roasted non-Dutched cocoa that looks reddish to start with." I went out and bought seven non-Dutched cocoa powders, ranging from Hershey's brand to the hippiest raw-food cocoa I could find at the local health-food co-op. Per Harold's instructions, I added measured amounts of an acid (buttermilk) to each cocoa powder and carefully examined the mixtures. After a battery of tests, I concluded that, to my untrained eye at least, they all looked the same. And, furthermore, although the cocoas did turn a warm brown color, they were most definitely *not* the bright hue of a red velvet cake.

Hoping that the cocoa powders just needed a bit more acid to turn bright red, I grabbed my copy of Fanny Farmer's velvet cake and turned on the oven. In my first test, I replaced half of the cornstarch in the original with natural cocoa powder. This yielded a brown cake that tasted like chocolate. Unshaken, I lessened the amount of cocoa powder and added a touch of apple cider vinegar to increase the acid, resulting in a cake with an undeniable red velvet flavor. Although the flavor was right, the color was auburn. Auburn! I was prepared for the cake to be brown, but not a gross upholstery color from the 1970s. Deflated, I reread an email that Rose Levy Beranbaum sent me when I proposed to her the idea of making a red velvet cake without food coloring. "You'll have to call it 'auburn velvet.' To my mind, calling it 'red' will disappoint if it's not red!" she wrote. She was right. Still determined to develop a red velvet cake as an homage to Lichtenstein, I took a second look at my bottle of red food coloring and decided that it might not be such a bad idea after all.

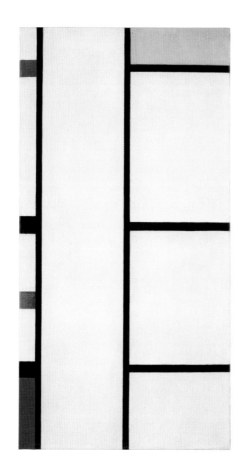

Piet Mondrian

Composition (No. III) Blanc-Jaune/Composition (No. III) with Red, Yellow, and Blue
1935–42
oil on canvas
39³/₄ in. x 20¹/₈ in.
SFMOMA, purchase through a gift of Phyllis Wattis, 98.298

———

Piet Mondrian (1872-1944) was a principal member of the Dutch avant-garde group De Stijl. He spent the better part of his career exploring the relationship between primary colors, black and white, geometric shapes, and line, all in search of universal harmony and balance. Though in reproduction Mondrian's paintings have a very graphic flatness, his finished canvases were hard-fought—the result of a labored process of painting, scraping, and repainting.

The first work of art executed on this canvas was made in Paris in 1935. When it was exhibited that year, it was known as *Composition (No. III) Blanc-Jaune* [Composition (No.III) White-Yellow]. After World War II prompted the artist to move to New York in 1940, he revisited the canvas, adjusting the placement and thickness of some of the lines and adding blue and red blocks to the left. Mondrian described his alterations to his seventeen "transatlantic" paintings—works that were begun in Europe and completed in the United States—as "bringing in a little boogie-woogie."

© 2013 Mondrian/Holtzman Trust c/o HCR International USA

MONDRIAN CAKE

MAKES ONE 16 BY 3 BY 3-INCH CAKE, SERVING 15
HANDS-ON TIME: 6 HOURS
FROM START TO FINISH: 2 DAYS

During those first few weeks visiting SFMOMA to brainstorm dessert ideas for the café, I would pass the two Mondrian pieces on display and think to myself, "I really should do something with these, but what in the world could I do with a Mondrian?" It wasn't until I was sitting with Leah at her kitchen table, browsing through a cookbook of

Victorian cakes, that I had a breakthrough. We were admiring the brilliant construction of the Battenberg cake, a traditional British cake that, when cut, looks like a pink and white checkerboard. It suddenly occurred to me that we could model a Mondrian cake on the

Battenberg cake. We rushed to the Blue Bottle kitchen and threw four loaf cakes into the oven—one white, one blue, one red, and one yellow—and I started sketching how I could cut them up and reassemble them into a Mondrian design held together with chocolate ganache. On paper it seemed easy enough, but as I got to cutting, ganaching, and squeezing the pieces together, I knew I was making either an incredibly exciting cake or a total disaster. I wrapped up the assembled piece and put it into the refrigerator to set up overnight. The next day I rushed in to see if my plan had worked. While it was far from perfect, cutting into the big, messy-looking cake and seeing the clear Mondrian pattern inside (pictured at left) was one of the highlights of my career in pastry.

NOTE: This recipe is for the Mondrian cake exactly how we make it at SFMOMA, using the same pans, tools, and methods that Leah, Tess, and I use in our work kitchen. Because this cake is so rooted in mathematics, I chose not to alter the recipe from our original—I wanted to teach you to make a cake with exactly the same proportions as the Mondrian cakes we make every day at the museum.

You'll need a few pieces of equipment to complete this recipe: a Pullman loaf pan, a cutting board at least 16 inches long, an 18 by 26-inch wire rack, an 18 by 26-inch rimmed baking sheet, a ruler, a sharp 12-inch serrated knife, a 13 by 18-inch wire rack, plastic wrap, parchment paper, and two 13 by 18-inch rimmed baking sheets.

DO AHEAD: The Mondrian cake is a multiday project that takes a bit of preparation before it can be assembled. The four cakes need to be baked and chilled for at least 3 hours before assembly, so consider making them a day or two ahead of time. They will keep for up to 5 days in the refrigerator or for up to 2 months in the freezer. The ganache is easiest to use when it is freshly made, but it can also be made ahead and easily rewarmed before using. It will keep for up to 1 week in the refrigerator. To store leftover cake, press plastic wrap against the cut sides and store for up to 3 days at room temperature or for up to 1 week in the refrigerator. If refrigerated, bring to room temperature before serving.

ABOVE AND BEYOND: If you're making this cake, you're already going above and beyond. But for absolute precision when slicing the cakes, at the café we rely on our Ateco adjustable dough divider (pictured below; see Resources, page 205). This tool helps us cut cake strips with perfectly straight edges and lines.

Rose's White Velvet Cake
(page 88; recipe doubled, see Variation)

Rose's White Velvet Cake
(page 88; tinted blue)

Rose's White Velvet Cake
(page 88; tinted yellow)

Rose's White Velvet Cake
(page 88; tinted red)

Chocolate Ganache (page 90)

STEP 1: CUTTING THE CAKE

To cut the cake, place an 18 by 26-inch wire rack in an 18 by 26-inch rimmed baking sheet and set aside.

Set the white cake on its side on a large (at least 16-inch) cutting board. Using a sharp 12-inch serrated knife, very carefully shave off the browned bottom of the loaf, removing less than $1/8$-inch, so that you have a flat, crustless side.

To cut off the top of the cake, spin the loaf 180 degrees so that the crustless bottom side is now facing the opposite direction. Measure 2 inches in from the bottom side and mark the measurement by scoring with the knife at the upper and lower edges of the loaf at both ends. Slice off the top of the cake, connecting the score marks and cutting as straight as possible. As the blade glides through the cake, make sure to slice straight down, not allowing the knife blade to veer off to the right or left.

Rotate the cake 90 degrees so that it's resting on a cut side and shave off the browned crust just as you did on the bottom. Rotate the cake 180 degrees and shave off the remaining browned side; leave the short ends untrimmed. You should have a white, crustless loaf cake measuring 16 by $3^1/2$ by 2 inches.

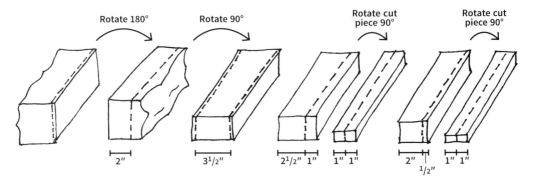

With the cake resting on a $3^1/2$-inch side, measure 1 inch from the edge and score with the knife at the upper and lower edges of the loaf. Using the same technique that you used to cut off the top of the cake, slice as straight as possible, connecting the score marks. You will now have 2 strips: one measuring 16 by 1 by 2 inches and one measuring 16 by $2^1/2$ by 2 inches. Flip the 1 by 2-inch strip onto a 2-inch side and cut it lengthwise in half, creating two 1 by 1-inch strips. Lay the strips across the wire rack, about an inch apart.

With the other piece resting on a $2^1/2$-inch side, measure $1/2$ inch from the edge and score with the knife at the upper and lower edges. Slice as straight as possible, connecting the score marks. Flip the $1/2$ by 2-inch strip onto a 2-inch side and cut lengthwise in half, creating two $1/2$ by 1-inch strips. Place on the wire rack, about an inch apart, along with the 2 by 2-inch strip that remains.

Trim the edges off of the smaller blue cake, as instructed previously, then cut the cake into two

16 by 1 by 1-inch strips. Set one of these strips on the wire rack. The remaining blue cake strip can be wrapped tightly in plastic wrap and stored in the freezer.

Repeat the same process with the yellow cake and the red cake, cutting them each into two 16 by 1 by 1-inch strips of each color. Cut one strip of each color in half lengthwise so that you have two yellow and two red $1/2$ by 1-inch strips. Place one strip of each color on the wire rack, about an inch apart, along with the other strips of cake. The remaining yellow and red cake strips can be wrapped tightly in plastic wrap and stored in the freezer.

STEP 2: ASSEMBLING THE CAKE

Before you begin assembly, review Tips for Mondrian Success (page 87).

So that you'll be able to easily wrap up the cake and transport it to the refrigerator, place a 13 by 18-inch rimmed baking sheet on the work surface with the long side parallel with the cake pieces. Pull out a 24-inch length of plastic wrap and center it along the length of the baking sheet, but leave the plastic attached to the roll. Place the sheet of parchment paper over the plastic wrap in the prepared baking sheet.

Prepare the ganache or, if you've made the ganache in advance, warm it to a pourable consistency (see Working with Chocolate Ganache, page 91).

Slowly pour or ladle ganache along the length of a cake strip, generously covering the top side of the cake. Use an offset spatula to smooth and spread the ganache, making sure the 3 exposed sides are fully enrobed (the bottom will remain uncoated). Coat all the strips in the same fashion, taking note of which one is yellow; once enrobed, it can be hard to distinguish it from the white strips. (After the cake has been assembled, the ganache that has dripped into the baking sheet can be scraped out, poured through a sieve to remove particles of cake, and used for the final coating of ganache.)

While the ganache is still fresh on the cake strips, begin assembling the cake. Carefully lift the 2 by 2-inch white cake strip, holding each end of the cake with your hands (this is the messy part!), and place it in the center of the prepared baking sheet with the uncoated side facing right. Place the blue cake strip to the left of the white cake strip, so that ganached sides of the two strips are touching. Gently but firmly use your hands to squeeze the pieces together along their length, and then spread ganache on any bare interior sides (the outside can remain bare, as the assembled cake will have a coating of ganache to finish).

Lay a 1 by 1-inch white cake strip on top of the blue strip so that ganached sides of the two strips are touching. Squeeze along the length of the cake to make sure the strips adhere, and then spread ganache on any bare interior sides.

Place the remaining 1 by 1-inch white cake strip on top of the 2 by 2-inch strip so that ganached sides of the two strips are touching, aligning it with the left edge of the 2 by 2-inch strip; it will be positioned directly in the center on top. Press firmly along the length of the cake to make sure the strips adhere, and then spread ganache on any bare interior sides.

Very carefully, as it is fragile, place the ganache-coated 1-inch side of the yellow cake strip against the left side of the uppermost 1 by 1-inch strip. Squeeze firmly along the length of the cake to make sure the strips adhere, and then spread ganache on any bare interior sides.

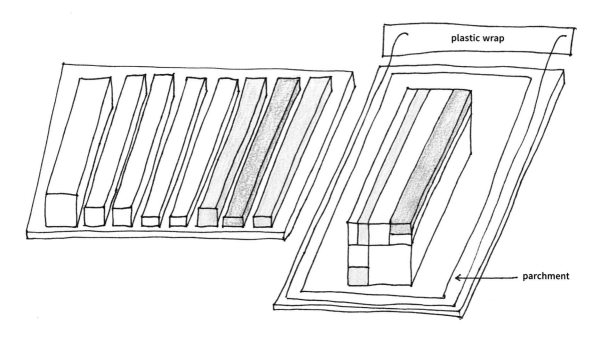

plastic wrap

parchment

Again, using great care, place the ganache-coated 1-inch side of a $^1/_2$ by 1-inch white strip against the left side of the yellow strip. Squeeze firmly along the length of the cake to make sure the strips adhere, and then spread ganache on any bare interior sides.

Carefully place the remaining $^1/_2$ by 1-inch white strip on top of the 2 by 2-inch white strip, laying it flat and ganache side down to the right of the 1 by 1-inch strip. Squeeze firmly along the length of the cake to make sure the strips adhere, and then spread ganache on the bare side.

Carefully place the red strip on top of the $^1/_2$ by 1-inch white strip, uncoated side facing up, in the last open space.

Give the cake a good squeeze up and down its length and width, using your hands and offset spatula as needed to form the cake into a perfect 3 by 3 by 16-inch loaf. Pull the parchment paper tightly up and around the sides of the cake, squeezing the sides together. Wrap the parchment up and over the top. Pull the plastic wrap up and over the top of the cake and wrap tightly. Refrigerate on the baking sheet for at least 2 hours, but preferably overnight.

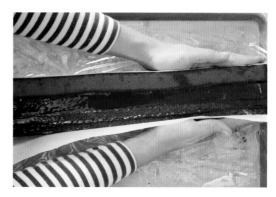

Using a rubber spatula, scrape the ganache from the baking sheet and strain through a fine-mesh strainer and refrigerate until needed.

STEP 3: FINISHING THE CAKE

Remove the cake from the refrigerator, unwrap it from the parchment paper and plastic wrap, and set it on the large cutting board. Using the serrated knife, trim and square off 1 side, making the surface level and flat. Rotate the cake 90 degrees and repeat with the 3 other sides.

Set a 13 by 18-inch wire rack in a 13 by 18-inch rimmed baking sheet. Place the cake lengthwise on the rack.

Warm the ganache once again to a pourable consistency (see Working with Chocolate Ganache, page 91) in a 2-cup liquid measuring cup if you plan to pour it instead of ladle it. The ganache should be smooth, shiny, and absolutely free of lumps. Pour or ladle a generous layer of ganache over the top of the cake, letting it run down the sides. Lightly tap the baking sheet to help distribute the ganache, using an offset spatula to help smooth the sides of the cake. Transfer the rack to a clean baking sheet, scrape up the ganache that dripped onto the baking sheet, and strain it through the sieve to use again. Refrigerate the cake, uncovered, until the ganache is firm, at least 2 hours.

Remove the cake from the refrigerator and cut a piece of parchment paper exactly the size of the top of the cake. Place it on the cake and, if needed, trim any overhanging edges with scissors. Grabbing the cake by the short ends, flip it over so that the parchment paper is on the bottom, and set it on the wire rack.

Apply another coat of ganache in the same manner as the first. Refrigerate the cake, uncovered, for at least 2 hours or up to 1 week.

Remove the cake from the refrigerator and transfer it to the large cutting board. Using the serrated knife, trim about $1/4$ inch off of the end to reveal the Mondrian design. Cut the cake into 1-inch slices and serve at room temperature.

TIPS FOR MONDRIAN SUCCESS

Your first Mondrian Cake will be thrilling but, inevitably, it will be less than perfect. Over the years, Leah, Tess, and I have gathered some tips and tricks that have helped us make the most perfect cakes possible.

STAY CALM AND WORK QUICKLY

There are a lot of steps to making a Mondrian Cake, but, believe it or not, it isn't a terribly difficult cake to make. Take it one step at a time and don't second-guess yourself.

MEASURE TWICE AND CUT ONCE

Measuring and slicing your cake strips as carefully and evenly as possible is what will earn you a geometrically perfect slice of square cake with straight lines between the color blocks. That being said, each of us has only ever made one or two Mondrians that we would consider perfect. It is cake, after all.

GANACHE IS THE GLUE

The most common flaw in a slice of Mondrian Cake are holes between the blocks, the result of air gaps between the cake strips. To avoid air gaps, make sure that all sides of contact are covered with ganache, the glue that holds everything together.

FREEZING CAN HELP

We've had luck freezing the cake strips overnight before assembly to make transferring the skinniest pieces a little easier. If your strip breaks, don't fret—just go ahead and reassemble it on the cake. Because of the way the finished cake is sliced for serving, it's rare that you will see such flaws.

KEEP UNGANACHED SIDES FACING OUT

In order to minimize the amount of ganache you use and to make assembly slightly less messy, try to position the unganached sides of the cake strips facing the outer edge of the cake.

STEP BACK FOR PERSPECTIVE

When your hands are covered in ganache and everything looks like a mess, it's easy to forget that you're simply assembling a grid. Sometimes taking a step back is the best way to reorient yourself and get a fresh perspective on the final assembly.

SMOOSHING HELPS

Along with a nice coating of fresh ganache, smooshing, believe it or not, helps make nice and neat lines. Again, it's all about avoiding air holes and creating the straightest possible lines.

Don't be discouraged if it looks like a mess once assembled. Everyone's Mondrian Cake is a mess from the outside. I like to think of the Mondrian design as a shiny, beautiful pearl inside a craggy, old oyster shell.

Rose's White Velvet Cake

MAKES ONE LOAF CAKE
HANDS-ON TIME: 15 MINUTES
FROM START TO FINISH: 1 1/4 HOURS

When teaching myself to bake, *The Cake Bible* by Rose Levy Beranbaum was my textbook. In the tiny kitchen of my first studio apartment, I pored through the pages, and Rose's fail-safe recipes, fun stories, and scientific approach laid the groundwork for my future career. For my twenty-fourth birthday, I threw myself a party, inviting my friends over to serve them all of my favorite cakes from my new bible. By far, the most crowd-pleasing one was Rose's White Velvet Cake with dark chocolate ganache poured over the top.

Nine years later, I was designing the Mondrian Cake for the SFMOMA café and needed a pure white cake that was both sturdy enough to be cut into thin strips and delicious enough to warrant the eight dollars I would have to charge for a slice of this labor-intensive cake. My mind went back to my early baking days and I knew there was only one cake that would fit the bill: Rose's White Velvet Cake. Indeed, it's the perfect cake, and the Mondrian Cake has become the most iconic dessert at our museum café. Just like my twenty-fourth birthday cake, it's paired with chocolate ganache and pleases crowds . . . only it's slightly more complicated to make.

NOTE: This recipe is for baking a loaf cake to make the Mondrian Cake. To make a standard round cake, you can bake the batter in an 8 by 3-inch round cake; the baking time will be 55 to 60 minutes.

DO AHEAD: Wrapped tightly in plastic wrap, the cake will keep for up to 5 days in the refrigerator or up to 2 months in the freezer.

---

4 1/2 large egg whites (5 oz / 135 g), at room temperature

1 cup (8.6 oz / 242 g) milk, at room temperature

2 1/4 teaspoons vanilla extract

2 1/3 cup (10.7 oz / 299 g) cake flour (see Note, page 28)

1 1/2 cups (10.6 oz / 300 g) sugar

4 teaspoons baking powder

3/4 teaspoon kosher salt

12 tablespoons (6 oz / 170 g) unsalted butter, cut into pieces and at room temperature

Red, yellow, and blue food coloring (see page 30)

Preheat the oven to 350°F. Butter and flour the sides of a 16 by 4 by 4-inch loaf pan (also called a Pullman loaf pan) and line the bottom with a parchment paper rectangle that has been cut to fit.

In a medium bowl, whisk together the egg whites, $^1/_2$ cup (4.3 oz / 121 g) of the milk, and the vanilla.

Sift the flour, sugar, baking powder, and salt into the bowl of a stand mixer fitted with the paddle attachment, and mix on low speed for 30 seconds. Add the remaining $^1/_2$ cup (4.3 oz / 121 g) of milk and mix on low speed until moistened, about 15 seconds. Add the butter and beat on medium speed for $1^1/_2$ minutes or until smooth and aerated. Scrape down the sides of the bowl with a rubber spatula. Add the egg mixture in 3 batches, mixing on medium speed for 20 seconds and then scraping down the bowl after each addition. This is the point at which to add the food coloring; add enough to tint the batter vivid red, yellow, or blue (the color doesn't change during baking). Mix on low speed for 20 seconds, scrape down the bowl, and then mix for 20 seconds longer to fully incorporate the coloring.

Transfer the batter to the prepared pan and smooth the surface with an offset spatula. Bake, rotating the pan midway through baking, until the cake springs back when gently pressed in the center, 45 to 50 minutes ($1^1/_4$ hours if the recipe is doubled). You can also test for doneness by listening to the cake: Remove the pan from the oven, set it on a wire rack, lower your ear to the cake, and listen. If you hear the cake snap, crackle, and pop, it needs a few more minutes in the oven. If it's quiet, it's done.

Let the cake cool on a wire rack for 30 minutes, and then run an offset spatula around the inside of the pan. Invert the cake onto the wire rack, lift off the pan, and remove the parchment. When the cake is cool enough to handle, after about 20 minutes, reinvert it so the top is facing up. Let cool completely, wrap tightly in plastic wrap and refrigerate for at least 3 hours before cutting.

VARIATION

For the white Mondrian loaf, double the recipe and omit the food coloring. Increase the baking time to about $1^1/_4$ hours.

Chocolate Ganache

MAKES 5²/₃ CUPS (51.4 OZ/1438 G)

HANDS-ON TIME: 10 MINUTES

FROM START TO FINISH: 10 MINUTES

The key to perfect ganache is high-quality chocolate and the thorough emulsification of the ingredients. I like to use an immersion blender (see page 23) to create a smooth, silky texture, but a food processor works, too.

DO AHEAD: Stored in an airtight container, the ganache will keep for up to 1 week in the refrigerator. See Working with Chocolate Ganache, opposite, for reheating instructions.

---

24 ounces (672 g) high-quality bittersweet chocolate (62% to 70% cacao), finely chopped

3 cups (25 oz / 696 g) heavy cream

¹/₄ cup plus 2 tablespoons (3.2 oz / 90 g) hot water (180°F to 190°F)

Put the chocolate in a medium heatproof bowl.

In a small, heavy-bottomed saucepan over medium-low heat, warm the cream, stirring occasionally, until it registers 180°F to 190°F on a digital thermometer and bubbles start to form around the edges. (Alternatively, put the cream into a microwavable liquid measuring cup or bowl and microwave at full power for about 60 seconds.)

Pour the hot cream over the chocolate and, using a rubber spatula, stir until the chocolate is mostly melted. Add the hot water and blend with an immersion blender or transfer to a food processor and process until the chocolate is completely melted and the mixture is smooth and shiny. (Alternatively, set the bowl over a saucepan of just simmered water and whisk until the chocolate is melted and the mixture is smooth.)

WORKING WITH CHOCOLATE GANACHE

Chocolate ganache is a simple combination of chocolate and heavy cream, milk, and/or water. When warm, it's a shiny, pourable liquid; room temperature, it's a deliciously spreadable frosting; or chilled, it can be rolled into balls and made into truffles. The key to working successfully with ganache lies in the temperature: heating it, cooling it, or letting it stand at room temperature until it's the perfect consistency for the specific dessert you're making.

Ganache can be kept for up to 1 week in the refrigerator, and is very easy to rewarm to a pourable consistency with the help of a microwave. Working in intervals of 10 to 20 seconds and stirring often, heat the ganache until it is free of lumps but not so hot that the edges start to burn. Reheating ganache is much harder without a microwave. Without a microwave, to keep ganache warm during use, put it into a glass liquid measuring cup and rest the cup in a bowl of warm water (110°F to 120°F).

There is no quick way to get chocolate ganache to room temperature (for the Kudless S'mores, page 111, for example), it just takes a little advance planning. Ganache must be made 3 to 4 hours ahead of time and left at room temperature until it is the smooth and spreadable texture of soft butter. Alternatively, it can be made ahead, refrigerated, and then left out at room temperature for about 4 hours to come to temperature.

Richard Diebenkorn
Ocean Park #122
1980
oil and charcoal on canvas
100 in. x 80 ⁵/₈ in.
SFMOMA, Charles H. Land
    Family Foundation Fund
    purchase, 80.389

———

Born in Oregon and raised in San Francisco, Richard Diebenkorn (1922–93) had become one of the region's leading painters and teachers before he moved to southern California in 1966 to accept a teaching position at UCLA. Soon thereafter, he launched a series of geometric abstractions called *Ocean Park*—a reference to a section of Santa Monica near the beach where he maintained a studio once occupied by painter Sam Francis. Resulting in some 150 pictures made from 1967 to 1988, *Ocean Park* marks the artist's most sustained investigation.

One of the largest works in the series, the luminous *Ocean Park #122* is composed of warm-toned horizontal bands of color that reward slow looking. Characteristic of Diebenkorn's canvases, it bears ample evidence of the artist's process: places where it has been painted, scraped away, and repainted, with the traces of earlier decisions visible in the surface of the finished canvas.

DIEBENKORN TRIFLE

MAKES 10 INDIVIDUAL TRIFLES
HANDS-ON TIME: 2 HOURS
FROM START TO FINISH: 8 HOURS

Although my love of Wayne Thiebaud's work runs deep, Richard Diebenkorn's oil paintings are what I want fill my house with; they're the paintings I would love to see when I wake up every morning. Much to my delight, the museum planned a special Diebenkorn gallery within one of its seventy-fifth anniversary shows, and I immediately knew which piece I would work with and exactly what dessert I would make for it. A huge painting from his *Ocean Park* series, *Ocean Park #122* is a composition of sunny, Southern California–colored horizontal stripes that, to me, looked just like an old-fashioned trifle.

A trifle is a British dessert traditionally made in a large footed glass dish with straight sides that showcase the layers of cake, cream, custard, and fruit. I envisioned individual trifles, and found simple glass cups to fill with génoise cake, lemon mousse, lemon curd, and pomegranate gelée. A génoise cake is a traditional Italian cake that has a light-as-a-feather texture and stays beautifully soft in frozen desserts. Creamy and concentrated lemon curd, which is heavenly on its own, is transformed into a light and airy mousse with just a few ingredients: yogurt adds a bit of tang and whipped cream adds lightness. For an added kick of summery flavor, I moistened the cake layers with simple syrup spiked with raspberry eau-de-vie. The trifle was a beautiful—and delicious—homage to the painting that I only wish I could have in my house.

NOTE: This recipe uses lemon curd in two ways: as a base for the mousse and straight-up as a layer in the trifle. If you make one full batch of Lemon Curd (page 49), you'll have all you need for the mousse and for layering.

DO AHEAD: I recommend assembling this trifle one day before serving, which allows the cake to soften and meld with the other layers in the dessert. The génoise cake needs to be baked and thoroughly chilled before assembly, so consider making it the day before that (two days before serving). Wrapped tightly in plastic wrap, it will keep for up to 5 days in the refrigerator or for up 2 months in the freezer. The lemon curd takes 3 to 4 hours to set, so consider preparing it while the cake is baking; it can be kept for up to 1 week in the refrigerator or for 4 months in the freezer. The simple syrup can be made shortly before assembling the trifle but, if made ahead of time, will keep for up to 3 weeks in the refrigerator. The lemon mousse and the pomegranate gelée should be made during the assembly of the trifle. Any leftovers can be stored in an airtight container or with the tops of the cups covered with plastic wrap for up to 2 days in the refrigerator.

ABOVE AND BEYOND: We use clear glass cups from CB2 (see Resources, page 205) and $2^1/2$-inch and 3-inch round cookie cutters for cutting the cake (the cup is slightly tapered, so two sizes are necessary).

GÉNOISE

6 large eggs (10.5 oz / 300 g)

$^1/4$ cup (1.8 oz / 50 g) sugar

$^1/2$ cup (2.5 oz / 70 g) all-purpose flour

$^1/2$ cup (2.2 oz / 62 g) cornstarch

$^1/4$ cup (2 oz / 57 g) unsalted butter, melted

2 teaspoons vanilla extract

—

$2^3/4$ cups (23.4 oz / 660 g) Lemon Curd (page 49), at room temperature, for filling

—

Simple Syrup (page 44) or
Simple Syrup with Raspberry Eau-de-Vie
(page 44; see Variation)

LEMON MOUSSE

2 gelatin sheets, or $1^1/_2$ teaspoons powdered gelatin

$^1/_4$ cup (2.1 oz / 60 g) water

$^3/_4$ cup (6.2 oz / 174 g) heavy cream

$^3/_4$ cup (6.5 oz / 182 g) plain whole-milk yogurt

1 cup (8.5 oz / 240 g) Lemon Curd (page 49), at room temperature

POMEGRANATE GELÉE

3 gelatin sheets, or $2^1/_4$ teaspoons powdered gelatin

1 cup (8.6 oz / 240 g) unsweetened pomegranate juice

2 tablespoons sugar

To make the génoise, preheat the oven to 350°F. Line an ungreased 13 by 18-inch rimmed baking sheet with parchment paper.

Bring 2 to 3 inches of water to a simmer in a saucepan.

In your mixer bowl or another clean, medium heatproof bowl, whisk together the eggs and sugar. Set the bowl on the saucepan, making sure the bottom does not touch the simmering water, and stir constantly until the sugar has dissolved and the mixture is slightly warm (about 110°F on a digital thermometer), 2 to 3 minutes.

Meanwhile, sift the flour and cornstarch into a small bowl. Combine the melted butter and vanilla in a medium bowl.

In the bowl of a stand mixer fitted with the whisk attachment, beat the eggs and sugar on low speed for 30 seconds. Increase the speed to medium and beat until the mixture is tripled in volume and pale yellow in color, 4 to 5 minutes. Measure out 1 cup (2.3 oz / 65 g) of the whipped egg mixture and gently whisk it into the butter mixture.

Transfer the remaining whipped egg mixture to a large bowl and evenly sift over one-half of the flour mixture. Using a rubber spatula or balloon whisk, quickly and gently fold the flour into eggs until no streaks of flour remain. Repeat with the remaining flour mixture. Fold in the butter mixture.

Pour the batter into the prepared baking sheet and smooth with an offset spatula. Bake until the cake is barely golden and pulls away from sides of the baking sheet, 15 to 20 minutes.

Let the cake cool in the baking sheet on a wire rack for 30 minutes. Run an offset spatula around the inside of the baking sheet and invert the cake onto the wire rack. Remove the parchment paper, then reinvert the cake so the top is facing up. Let cool to room temperature, and then return the cake to the baking sheet. Wrap the baking sheet tightly in plastic wrap and refrigerate until the cake is cold, at least 3 hours.

Have ready ten 13-ounce straight-sided clear glass cups on a rimmed baking sheet.

Unwrap the génoise. Using a round cookie cutter of the same diameter as the bottom of the cups, cut out 10 circles from the génoise, reserving the remaining half of the cake for the second layer of circles. It's important that the circles fit tightly in the bottom of the cups because any space will allow the mousse to seep between the cup and the cake. Put a circle in each cup, and then brush the cake with simple syrup.

To make the mousse, if you're using gelatin sheets, fill a medium bowl with ice water and submerge the sheets in the water. If you're using powdered gelatin, pour the water into a small bowl and sprinkle the gelatin evenly over the surface. Let either stand for 5 to 10 minutes.

Meanwhile, in the bowl of a stand mixer fitted with the whisk attachment, whip the cream on medium speed until it holds medium-soft peaks, about 2 minutes. Alternatively, whip the cream in a large bowl with a hand mixer or whisk. Set aside in the refrigerator.

If using gelatin sheets, lift the softened sheets out of the bowl, and squeeze out the excess water. Place them or the bloomed powdered gelatin in a microwavable bowl or in a small saucepan and microwave at full power for 5 to 10 seconds or warm over low heat for 30 seconds to 1 minute, stirring often, until the mixture is fluid. Transfer to a medium bowl. Whisk the yogurt into the gelatin mixture in 3 batches, mixing until smooth after each addition. Whisk in the lemon curd, and then fold in the whipped cream until no white streaks remain.

Use a spoon or a piping bag fitted with a $1/2$-inch plain tip to distribute the mousse onto the cake layer in the cups, dividing it evenly. You should have about a 1-inch layer of mousse in each cup.

Using a round cookie cutter of the same diameter as the midsection of the cups, cut out 10 circles from the génoise. Place a circle on top of the mousse in each cup, and then brush the cake with simple syrup.

Stir the lemon curd to break up any lumps. Transfer to a piping bag fitted with a $1/2$-inch plain tip or a liquid measuring cup, and then pour curd on top of the cake layer in each cup to a depth of about $1/2$ inch. Refrigerate for at least 30 minutes while you make the gelée.

To make the pomegranate gelée, if you're using gelatin sheets, fill a medium bowl with ice water and submerge the sheets in the water. If you're using powdered gelatin, pour $1/4$ cup (2.1 oz / 60 g) of the pomegranate juice into a small bowl and sprinkle the gelatin evenly over the surface. Let either stand for 5 to 10 minutes.

In a small saucepan over medium heat, warm the remaining $3/4$ cup (6.4 oz / 180 g) of pomegranate juice and the sugar, stirring, until the sugar dissolves, about 5 minutes. Remove from the heat. If using gelatin sheets, lift the softened sheets out of the bowl, squeeze out the excess water, and stir the gelatin into the juice mixture until dissolved. If using powdered gelatin, add the bloomed gelatin to the juice mixture and stir until dissolved. Let cool until the gelée registers about 95°F on a digital thermometer.

Divide the gelée evenly among the cups. To avoid creating a big hole in the lemon curd when you add the gelée, hold a spoon just above the curd and slowly pour the gelée into it, letting the liquid run over the spoon and fall gently onto the curd, creating a perfect little stripe of red.

Loosely cover the cups with plastic wrap and refrigerate for at least 5 hours before serving; the trifle is most delicious when the cake has had time to soften and meld with the other layers. Serve chilled.

Rineke Dijkstra
De Panne, Belgium,
  August 7, 1992
1992
Chromogenic print
66^1/$_8$ in. x 55^{11}/$_{16}$ in.
Courtesy the artist and
  Marian Goodman
  Gallery, New York & Paris
——
The first piece Dutch photographer Rineke Dijkstra (born 1959) considers truly important to her is an image of herself standing in a tiled shower in a striped bathing suit titled *Self-Portrait, Marnixbad, Amsterdam, Netherlands, June 19, 1991*. The following summer, Dijkstra, who had been doing editorial work, took her 4 x 5 camera to Hilton Head. There she began photographing adolescent bathers, pursuing the subject for the next decade at beaches in Belgium, Croatia, Poland, the United Kingdom, the Ukraine, and again in the United States. Of all of the works in the *Beach Portraits* series, the tense dark-haired girl in a striped one-piece in *De Panne, Belgium*, most directly echoes the self-portrait. Dijkstra has continued to make large-scale color images of people at inherently transitional times of life, from young Israeli soldiers and Portuguese bullfighters to new mothers just after giving birth.

DIJKSTRA ICEBOX CAKE

MAKES 4 INDIVIDUAL ICEBOX CAKES
HANDS-ON TIME: 30 MINUTES
FROM START TO FINISH: 13 HOURS

Rineke Dijkstra is a contemporary photographer whose images I mimicked for a short time as a photography student. Cleaning out a closet, I recently stumbled across the old photos: portraits of myself in a vintage bathing suit made soggy by a dip in our backyard hot tub, my face flushed from the shock of leaping out of the hot water onto the rain-soaked grass. Those self-portraits and the Dijkstra originals that inspired them bring back strong memories of my senior year in college.

For the Dijkstra retrospective at SFMOMA, I knew that our dessert would be based on one of her beach portraits, the photos that had captivated me in college. Her harshly lit, swimsuit-clad subjects seemed awkward and in conflict with the quiet, cold-looking beaches on which they were standing, and I wanted to create both a dessert and a serving plate that would capture the same kind of disconnect. We all loved the graphic black and white stripes of the bathing suit on the girl in *De Panne, Belgium, August 7, 1992*, so Leah and Tess started testing an icebox cake—just like the classic Cool Whip concoction—by layering extra-dark chocolate sablé cookies with whipped cream. I grabbed my camera and headed out to the seashore to photograph a setting similar to the one in the original—a soft blue sky, strong horizon line, and saturated sand—to turn into photo coasters for use as individual plates. Once completed, the icebox cake atop the photo coaster was an eye-catching and delicious homage to one of my favorite photographs—and a more inspired tribute to Dijkstra than my gangly legs hanging out of a saggy bathing suit.

DO AHEAD: This cake must be assembled at least 12 hours before serving for the cookies to soften and become a delicious and forkable cake. The chocolate sablé dough must be rolled out, cut, and chilled before baking, so consider making it the day before that (two days before serving). The whipped cream should be made just before the ice box cake is assembled. Stored in an airtight container, the icebox cakes will keep for up to 2 days in the refrigerator.

ABOVE AND BEYOND: This dessert is delicious no matter what you serve it on. But it's really easy, quick, and satisfying to take your own photos and then have them made into coasters; see Resources (page 205) for more information. When not topped with dessert, beach scene coasters are a charming conversation-starter for your next cocktail party.

Chocolate Sablé Dough (page 168; see Variation)
1^1/$_2$ cups (12.4 oz / 348 g) cold heavy cream
2 tablespoons confectioners' sugar

Set the sablé dough on a large sheet of parchment paper and press it into a flat, even, rectangle measuring about 5 by 6 inches. Lay a second sheet of parchment paper on top and roll out the dough to an even ^{1}/$_8$ to ^{1}/$_4$-inch thickness. Remove the top sheet of parchment and, using a 2^1/$_2$-inch round cookie cutter, cut out circles of dough; you will need a total of 24 cookies. The dough will be soft, so don't try to remove the circles until after chilling. Slide the parchment paper with the dough onto a baking sheet, cover with plastic wrap, and refrigerate until the dough is cold and firm, at least 45 minutes or up to 2 days. The longer the dough chills, the less it will spread during baking.

Position racks in the upper and lower thirds of the oven. Preheat the oven to 350°F. Line 2 baking sheets with parchment paper.

Use a small metal spatula to transfer the dough circles to the prepared baking sheets, spacing them about 1 inch apart. Because this dough toughens too much when rerolled, we save any cookie dough scraps and bake them as snacks for our café employees. They are best baked on their own baking sheet, with the baking time reduced by 1 to 2 minutes.

Bake until crisp, about 6 minutes, rotating the baking sheets midway through baking. (Note: because the sablés don't change color during baking, it's wise to bake a test batch of one or two cookies to check baking time for your oven before committing your whole batch; see Baking Times, page 25.) Let cool on the baking sheets for 10 minutes, and then transfer the cookies to a wire rack. Let cool to room temperature.

In the bowl of a stand mixer fitted with the whisk attachment, whip the cream and confectioners' sugar on medium speed until the cream holds medium-soft peaks, about 2 minutes. Alternatively, whip the cream and confectioners' sugar in a large bowl with a hand mixer or whisk. If you're not ready to use the whipped cream, cover with plastic wrap and refrigerate for up to 1 hour.

Set a cookie on your work surface; have the rest of them nearby. Fit a piping bag with a $1/2$-inch plain tip and fill the bag about halfway with whipped cream. Position the tip about $1/4$ inch above the cookie and, holding the bag stationary and perpendicular to the surface, pipe whipped cream onto the cookie until the cream forms a circle about $1/4$ inch thick that reaches the edge of the cookie. Top with a second cookie. Repeat the layering until you have a stack of 6 cookies separated by 5 layers of cream (do not pipe cream onto the sixth cookie). Repeat with the remaining cookies and whipped cream; refill the piping bag as needed.

Place the stacks on a large plate and cover carefully with plastic wrap. Refrigerate for at least 12 hours to let the layers meld into a forkable cake. Serve chilled.

Frida Kahlo
Frieda and Diego Rivera
1931
oil on canvas
39³/₈ in. x 31 in.
SFMOMA, Albert M. Bender
   Collection, gift of Albert
   M. Bender, 36.6061

———

Adapting the form of a traditional marriage portrait, Mexican artist Frida Kahlo (1907–54) made this painting of herself and famed muralist Diego Rivera during the first of two extended stays in the Bay Area, where Rivera painted murals in 1931 and again in 1940. Although she has gone on to be one of the most enduringly popular painters of all time, here Kahlo shows her new husband as the artist. He wears workman's clothes and boots and carries brushes and a palette as she stands deferentially by his side.

The painting is dedicated to the couple's friend and longtime supporter Albert M. Bender. The banderole held by a bird reads, in Spanish: "Here you see us, me, Frieda Kahlo, with my beloved husband Diego Rivera. I painted these portraits in the beautiful city of San Francisco, California, for our friend Mr. Albert Bender, and it was in the month of April of the year 1931."

© 2013 Banco de Mexico Diego Rivera & Frida Kahlo Museums Trust, Mexico, D.F. / Artists Rights Society (ARS), New York

KAHLO WEDDING COOKIES

MAKES ABOUT 80 COOKIES
HANDS-ON TIME: 45 MINUTES
FROM START TO FINISH: 6 HOURS

In 2002, I took a trip to Mexico for Día de los Muertos. I decided to immerse myself in all things Frida Kahlo. Armed with the 500-page biography by Hayden Hererra, I explored her Mexico City neighborhoods and made a pact to grow my hair long, braiding it into nests of ribbons and flowers, just like Frida. Years later, when planning new desserts for SFMOMA's seventy-fifth anniversary show, I spent a lot of time looking at Frida Kahlo's *Frieda and Diego Rivera*, one of the most beloved paintings on the SFMOMA walls. Although I'm captivated by the piece as a whole, what I love the most about it are the tiny little details: the bird with the ribbon; the lovely way Frida wrote the year, 1931, in the inscription; and her tiny turquoise shoes embellished with a sweet floral pattern. All of those details seemed perfect to bring together as a takeaway sweet, our first dessert packaged for enjoying outside of the Rooftop Garden. We decided to fill a decorated box with Mexican wedding cookies that we made using *nocino*, an Italian walnut liqueur, to enhance the toasted walnut flavor. Formed into little balls and tucked into the box, the cookies would be like little jewels, and a perfect homage to the wedding of Frida and Diego.

To design the package, I enlisted the help of Holly Bobisuthi, an incredible artist specializing in printmaking and metal arts, who, coincidentally, has waist-length hair woven into elaborate crowns around her head—the very embodiment of the person I wanted to become (but never did) during my Frida holiday! Holly created a lovely two-color linocut design, perfectly aligned so that the bow of the pink ribbon that we had printed with the wedding inscription would nestle right into the bird's beak. She even incorporated the turquoise and red color scheme of Frida's shoes into a sticker for sealing the package. Stamped with a tiny halo of flowers encircling the number 1931, the sticker—inspired by that tiny element that I loved so much in Frida's painting—was the perfect finishing touch to the beautiful presentation.

NOTE: If *nocino* is not available, vanilla extract can take its place. The key to creating a nice, spherical cookie is to thoroughly chill the dough before baking. The bottoms will flatten slightly, but the cookies will stay round otherwise.

DO AHEAD: Stored in an airtight container, the toasted walnuts can be frozen for up to 2 months. The cookie dough must be chilled before and after shaping; at either stage, it can be refrigerated, covered tightly with plastic wrap, for up to 5 days. Stored in an airtight container, the baked, unsugared cookies will keep for up to 4 days at room temperature.

ABOVE AND BEYOND: The Kahlo Wedding Cookies are absolutely delicious on their own, but if you want to capture the details of the *Frieda and Diego Rivera* painting as we do at the museum, it's all about the packaging. See Resources on page 205 for ordering the materials to create your own box, craft paper sticker, and custom ribbon, and download templates to make your own bird and sticker stamps from www.modernartdesserts.com.

---

1 cup (4 oz / 114 g) walnuts

1/2 cup (2 oz / 57 g) confectioners' sugar, plus more for rolling

1 cup (8 oz / 227 g) unsalted butter, at room temperature

1 teaspoon Maldon sea salt (see page 31)

1 tablespoon *nocino* (see Note, above)

1 3/4 cups (8.6 oz / 245 g) all-purpose flour

In a medium, heavy-bottomed skillet, toast the walnuts over medium heat, shaking often, until fragrant and lightly browned, about 5 minutes. Transfer the walnuts to a bowl or plate and freeze until thoroughly chilled, at least 1 hour or for up to 2 months.

Place the frozen walnuts (they're more easily processed when they're cold) and $1/4$ cup (1 oz / 28 g) of the confectioners' sugar in a food processor and pulse until the mixture resembles coarse sand.

Combine the flour and walnut mixture in a medium bowl and set aside. In the bowl of a stand mixer fitted with the paddle attachment, beat the butter on low speed until smooth, 1 to 2 minutes. Sift in the remaining $1/4$ cup (1 oz / 28 g) of confectioners' sugar, add the salt, and mix on low speed until combined. Scrape down the bowl with a rubber spatula, and then beat on medium speed until the mixture is light and fluffy, 4 to 5 minutes. Add the *nocino* and beat until incorporated, about 20 seconds. Scrape down the bowl, then add the flour mixture and mix on low speed just until the dough is uniform, about 15 seconds. Cover the bowl tightly with plastic wrap and refrigerate for at least 3 hours or up to 5 days.

Portion the chilled dough into teaspoon-sized (0.25 oz / 7 g) pieces, and then roll each piece into a ball between your hands. Set the balls on a large plate, cover with plastic wrap, and refrigerate for at least 30 minutes, or up to 1 week.

Position racks in the upper and lower thirds of the oven. Preheat the oven to 350°F. Line 2 baking sheets with parchment paper.

Place the chilled balls on the prepared baking sheets, spacing them about 1 inch apart. Bake, rotating the baking sheets midway through baking, until the cookies are fragrant and lightly golden around the edges, 10 to 12 minutes.

Let the cookies cool for a few minutes on the baking sheets, and then use a spatula to transfer them to a wire rack to finish cooling. Once the baking sheets are no longer warm, bake the remaining dough balls and let the cookies cool completely.

Just before serving, sift about $1/2$ cup (2 oz / 57 g) of confectioners' sugar into a medium bowl. Roll the cooled cookies in the sugar until coated on all sides.

Barnett Newman
Zim Zum I
1969
weathering steel
96 in. x 72^1/$_2$ in. x 180 in.
SFMOMA, purchase through a gift of
   Phyllis Wattis, 98.295

Known best for deceptively simple paintings characterized by vertical lines, or "zips," abstract expressionist Barnett Newman (1905–70) also occasionally made sculpture. *Zim Zum I*, the last fabricated during his lifetime, consists of two staggered zigzag walls that one can walk through. Both its title and form refer to the kabbalistic notion of a divine contraction that enabled God to make space for the creation of the universe.

Zim Zum I was constructed at Lippincott, in North Haven, Connecticut, a foundry established in 1966 that allowed artists to work on an industrial scale. Newman made the piece to include in the Hakone Open-Air Museum's *First International Exhibition of Modern Sculpture*. His original specifications for the piece indicated that it should be twelve rather than eight feet high. However, at that scale, it would have been too costly to ship to Japan. Fifteen years after the artist's death, his estate had the larger version fabricated, which was shown for the first time in New York in 1992.

BUILD YOUR OWN NEWMAN

MAKES 4 EDIBLE SCULPTURES
HANDS-ON TIME: 30 MINUTES
FROM START TO FINISH: 1 HOUR

After Richard Serra put the kibosh on the cookie plate inspired by his work (see page 16), I was determined to design another assemble-it-yourself cookie project. *Zim Zum I*, the large weathered-steel sculpture that often becomes a hide-and-seek passageway for the young visitors to the Rooftop Garden, was the perfect muse. We measured the panels of the sculpture and scaled them down, making salted chocolate sablé cookies in a similar rust-brown color and in, proportionally, the same dimensions as the original. At the café, we serve a stack of 8 cookies and a little crock of chocolate ganache that can be used to hold them together.

Assembling the cookie replica of *Zim Zum I* is a pretty challenging feat under ordinary circumstances, but for the photo in this book, I was determined to have the assembled cookies photographed with the sculpture behind them. What I didn't realize was that, in order to get this photograph, we would need to climb two ladders up to the roof of the SFMOMA, perch a sheet pan over the ledge, and I would have to assemble the cookies in hurricane force winds while simultaneously holding lighting equipment. Let's just say assembling your own *Zim Zum I* on the roof of your home is not advised; these cookies will taste just as delicious from the comfort of your cozy kitchen.

NOTE: This recipe yields a few more cookies than are needed for the 4 sculptures—perfect for snacking on as you build your masterpieces. If you have any extra chocolate ganache, you can either assemble more sculptures or use it to make some hot chocolate (Fuller Hot Chocolate, page 191) to eat with your cookies.

DO AHEAD: Covered with plastic wrap, the rolled and cut sablé dough will keep for up to 2 days in the refrigerator. Stored in an airtight container, the baked sablés will keep for up to 2 days at room temperature. The ganache can be made ahead and stored in an airtight container in the refrigerator for up to 1 week. See Working with Chocolate Ganache, page 91, for reheating instructions.

Chocolate Sablé Dough (page 168)

CHOCOLATE GANACHE

4 ounces (112 g) high-quality bittersweet chocolate (62% to 70% cacao), finely chopped

$^1/_2$ cup (4.1 oz / 116 g) heavy cream

Set the sablé dough on a large sheet of parchment paper and press it into a flat, even, rectangle measuring about 5 by 6 inches. Lay a second sheet of parchment paper on top and roll out the dough to an even $^1/_8$ to $^1/_4$-inch thickness. Remove the top sheet of parchment and, using a large knife or pizza wheel, cut the dough into $1^1/_2$ by 3-inch rectangles. The dough will be soft, so don't try to remove the rectangles until after chilling. Slide the parchment paper with the dough onto a baking sheet, cover with plastic wrap, and refrigerate until the dough is cold and firm, at least 45 minutes or up to 2 days. The longer the dough chills, the less it will spread during baking.

Position racks in the upper and lower thirds of the oven. Preheat the oven to 350°F. Line 2 baking sheets with parchment paper.

Use a small metal spatula to transfer the dough squares to the prepared baking sheets, spacing them about 1 inch apart. Because this dough toughens too much when rerolled, we save any cookie dough scraps and bake them as snacks for our café employees. They are best baked on their own baking sheet, with the baking time reduced by 1 to 2 minutes.

Bake until crisp, about 7 minutes, rotating the baking sheets midway through baking. (Note: because the sablés don't change color during baking, it's wise to bake a test batch of one or two cookies to check baking time for your oven before committing your whole batch; see Baking Times, page 25.) Let cool on the baking sheets for 10 minutes, and then transfer the cookies to a wire rack. Let cool to room temperature.

To make the ganache, put the chocolate in a medium heatproof bowl.

In a small, heavy-bottomed saucepan over medium-low heat, warm the cream, stirring occasionally, until it registers 180°F to 190°F on a digital thermometer and bubbles start to form around the edges. (Alternatively, put the cream into a microwavable liquid measuring cup or bowl and microwave at full power for about 60 seconds.)

Pour the hot cream over the chocolate and, using rubber spatula, stir until the chocolate is mostly melted. Blend with an immersion blender or transfer to a food processor and process until the chocolate is completely melted and the mixture is smooth and shiny. (Alternatively, set the bowl over a saucepan of just simmered water and whisk until the chocolate is melted and the mixture is smooth.)

To assemble, pour the ganache into a shallow bowl with a diameter of at least 3 inches. Dip the long edge of 1 cookie into the ganache, and then dip the 2 long edges of another cookie into the ganache. Stand the cookies upright and bring them together at a right angle, connecting the ganache-dipped edge of the first cookie with one of the dipped edges of the second cookie, and hold together until the ganache starts to set, about 1 minute. Repeat with 2 more cookies and ganache so that you have 2 freestanding sets. Now bring together the 2 ganache-dipped edges of each set, creating a four-panel zigzag.

Repeat with 4 more cookies and ganache to create another four-panel zigzag. To complete the sculpture, position the zigzags about 2 inches from each other at the widest point, with the end panels facing in.

Repeat with the remaining cookies and ganache until you've built 4 edible Newmans.

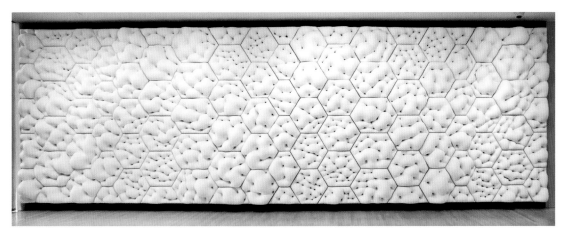

Andrew Kudless
P_Wall (detail)
2006/2009
plaster
144 in. x 546 in. x 18 in. (365.76 cm x
    1386.84 cm x 45.72 cm)
SFMOMA, Accessions Committee Fund
    purchase, 2009.125

For a 2009 exhibition called *Sensate: Bodies and Design*, SFMOMA commissioned *P_Wall*—a globular, 45-foot-long wall relief by Andrew Kudless (born 1975). The piece consists of hexagonal plaster tiles, each individually made at Matsys, Kudless's Bay Area design studio. By using elastic Lycra draped between wooden dowels as a flexible mold for the wet plaster, the tiles bulge and pucker, taking on a very organic quality.

According to Kudless, *P_Wall* owes a debt to the experimental concrete work of Spanish architect Miguel Fisac, who was active in the 1960s and 1970s, and reflects the integration of "form, growth, and behavior." Installed on a gallery wall, the piece subverts the expectation of a pristine white space, transforming it into something that almost appears to live and breathe.

KUDLESS S'MORES

MAKES NINE S'MORES
HANDS-ON TIME: 2 HOURS
FROM START TO FINISH: 5 TO 6 HOURS

In 2011, SFMOMA presented works by emerging artists in a yearlong, continually evolving show called *The More Things Change*. Through the window of the gallery, Leah spotted *P_Wall*, Andrew Kudless's undulating sculpture of hexagonal white plaster tiles, being installed in view of the café. The wall was being turned into a giant marshmallow right before her eyes.

Billowy and bright white, marshmallows are a great element in a few of our art-inspired desserts, but we weren't quite sure how to implement them for *P_Wall*. Just-made marshmallow is too sticky and uncooperative to capture the undulation of the sculpture, and if we poured it flat and cut it into hexagons, the effect would be too static. Then one day at the Powell Street BART station, I noticed that the hexagonal tiles lining the walls were similar to those in *P_Wall*. Realizing the wavelike appearance was a result of the tiles being grouped en masse, I knew we needed a grouping of marshmallow hexagons to mimic Kudless's effect.

Leah had a hard plastic candy mold with a repeating hexagonal design that we greased and generously dusted with a mixture of cornstarch and confectioners' sugar. Then we poured in the marshmallow and waited for it to set. It took a bit of wrestling to remove it, but even with the imperfections in our first batch, we could see that the marshmallow was a perfect edible representation of Kudless's piece.

And what better to pair with marshmallows and chocolate than graham crackers? I think homemade graham crackers are pretty magical, and though they might seem hard to make, they're actually really simple. With these components, we put together open-faced s'mores that were fun and tasty tributes to *P_Wall*.

NOTE: Once the marshmallows have set, they are still quite sticky. The best way to conquer the stickiness is to be generous with the cornstarch and confectioners' sugar mixture, dusting your hands, tools, and all marshmallow surfaces. Note that this recipe makes more marshmallows than you need for the s'mores. Since the marshmallows are best made in this batch size and have a 1 month shelf life, consider using the leftovers for the Fuller Hot Chocolate (page 191) or a nonboozy version of the Koons White Hot Chocolate (page 185).

This recipe requires an accurate thermometer for taking the temperature of the sugar syrup. Instant-read thermometers are notoriously inaccurate (which is why I love my thermocouple; see page 25), so if you own an instant-read thermometer, it's good practice to check its calibration before beginning. Simply bring a small pot of water to a boil and verify that the thermometer registers 212°F (at sea level) when inserted into the water.

DO AHEAD: S'mores are best assembled and then eaten right away. All of the components should be prepared ahead of time and then assembled just before serving. The marshmallows take 3 to 4 hours to set, but can be made up to a month in advance and, in fact, the curing time gives them an even better texture. Stored in an airtight container, the marshmallows will keep for 1 month at room temperature. The graham cracker dough needs at least 45 minutes to chill before baking, but the rolled and cut dough will keep for up to 2 days in the refrigerator and should be baked and cooled just before assembling the s'mores. Stored in an airtight container, the baked crackers will keep for 1 day at room temperature. The chocolate ganache needs to be made 3 to 4 hours prior to assembly and used at room temperature for the smoothest spreading (see Working with Chocolate Ganache, page 91). Stored in an airtight container, the ganache will keep for up to 1 week in the refrigerator.

ABOVE AND BEYOND: These s'mores are delicious no matter their shape, but if you want to create *P_Wall* s'mores just as we did at the museum, cut the rolled-out cracker dough into 2 by 3-inch rectangles and bake as directed. To form the marshmallows, you'll need a chocolate mold with hexagonal shapes (each mold makes two 2 by 3-inch marshmallows, see Resources, page 205); butter the molds and generously dust with the cornstarch mixture. Pour in enough marshmallow to fill the molds and smooth with a greased or wet offset spatula. Let sit for 1 to 2 hours. Once set, generously dust with the cornstarch mixture, remove the marshmallow, dust again with the cornstarch mixture, and invert the marshmallow so the design is facing up. Using a knife or scissors dusted with the cornstarch mixture, cut each sheet of marshmallow into two 2 by 3-inch pieces. To assemble, spread a generous amount of ganache on the flat side of each cracker, top with a marshmallow, and serve open-faced.

CHOCOLATE GANACHE

4 ounces (112 g) high-quality bittersweet chocolate (62% to 70% cacao), finely chopped

$^1/_2$ cup (4.1 oz / 116 g) heavy cream

MARSHMALLOWS

5 gelatin sheets, or $3^3/_4$ teaspoons powdered gelatin

$^1/_3$ cup (2.9 oz / 80 g) water, if using powdered gelatin, plus 3 tablespoons water

$^1/_4$ cup (1.1 oz / 31 g) cornstarch

$^1/_4$ cup (1 oz / 28 g) confectioners' sugar

$^3/_4$ cup (5.3 oz / 150 g) granulated sugar

$1^1/_2$ teaspoons vanilla extract

$^1/_4$ cup plus 2 tablespoons (2.9 oz / 82 g) light agave syrup

$^1/_2$ teaspoon vanilla extract

Pinch of kosher salt

GRAHAM CRACKERS

$1^1/_2$ cup (7.4 oz / 210 g) all-purpose flour

$^2/_3$ cup (3.2 oz / 92 g) whole wheat flour

$^1/_2$ teaspoon baking soda

1 teaspoon ground cinnamon

$^1/_3$ cup (2.4 oz / 66 g) granulated sugar

$^1/_3$ cup (3 oz / 72 g) packed light brown sugar

$^1/_2$ teaspoon Maldon sea salt (see page 31)

15 tablespoons (7.5 oz / 210 g) unsalted butter, at room temperature

3 tablespoons honey

To make the ganache, put the chocolate in a medium heatproof bowl.

In a small, heavy-bottomed saucepan over medium-low heat, warm the cream, stirring occasionally, until it registers 180°F to 190°F on a digital thermometer and bubbles start to form around the edges. (Alternatively, put the cream into a microwavable liquid measuring cup or bowl and microwave at full power for about 60 seconds.)

Pour the hot cream over the chocolate and, using rubber spatula, stir until the chocolate is mostly melted. Blend with an immersion blender or transfer to a food processor and process until the chocolate is completely melted and the mixture is smooth and shiny. (Alternatively, set the bowl over a saucepan of just simmered water and whisk until the chocolate is melted and the mixture is smooth.) Cover the bowl with plastic wrap and let the ganache sit at room temperature until it is smooth and spreadable, 3 to 4 hours.

To make the marshmallows, if you're using gelatin sheets, fill a medium bowl with ice water and submerge the sheets in the water. If you're using powdered gelatin, pour the $1/3$ cup (2.9 oz / 80 g) of water into a small bowl and sprinkle the gelatin evenly over the surface. Let either stand for 5 to 10 minutes. Meanwhile, sift the cornstarch and confectioners' sugar into a small bowl.

Line an 8 by 8-inch baking pan with 2 sheets of parchment or waxed paper, laying the sheets perpendicular to each other so that the bottom and all sides of the pan are covered. Sift enough cornstarch mixture into the prepared pan to completely and generously cover the bottom. Reserve the remaining cornstarch mixture.

In a small saucepan over medium-high heat, stir together the remaining 3 tablespoons of water, the granulated sugar, agave syrup, vanilla, and salt. Bring the mixture to a boil without stirring and cook until the temperature registers 238°F to 240°F on a digital thermometer.

Meanwhile, if using gelatin sheets, lift the softened sheets out of the bowl, squeeze out the excess water, and put the gelatin in the bowl of a stand mixer fitted with the whisk attachment. If using powdered gelatin, pour the dissolved mixture directly into the mixer bowl. Add the vanilla extract to the mixer bowl.

With the mixer turned off, pour all of the hot sugar syrup over the gelatin. Whip on low speed for 30 seconds, increase the medium speed and beat for 30 seconds, and then increase the speed to high and whip for 10 to 11 minutes until the mixture is smooth, glossy, and holds medium-firm peaks. It won't begin to resemble marshmallow until around the 5-minute mark.

Working quickly, transfer the mixture to the prepared pan and smooth the surface with a greased offset spatula. Let stand at room temperature for 3 to 4 hours until set.

Meanwhile, to make the graham crackers, sift the flours, baking soda, and cinnamon into a medium bowl. If any bran flakes from the whole wheat flour were sifted out, whisk them back into the flour mixture. Combine the granulated sugar, brown sugar, and salt in a second medium bowl and mix well.

In the bowl of a stand mixer fitted with the paddle attachment, beat the butter and honey on low speed until smooth, 1 to 2 minutes. With the mixer running on low speed, add the sugar mixture in a slow, steady stream and mix until well combined, about 20 seconds. Scrape down the bowl with a rubber spatula, and then beat on medium speed until the mixture is light and fluffy, 4 to 5 minutes.

Scrape down the bowl, and then add the flour mixture. Mix on low speed just until the dough is uniform, about 15 seconds, scrape down the sides of the bowl and mix for another minute.

Set the dough on a large sheet of parchment paper and press it into an even, flat rectangle measuring about 5 by 6 inches. Lay a second sheet of parchment paper on top and roll out the dough to an even $1/8$ to $1/4$-inch thickness. Slide the parchment paper with the dough onto a baking sheet and refrigerate until firm, at least 45 minutes or up to 2 days. The dough will be sticky, so don't try cut out shapes until after chilling. The longer the dough chills, the less it will spread during baking.

Position racks in the upper and lower thirds of the oven. Preheat the oven to 350°F. Line 2 rimmed baking sheets with parchment paper.

Remove the top sheet of parchment from the dough and, using a chef's knife or pizza wheel, cut the dough into 2 by 3-inch rectangles.

Use a small metal spatula to transfer the rectangles to the prepared baking sheets, spacing them about 1 inch apart. Because this dough toughens too much when rerolled, we save any cookie dough scraps and bake them as snacks for our café employees. They are best baked on their own baking sheet, with the baking time reduced by 1 to 2 minutes.

Bake, rotating the baking sheets midway through baking, until the crackers are an even golden brown, about 14 minutes. Let cool on the baking sheets for 10 minutes, and then transfer the crackers to a wire rack. Let cool to room temperature.

Returning to the marshmallows, sift a generous amount of the reserved cornstarch mixture over the surface of the marshmallow. Remove from the pan by running a knife along any stuck edges, and then carefully peel away the parchment paper. Cover all of the edges with the cornstarch mixture. Using a knife or scissors dusted with the cornstarch mixture, cut the marshmallow into 2 by 3-inch rectangles. Generously dust all cut edges with cornstarch mixture to prevent sticking.

To assemble, smear a generous amount of ganache on the flat side of each of 9 crackers. Place a marshmallow on top of the ganache, top with another cracker, and serve immediately.

© 2013 The Andy Warhol Foundation for the Visual Arts / Artists Rights Society (ARS), New York

Andy Warhol
Red Liz
1963
synthetic polymer paint and silkscreen ink on canvas
40 in. x 40 in.
SFMOMA, fractional purchase and bequest of Phyllis Wattis, 98.563

———

Born and raised in Pittsburgh and trained as commercial artist, Andy Warhol would go on to become one of the most influential artists of the twentieth century. Warhol epitomized Pop by eroding boundaries between high and low art—embracing techniques associated with mechanical reproduction for images drawn largely from consumer culture.

Warhol was obsessed with fame and glamour, and among his favorite subjects were Marilyn Monroe, Jackie Kennedy, and Elizabeth Taylor. *Red Liz* is one of dozens of canvases Warhol made in the early 1960s based on an MGM publicity still of the actress. Using silkscreen, he produced the same image in multiple variations—in silver and black, in different color combinations, and with more or less degrees of smudginess. Warhol finally met Taylor in Rome in 1973, when he was invited to be a part of the cast of *The Driver's Seat*, in which she starred.

WARHOL GELÉE

MAKES SIXTEEN 2-INCH SQUARES
HANDS-ON TIME: 1 HOUR, 45 MINUTES
FROM START TO FINISH: 5 HOURS

Maybe it's because his work is so iconic, or perhaps it's because his pieces don't usually include "edible" colors, but I have had more failed attempts at desserts based on Andy Warhol than on any other artist. One day, Leah and I were standing in front of Warhol's *Self-Portrait* at the museum, talking about what the colors—navy blue, red, and green— might translate to as flavors. We were interested in a dessert with layers that referenced the process of screen printing, but it wasn't until I suggested gelée as the format that the idea really came together. We tried to turn *Self-Portrait* into a Bloody Mary gelée using blue curaçao as a blue-colored vodka substitute, Campbell's Tomato Soup for the red, and celery-horseradish juice for the green. Needless to say, the results were disgusting.

It wasn't until Warhol's *Red Liz* appeared in an exhibition called *Contemporary Painting: 1960 to the Present* that we finally had the perfect Warhol inspiration for a dessert. The red, pink, turquoise, and black screen print of the lovely Elizabeth Taylor just begged to be turned into stripes of strawberry, rose, and mint gelée served on a dramatic black plate.

This recipe uses fresh strawberries to make a beautiful ruby-red gelée that's more pure and delicious than anything made from a box. The key to getting jewel-like clarity in your gelée is to gently cook the berries and then let the juice strain out without mashing the pulp.

NOTE: Rose water, a clear distillate of rose petals, can be found in Middle Eastern markets and often in health-food stores. It's fairly potent and can be overpowering—when used with a heavy hand, it sometimes reminds me of grandmotherly perfume. But when used sparingly, rose water adds a very lovely and subtle floral flavor.

DO AHEAD: The finished gelée, uncut or cut, can be stored in an airtight container or wrapped tightly in plastic wrap for up to 1 week in the refrigerator.

ABOVE AND BEYOND: To incorporate the black color from *Red Liz*, we serve the striped gelée on a rectangular onyx-colored Heath Ceramics plate (see Resources, page 205).

STRAWBERRY GELÉE

2 pounds (908 g) fresh strawberries

2 cups (17 oz / 475 g) water,
plus ³/₄ cup (6.4 oz / 180 g) water if using powdered gelatin

1 cup (7.1 oz / 200 g) sugar

¹/₄ cup (2.1 oz / 60 g) fresh lemon juice

10 gelatin sheets, or 2¹/₂ tablespoons powdered gelatin

ROSE MILK GELÉE

3¹/₂ gelatin sheets, or 2¹/₂ teaspoons powdered gelatin

¹/₄ cup (2.1 oz / 60 g) water, if using powdered gelatin

2 cups (17.3 oz / 484 g) whole milk

2 tablespoons sugar

1 tablespoon rose water

Red food coloring (see page 30)

MINT MILK GELÉE

1³/₄ gelatin sheets, or 1¹/₄ teaspoons powdered gelatin

¹/₄ cup (2.1 oz / 60 g) water, if using powdered gelatin

1 cup (8.6 oz / 242 g) whole milk

1 tablespoon sugar

¹/₂ cup (0.35 oz / 10 g) loosely packed fresh spearmint leaves

Turquoise food coloring (see page 30)

To make the strawberry gelée, wash, dry, and hull the strawberries. Cut the berries in half or quarter them if they are especially big.

Combine the strawberries, 2 cups of the water, sugar, and lemon juice in a medium saucepan and bring to a simmer over medium-low heat, stirring to help the sugar dissolve. Turn down the heat to low, cover, and simmer until the berries are soft, 8 to 10 minutes. Remove from the heat and let the berries rest for 5 minutes.

Transfer the berry mixture to a fine-mesh strainer set over a medium bowl. Let stand for 5 minutes to allow the juice to drain from the berries; don't press on the fruit to extract additional liquid. You should have 4 cups (34 oz / 950 g) of strained strawberry juice.

Meanwhile, if you're using gelatin sheets, fill a medium bowl with ice water and submerge the sheets in the water. If you're using powdered gelatin, pour the $^3/_4$ cup (6.4 oz / 180 g) water into a small bowl and sprinkle the gelatin evenly over the surface. Let either stand for 5 to 10 minutes.

In a small saucepan over medium heat, warm the strawberry juice until it is slightly warm (about 110°F on a digital thermometer), 1 to 2 minutes. Remove from the heat. If using gelatin sheets, lift the softened sheets out of the bowl, squeeze out the excess water, and stir the gelatin into the warm juice until dissolved. If using powdered gelatin, add the bloomed gelatin to the warm juice and stir until dissolved. Pour one-half of the strawberry mixture into an 8-inch square baking dish or cake pan, reserving the remaining mixture at room temperature. Skim off any bubbles with a spoon and refrigerate until firm, about 1 hour.

After about 30 minutes of chilling, make the rose gelée. If you're using gelatin sheets, fill a medium bowl with ice water and submerge the sheets in the water. If you're using powdered gelatin, pour the water into a small bowl and sprinkle the gelatin evenly over the surface. Let either stand for 5 to 10 minutes.

In a small saucepan over medium heat, warm the milk, sugar, and rose water, stirring occasionally. When the mixture begins to bubble around the edges and registers 180°F to 190°F on a digital thermometer, remove the pan from the heat. Add just enough red food coloring to tint the mixture a bubblegum-pink color. If using gelatin sheets, lift the softened sheets out of the bowl, squeeze out the excess water, and stir the gelatin into the warm milk mixture until dissolved. If using powdered gelatin, add the bloomed gelatin to the warm milk mixture and stir until dissolved. Transfer to a 1-quart liquid measuring cup and let cool to 110°F to 120°F.

Remove the baking dish from the refrigerator. To avoid creating a big hole in the strawberry layer when you add the rose gelée, hold a cooking spoon just above the strawberry layer and slowly pour the rose gelée into it (see photo, page 121), letting the liquid run over the spoon and fall gently onto the strawberry layer. Skim off any bubbles with a spoon and refrigerate until firm, about 1 hour.

Using the same technique, pour the remaining strawberry gelée over the rose layer. (If the strawberry gelée is no longer pourable, warm it to 110°F to 120°F). Skim off any bubbles with a spoon and refrigerate until firm, about 1 hour.

After about 30 minutes of chilling, make the mint gelée. If you're using gelatin sheets, fill a medium bowl with ice water and submerge the sheets in the water. If you're using powdered gelatin, pour the water into a small bowl and sprinkle the gelatin evenly over the surface. Let either stand for 5 to 10 minutes.

Meanwhile, in a small saucepan over medium heat, warm the milk, sugar, and mint leaves, stirring occasionally. When the mixture begins to bubble around the edges and registers 180°F to 190°F on a digital thermometer, remove the pan from the heat, cover, and let the mixture steep for 10 minutes. Strain through a fine-mesh sieve set over a 2-cup liquid measuring cup; discard the mint. Add just enough turquoise food coloring to tint the mixture a mint-green color. If using gelatin sheets, lift the softened sheets out of the bowl, squeeze out the excess water, and stir the gelatin into the warm milk mixture until dissolved. If using powdered gelatin, add the bloomed gelatin to the warm milk mixture and stir until dissolved. Let cool to 110°F to 120°F.

Again using the spoon technique, pour the mint gelée over the second strawberry layer. Skim off any bubbles with a spoon and refrigerate until fully set, at least 3 hours, but preferably overnight.

To serve, fill a dish or roasting pan slightly larger than the baking dish with 1 to 2 inches of warm water. Place the baking dish in the warm water for 15 to 20 seconds, taking care not to let the water flow onto the gelée. Remove the baking dish from the water bath and run an offset spatula around the inside edge to loosen the gelée. Invert a serving platter over the baking dish, and, holding the two together, invert both the baking dish and platter. Lift off the baking dish. Cut the gelée into 2-inch squares and serve.

WARHOL GELÉE

Rosana Castrillo Díaz
Untitled
2009
mica acrylic on wall
13 ft. 6 in. x 91 ft. 9 in.
SFMOMA, commissioned through a gift of Robert and
  Claudia Allen and the Mary Heath Keesling Fund, 2009.85

SFMOMA's Rooftop Garden was built on top of a parking garage just east of the main building, and in order to connect it to the museum, Jensen Architects designed a footbridge. The museum then invited San Francisco artist and 2006 SECA Art Award recipient Rosana Castrillo Díaz (born Spain, 1971) to activate it with a new piece.

After carefully studying the site—a sloped, ninety-three-foot-long bridge with a solid wall on the south side and windows on the north—the artist knew that she wanted to convey a sense of movement. She looked at marbles by Camille Claudel and Renaissance artists, particularly folds of drapery, as a source of inspiration. Given the length of the wall, it is impossible to fully take in the work as a whole. Rather, the subtle abstracted image, made with four shades of matte and reflective white paint, reveals itself experientially as one walks along the ramp, shifting as its forms either distinguish themselves or visually collapse depending on changes in the light and one's own vantage point.

CASTRILLO DÍAZ PANNA COTTA

MAKES 8 INDIVIDUAL PANNA COTTAS
HANDS-ON TIME: 1 HOUR
FROM START TO FINISH: 5^1/$_2$ HOURS

For the opening of SFMOMA's Rooftop Garden, the museum invited San Francisco artist Rosana Castrillo Díaz to make a new piece for the footbridge leading to the garden's Pavilion. Subtle and elegant, the undulating forms that Rosana Castrillo Díaz painted in shimmery earth tones are illuminated by the sunlight that filters through the facing windows of the footbridge. We captured the mural's sparkle by using Luster Dust, an edible decoration, in this layered dessert of two types of panna cotta: one made with coffee and crème fraîche, the other flavored with maple syrup and yogurt. Panna cotta, a traditional Italian dessert of sweetened cream and gelatin, can range from a barely solidified, super-silky pudding to a rubbery, aspic-style block. My taste is decidedly in the barely solidified camp, and I prefer panna cotta so soft that it can't be unmolded—it has to be eaten from a cup.

For color and flavor contrast, we added a thin layer of Nocino Gelée between the panna cotta layers as well as on top to garnish the dessert. (*Nocino* is an Italian green walnut liqueur; if you prefer, substitute the dark-hued liqueur of your choosing.)

DO AHEAD: Stored in an airtight container or with each cup covered tightly with plastic wrap, the panna cottas will keep for up to 1 week in the refrigerator.

ABOVE AND BEYOND: I call for 8-ounce cups in this recipe, but at the museum, we use small 4-ounce cups; see Resources (page 205) for ordering information. To create panna cotta layers that mimic the waves of the Castrillo Díaz mural, prop up each unfilled cup on a wedge approximately $^1/_4$ inch high (two stacked ice-pop sticks work well) on a silicone baking mat–lined baking sheet to prevent slipping. Pour the first layer of panna cotta into the angled cups and refrigerate until set. Prepare the Nocino Gelée, stirring in a pinch of Luster Dust (see Resources, page 205) for optional sparkle; add 2 to 3 tablespoons of gelée to each cup, still angled, and refrigerate until set. Remove the wedges before filling cups with the second layer of panna cotta and final gelée layer.

COFFEE PANNA COTTA

2 gelatin sheets, or $1^1/_2$ teaspoons powdered gelatin

$^1/_4$ cup (2.1 oz / 60 g) water, if using powdered gelatin

$1^1/_2$ cups (12.4 oz / 348 g) heavy cream

$^1/_2$ cup (3.5 oz / 100 g) sugar

$^1/_2$ cup (4.3 oz / 120 g) strong brewed coffee

$^3/_4$ cup (6.4 oz / 180 g) crème fraîche (page 131)

NOCINO GELÉE

$1^1/_2$ gelatin sheets, or 1 teaspoon powdered gelatin

$^1/_4$ cup (2.1 oz / 60 g) water, if using powdered gelatin

$^1/_4$ cup (2.1 oz / 60 g) *nocino*

2 tablespoons sugar

MAPLE-YOGURT PANNA COTTA

2 gelatin sheets, or $1^1/_2$ teaspoons powdered gelatin

$^1/_4$ cup (2.1 oz / 60 g) water, if using powdered gelatin

$1^1/_2$ cups (12.4 oz / 348 g) heavy cream

$^1/_2$ cup (5.8 oz / 162 g) maple syrup

$^3/_4$ cup (6.5 oz / 182 g) plain whole-milk yogurt

Set eight 8-ounce clear glass cups on a baking sheet.

To make the coffee panna cotta, if you're using gelatin sheets, fill a medium bowl with ice water and submerge the sheets in the water. If you're using powdered gelatin, pour the cold water into a small bowl and sprinkle the gelatin evenly over the surface. Let either stand for 5 to 10 minutes.

Combine the cream and sugar in a small saucepan over medium heat, stirring occasionally to help the sugar dissolve. When the mixture begins to bubble around the edges and registers 180°F to 190°F on a digital thermometer, remove the pan from the heat. If using gelatin sheets, lift the softened sheets out of the bowl, squeeze out the excess water, and stir the gelatin into the warm cream mixture until dissolved. If using powdered gelatin, add the bloomed gelatin to the warm cream mixture and stir until dissolved. Add the coffee and stir to combine.

Transfer the mixture to a medium bowl and whisk in the crème fraîche. Strain through a fine-mesh sieve set over a 1-quart liquid measuring cup, then pour the mixture into the cups, dividing it evenly. Refrigerate for about 2 hours, until firm.

After about $1^1/_2$ hours of chilling, prepare the gelée. Soften the gelatin sheets or bloom the powdered gelatin as described above. Let either stand for 5 to 10 minutes.

In a small saucepan over medium heat, warm the *nocino* and sugar, stirring, until the sugar dissolves, about 5 minutes. Remove from the heat. If using gelatin sheets, lift the softened sheets out of the bowl, squeeze out the excess water, and stir the gelatin into the *nocino* mixture until dissolved. If using powdered gelatin, add the bloomed gelatin to the *nocino* mixture and stir until dissolved. (If you're going above and beyond and using Luster Dust, stir in a pinch now.) Let cool to about 95°F.

Distribute one-half of the gelée mixture over the chilled panna cottas, dividing it evenly. Return the panna cottas to the refrigerator to chill for about 30 minutes; reserve the remaining gelée mixture at room temperature.

To make the maple-yogurt panna cotta, soften the gelatin sheets or bloom the powdered gelatin as described above. Let either stand for 5 to 10 minutes.

In a small saucepan over medium heat, warm the cream and maple syrup, stirring occasionally. When the mixture begins to bubble around the edges and registers 180°F to 190°F on a digital thermometer, remove the pan from the heat. If using gelatin sheets, lift the softened sheets out of the bowl, squeeze out the excess water, and stir the gelatin into the warm cream mixture until dissolved. If using powdered gelatin, add the bloomed gelatin to the warm cream mixture and stir until dissolved.

Transfer the mixture to a medium bowl and whisk in the yogurt. Strain through a fine-mesh sieve set over a 1-quart liquid measuring cup. Pour the mixture into the cups over the gelée layer, dividing it evenly. Refrigerate for 2 hours or until set.

If the reserved gelée has begun to firm up, transfer it to a microwavable bowl and heat on full power for 5 to 10 seconds, until liquefied. Divide the gelée evenly among the panna cottas, then return the cups to the refrigerator. Let chill for at least 30 minutes before serving.

Richard Avedon
*Ronald Fischer, beekeeper, Davis,
  California, May 9, 1981*
gelatin silver print
59⅝ in. x 47⅛ in.
© The Richard Avedon Foundation
—

In 1979, Richard Avedon (1923–2004)—already famous for his pictures of cultural icons—embarked on a project that would become a book and exhibition titled *In the American West*. Over the next five years, Avedon traveled through the western states creating portraits of coal miners, farmers, drifters, criminals, carnies, and other intriguing characters. In some cases, he photographed people he stumbled across. In other cases, he sought out particular types.

According to Laura Wilson, who wrote about the making of the series in *Avedon at Work in the American West*, Ronald Fischer responded to Avedon's notice in a beekeepers' journal for a person willing to be photographed covered with bees. Avedon was fascinated by Fischer's appearance, saying "he had a quality so exceptional, so like a dream." In order to get this Zen-like image, Avedon shot more than 100 sheets of film in front of a backdrop set against a barn.

AVEDON PARFAIT

MAKES 16 INDIVIDUAL PARFAITS
HANDS-ON TIME: 1 HOUR
FROM START TO FINISH: 3 HOURS

Just a few months after the café opened in 2009, a Richard Avedon retrospective opened as the big summer exhibition. I was delighted to be able to spend time admiring the work of one of my very favorite photographers, and I hoped that I'd find inspiration for an Avedon dessert in the galleries.

Ronald Fischer, beekeeper, Davis, California, May 9, 1981, is an unsettling photograph, and the one that I've always considered the most iconic from Avedon's series *In the American West*. The most startling aspect of the photo are the bees clumped on the vulnerable parts of the subject's body: on his ear, around his neck, and in his armpit. Playing off the pale color of the beekeeper's skin and the claustrophobic feeling of being enveloped in bees, I envisioned a white chocolate box, reminiscent of a beekeeper's beehive, that would encase a frozen dessert. With zero experience working with chocolate (other than ganache), I called on my friend Boris Portnoy, a hotshot pastry chef from San Francisco who earned his chocolate chops at the Valrhona chocolate academy in France. Boris gave me a tutorial on tempering chocolate and advice on the construction of my box. Then my talented friend Courtney Utt designed a cocoa transfer sheet using the bees from the photo as the models for her own illustrations, allowing me to transfer Avedon's bees right onto the chocolate.

Without a doubt, the Avedon Parfait is one of the desserts of which I am the most proud, but the chocolate boxes were truly a pain to execute. I've modified this recipe, replacing the tempered chocolate panels with white chocolate ganache for pouring over the cubes of parfait. This simplified version incorporates the same flavors as the original but is a snap to make at home.

NOTE: This recipe requires an accurate thermometer for taking the temperature of the sugar syrup. Instant-read thermometers are notoriously inaccurate (which is why I love my thermocouple; see page 25), so if you own an instant-read thermometer, it's good practice to check its calibration before beginning. Simply bring a small pot of water to a boil and verify that the thermometer registers 212°F (at sea level) when inserted into the water.

Essential oils, sold in some herbal shops and natural foods markets, are highly concentrated distillations of herbs, flowers, or spices. As long as they are steam-distilled and labeled food grade, they're safe to use in cooking. If you can't find cardamom essential oil, add 3 whole green cardamom pods when heating the milk; let the mixture steep, covered, for 10 minutes; and then strain the milk over the white chocolate.

DO AHEAD: This dessert has a few different components that require preparation before it can be assembled. The crème fraîche needs to sit out overnight and should be prepared at least 2 days before the dessert is to be eaten. Stored in an airtight container, crème fraîche will keep for up to 1 week in the refrigerator. The parfaits need to chill for at least 4 hours before serving, but can be made ahead and stored in an airtight container in the freezer for up to 1 week. The white chocolate ganache can be made ahead and stored in an airtight container in the refrigerator for up to 1 week. See Working with Chocolate Ganache, page 91, for reheating instructions.

ABOVE AND BEYOND: If you want to make the Avedon Parfait just as we did at the museum, use a 2-inch flexible cube mold for shaping the parfait (see Resources, page 205). Sources for ordering custom chocolate transfer sheets using the template are in Resources (page 205), and you can download a template for the bee box from www.modernartdesserts.com. For instructions on tempering the chocolate and creating the walls of the bee box, see Tempering White Chocolate, page 132.

HONEY-PISTACHIO PARFAIT

2¹/₂ gelatin sheets, or 1³/₄ teaspoons powdered gelatin

¹/₄ cup (2.1 oz / 60 g) water, if using powdered gelatin, plus ¹/₂ cup (4.2 oz / 120 g) water

1 cup (8.5 oz / 240 g) Crème Fraîche (page 131)

²/₃ cup (5.5 oz / 153g) cold heavy cream

6 large egg yolks (4 oz / 114 g)

¹/₄ cup (1.8 oz / 50 g) sugar

2 tablespoons honey

¹/₂ teaspoon kosher salt

¹/₄ cup (1.4 oz / 38 g) chopped shelled pistachios, unsalted

WHITE CHOCOLATE GANACHE WITH CARDAMOM

10 ounces (280 g) white chocolate, coarsely chopped

¹/₂ cup (4.3 oz / 121 g) whole milk

2 drops cardamom essential oil (see Note, page 128)

To make the parfait, line an 8-inch square cake pan with plastic wrap.

If you're using gelatin sheets, fill a medium bowl with ice water and submerge the sheets in the water. If you're using powdered gelatin, pour the ¹/₄ cup (2.1 oz / 60 g) of water into a small bowl and sprinkle the gelatin evenly over the surface. Let either stand for 5 to 10 minutes.

In the bowl of a stand mixer fitted with the whisk attachment, whip the crème fraîche and cream on medium speed until the mixture holds soft peaks, about 2 minutes. Alternatively, whip the crème fraîche and the cream in a large bowl with a hand mixer or whisk. Transfer to a bowl, cover, and refrigerate until ready to use, up to 1 hour.

In a small saucepan over medium-low heat, warm the ¹/₂ cup (4.2 oz / 120 g) of water, sugar, honey, and salt and cook, swirling occasionally, until the sugar dissolves, and then continue simmering without stirring until the syrup registers 230°F on a digital thermometer. Meanwhile, wash and dry the mixer bowl and add the yolks. Using the whisk attachment, whip the yolks on medium speed until lightened in color, 3 to 4 minutes.

Immediately transfer the syrup to a heatproof liquid measuring cup. With the mixer running on medium-low speed, add the hot sugar syrup to the yolks in a thin, steady stream; aim to pour it into the small space between the mixer bowl and the whisk.

If using gelatin sheets, lift the softened sheets out of the bowl and squeeze out the excess water. While the yolk mixture is still hot, add the sheets or the bloomed powdered gelatin to the bowl and whip on low speed until the gelatin has dissolved and the mixture has cooled to room temperature, about 5 minutes.

Remove the bowl from the mixer. Using a flexible rubber spatula, gently but thoroughly fold in the whipped crème fraîche and the pistachios until no streaks of color remain. Pour the mixture into the prepared baking pan and smooth with an offset spatula. Cover in plastic wrap and freeze until firm, about 2 hours.

To make the ganache, put the chocolate in a medium heatproof bowl.

In a small, heavy-bottomed saucepan over medium-low heat, warm the milk, stirring often, until it registers 180°F to 190°F on a digital thermometer and bubbles start to form around the edges. (Alternatively, put the cream into a microwavable liquid measuring cup or bowl and microwave at full power for about 60 seconds.)

Pour the hot milk over the chocolate and add the cardamom oil. Stir or blend with an immersion blender until the chocolate is melted and the ganache is smooth.

Invert the frozen parfait from the pan onto a cutting board, remove the plastic wrap and, using a large knife, cut the block into 2-inch squares. Use immediately or return to the freezer until ready to use.

If you've made the ganache in advance, warm it to a pourable consistency (see Working with Chocolate Ganache, page 91). When re-warming ganache, take care to heat it only just enough to melt all of the lumps—if the ganache is too warm when poured over the parfait, there's a risk it could melt the frozen pieces.

To assemble, place the parfait squares on wire rack set in a rimmed baking sheet. Pour the ganache over the top, letting it drip down and coat the sides. Using a spatula, transfer each parfait to a serving plate and serve immediately.

USING A BEE TRANSFER SHEET AND ASSEMBLING THE BOX

Place a plain piece of acetate (or the back side of a chocolate transfer sheet) on an inverted rimmed baking sheet, and pour a thin layer of the tempered chocolate onto the sheet. Using an off-set spatula, spread the chocolate into a thin, even layer over the surface. Place a chocolate transfer sheet, bee design side down, onto the chocolate. Using a large knife, gently score the soft chocolate into 2 by 2-inch squares. Let cool at comfortable room temperature (65°F to 75°F) until set.

Once cooled, gently pull the acetate off of the tempered chocolate. Use a large hot knife to carefully trim the chocolate panels along the score lines. Apply one panel to each of the five exposed sides, the stickiness of the parfait will be the glue that keeps the panels in place.

MAKING CRÈME FRAÎCHE

Crème fraîche is sold in tiny little tubs at exorbitant prices in gourmet grocery stores and cheese shops. I used to avoid any recipe calling for crème fraîche, knowing that if I messed something up, I would be annoyed by how much money I had lost. To spare you from winding up in that same sad predicament, I'm here to tell you that crème fraîche is super easy to make at home. With some high-quality cream, a touch of buttermilk, and a few hours, you can have as much as your heart desires. (Stored in an airtight container, crème fraîche will keep for up to 1 week in the refrigerator.)

1 cup (8.3 oz / 232 g) heavy cream
1 tablespoon buttermilk

Whisk together the cream and buttermilk in a small bowl or container. Cover and let stand overnight at cool room temperature until thickened.

Refrigerate until cool, at least 3 hours.

TEMPERING WHITE CHOCOLATE

When I think about perfectly tempered chocolate, I envision a beautiful chocolate truffle with a thin, shiny shell that breaks with a satisfying crack to reveal the soft center within. The process called tempering is what produces that beautiful chocolate sheen and snap.

Tempering isn't always necessary. Chocolate can simply be melted, poured, and then left to firm up, but the results will be soft and prone to blooming, the unsightly—but totally harmless—rising of cocoa butter to the surface that looks like mold. Chocolate used in ganache doesn't need to be tempered because the addition of cream creates a soft or pourable consistency anyway. But, if you're after that crispy crunch in your dessert or confections, tempering is necessary—and totally doable.

The tempering method that I describe here is called seeding, and involves only three steps: melting the chocolate, cooling it down, and then bringing it back up to a workable temperature. The trickiest parts are taking very accurate temperatures and working quickly.

NOTE: Different types of chocolates require slightly different temperatures to reach temper. Information about temperatures can be found on the Internet and often on the package of professional-grade chocolates; you can also check with the manufacturer. The temperature ranges that I've specified here are for tempering white chocolate.

8 ounces (227 g) high-quality white chocolate pastilles or coarsely chopped white chocolate, such as El Rey Icoa (see Resources, page 205), plus more as needed

Bring an inch or two of water to simmer in a medium saucepan, and then turn off the heat. Put 6 ounces (168 g) of the chocolate in a clean, dry heatproof bowl and set the bowl over water in the pan; the bottom of the bowl should not touch the water. Let the chocolate melt, stirring often with a clean flexible rubber spatula until the temperature registers 113°F to 118°F on a digital thermometer. (Alternatively, put 6 ounces of the chocolate in a microwavable bowl and heat at full power in 10-second intervals, stirring often, until melted and the temperature registers 113°F to 118°F.) Meanwhile, fill another bowl with ice water.

Set the bowl containing the chocolate over the ice water; make sure that the bottom of the bowl is not touching the water. Add the remaining 2 ounces (56 g) of chocolate and stir constantly to melt the chocolate and bring the temperature down to 79°F to 81°F. This process should take about 10 minutes; if needed, add a little more chocolate to the bowl.

Now set the bowl back over the warm water in the saucepan and bring the temperature of the chocolate up to 82°F to 83°F. (If using a microwave, heat at full power in 2- to 3-second intervals, stirring often, until the temperature registers.) Remove any unmelted chocolate pieces (they can be saved for later use) and use the tempered chocolate right away.

Let the tempered chocolate cool at comfortable room temperature (65°F to 75°F) until set. Any chocolate that is either bloomed or left over can be saved and tempered again. (Store tempered chocolate in an airtight container at cool room temperature.)

Luc Tuymans
St. Valentine
1994
oil on canvas
18¹/₂ in. x 16 in.
Collection of J. Asselman

———

Luc Tuymans (born 1958) is one of the most enigmatic and influential painters working today. Working in the tradition of northern European painting, while at the same time attuned to contemporary conditions, Tuyman takes on subjects as fraught as memory, history, and politics though evocative, thinly painted pictures that seem to materialize and dematerialize at the same time. His work was the subject of *Artforum*'s November 2004 issue, "The Tuymans Effect," which addressed the appeal and impact of the Belgian artist and his work.

There is an intentional ambiguity in *St. Valentine* (1994). The artist has noted that "the heart can be the sign of love, but at the same time . . . it can also be the sign of death." If Tuyman's curvilinear image alludes to a Valentine's Day greeting, something edible, or perhaps a heart-shaped ashtray, its reference remains unresolved.

TUYMANS PARFAIT

MAKES 16 INDIVIDUAL PARFAITS
HANDS-ON TIME: 1 ¹/₂ HOURS
FROM START TO FINISH: 5 HOURS

Leah was working in the kitchen one day when she overheard "This is shit!" coming from the coffee bar. She peeked around the corner to discover Luc Tuymans, a Belgian painter whose retrospective was about to open at the museum, glaring at our Mondrian Cake, the exhibition cocurator, Madeleine Grynsztejn, by his side. Leah gathered her gumption, marched out to introduce herself, and asked Tuymans if he had a piece of art that he would like to see turned into a dessert. A grumpy reply was imminent, but Madeleine came to the rescue, enthusiastically suggesting his painting *St. Valentine*, as Valentine's Day was just around the corner. Tuymans seemed unconvinced, but his mood softened as he described the piece to Leah.

Leah phoned me immediately, and by the time I arrived at the museum, Tuymans had started dropping by the kitchen to check on our progress. By his third or fourth visit, I started to crumble under the stress of trying to figure out a Valentine's Day dessert based on a gray painting. I was adamant that it *not* be in the shape of a heart—too corny for such a somber painting, and I wasn't interested in making holiday themed desserts for our café—but Leah unearthed a wide variety of heart-shaped bakeware anyway. Most were too cute, but there was one mold with dreary, sad little heart-shaped cups that were just perfect for a *St. Valentine* sweet. With still no idea what to put into the molds, I fell asleep that night pondering how to incorporate a grayish purple hue into the dessert. In the middle of the night, a flash of inspiration came to me: a coulis made of agar and crème de violette, a purple, violet-flavored liqueur.

The next day, I whipped up a batch of the coulis from my dream while Leah baked Earl Grey shortbread in the bottom of the molds. We concocted a simple and tangy crème fraîche parfait, poured it over the shortbreads, and then put the molds into the freezer. Depanned and nestled into a pool of the coulis, the parfaits were a perfect homage to the painting, but it was too late for the artist to see. Tuymans had already returned to Belgium.

NOTE: The sablé recipe makes more cookies than you need for the parfaits, but as long as you're going through the effort, it's worthwhile to have extras to nibble on. To infuse the dough with Earl Grey flavor, I grind up tea leaves and steep them in just a bit of melted butter. It's a rule of thumb that loose-leaf tea is of higher quality than tea in tea bags, but there are exceptions to this rule, of course, so if you have good-quality Earl Grey in bags, you can empty out a bag and use the tea in this recipe.

DO AHEAD: This dessert has a few different components that require preparation before it can be assembled. The crème fraîche needs to sit out overnight and should be prepared at least 2 days before the dessert is to be eaten. Stored in an airtight container, it will keep for up to 1 week in the refrigerator. The coulis must chill for at least 3 hours before processing, but can be made ahead and stored in an airtight container for up to 1 week. The parfaits need to chill for at least 4 hours before serving, but can be made ahead and stored in an airtight container in the freezer for up to 1 week. The mixed, rolled, and cut Earl Grey sablé dough must cool for at least 45 minutes before baking and can be stored in the refrigerator for 2 days. Stored in an airtight container, the baked cookies will keep for up to 1 day at room temperature.

ABOVE AND BEYOND: Leah can't recall where she got our heart-shaped molds, but Wilton makes some that are similar, just a little more cheery than I like (see Resources, page 205, for ordering information; be sure to use metal or silicone molds). To bake the sablés in the molds, instead of rolling out the dough, drop a teaspoon-sized piece into each mold and, using your fingers, press it evenly into the bottom; the dough should be about $1/4$ inch thick. Bake at 325°F for about 7 minutes. Let cool to room temperature in the molds, and then refrigerate until cold.

Prepare the parfait, divide it evenly among the cookie-lined molds, and freeze until firm, about 2 hours. Unmold the hearts and nestle, cookie side down, in a pool of coulis. (Stored in an airtight container, the unmolded parfaits will keep for up to 1 week in the freezer.)

VIOLET COULIS
$1^1/3$ cup (11.1 oz / 315 g) water

4 tablespoons sugar

Grated zest of 2 lemons

2 tablespoons agar flakes
(see Note, page 142)

1 cup (8.6 oz / 240 g) crème de
violette liqueur

EARL GREY SABLÉS
7 tablespoons (3.5 oz / 100 g)
unsalted butter, at room temperature

1 teaspoon loose-leaf Earl Grey tea,
finely ground

1 cup (4.9 oz / 140 g) all-purpose flour

$1/4$ teaspoon baking soda

$1/2$ cup (3.5 oz / 100 g) sugar

$1/4$ teaspoon Maldon sea salt (see page 31)

CRÈME FRAÎCHE PARFAIT
$2^1/2$ gelatin sheets, or $1^3/4$ teaspoons
powdered gelatin

$1/4$ cup (2.1 oz / 60 g) water,
if using powdered gelatin, plus
$1/2$ cup (4.3 oz / 120 g) water

1 cup (8.5 oz / 240 g) Crème Fraîche
(page 131)

$2/3$ cup (5.4 oz / 153 g) cold heavy cream

1 cup (7.1 oz / 200 g) sugar

$1/2$ teaspoon kosher salt

6 large egg yolks (4 oz / 114 g)

To make the coulis, in a small saucepan over medium-low heat, bring the water, sugar, zest, and agar flakes to a boil, stirring constantly. Cook, still stirring, until the agar is completely dissolved and the mixture thickens into a clear gel with no visible agar pieces, about 8 minutes. Stir in the crème de violette and cook for 1 minute longer.

Strain the mixture through a fine-mesh sieve set over a small bowl. Cover with plastic wrap and refrigerate until firm, at least 4 hours or up to 1 week.

To make the sablés, in a small saucepan over medium heat or in a microwavable bowl at full power, melt 5 tablespoons (2.5 oz / 70 g) of the butter. Stir in the tea and let steep for 10 minutes.

Sift the flour and baking soda into a medium bowl.

In the bowl of a stand mixer fitted with a paddle attachment, beat the unstrained tea-infused butter and the remaining 10 tablespoons (5 oz / 140 g) room-temperature butter on low speed until smooth, 1 to 2 minutes. With the mixer running, add the sugar in a slow, steady stream, followed by the salt, and mix on low speed until well combined. Scrape down the bowl with a rubber spatula and beat on medium speed until the mixture is light and fluffy, 4 to 5 minutes.

Scrape down the bowl, and then add the flour mixture. Mix on low speed just until the dough is uniform, about 15 seconds, scrape down the sides of the bowl and mix for another minute.

Set the dough on a large sheet of parchment paper and press it into an even, flat rectangle measuring about 5 by 6 inches. Lay a second sheet of parchment paper on top and roll out the dough to an even $1/8$ to $1/4$-inch thickness. Remove the top sheet of parchment and, using a large knife or pizza wheel, cut the dough into 2-inch squares. The dough will be soft, so don't try to remove the squares until after chilling. Slide the parchment paper with the dough onto a baking sheet, cover with plastic wrap, and refrigerate until the dough is cold and firm, at least 45 minutes or up to 2 days. The longer the dough chills, the less it will spread during baking.

To make the parfait, line an 8-inch square cake pan with plastic wrap.

If you're using gelatin sheets, fill a medium bowl with ice water and submerge the sheets in the water. If you're using powdered gelatin, pour the $1/4$ cup (2.1 oz / 60 g) of water into a small bowl and sprinkle the gelatin evenly over the surface. Let either stand for 5 to 10 minutes.

In the bowl of a stand mixer fitted with the whisk attachment, whip the crème fraîche and cream on medium speed until the mixture holds soft peaks, about 2 minutes. Alternatively, whip the crème fraîche and the cream in a large bowl with a hand mixer or whisk. Transfer to a bowl, cover, and refrigerate until ready to use, up to 1 hour.

In a small saucepan over medium-low heat, warm the remaining $1/2$ cup (4.2 oz / 120 g) of water, the sugar, and salt and cook, swirling occasionally, until the sugar dissolves, and then continue simmering without stirring until the syrup registers 230°F on a digital thermometer. Meanwhile, wash and dry the mixer bowl and add the yolks. Using the whisk attachment, whip the yolks on medium speed until lightened in color, 3 to 4 minutes.

Immediately transfer the syrup to a heatproof liquid measuring cup. With the mixer running on medium-low speed, add the hot sugar syrup to the yolks in a thin, steady stream; aim to pour it into the small space between the mixer bowl and the whisk.

If using gelatin sheets, lift the softened sheets out of the bowl and squeeze out the excess water. While the yolk mixture is still hot, add the sheets or the bloomed powdered gelatin to the bowl and whip on low speed until the gelatin has dissolved and the mixture has cooled to room temperature, about 5 minutes.

Remove the bowl from the mixer. Using a flexible rubber spatula, gently but thoroughly fold in the whipped crème fraîche until no streaks of color remain. Pour the mixture into the prepared baking pan and smooth with an offset spatula. Cover in plastic wrap and freeze until firm, about 2 hours.

To bake the sablés, position racks in the upper and lower thirds of the oven. Preheat the oven to 350°F. Line 2 rimmed baking sheets with parchment paper.

Use a small metal spatula to transfer the chilled dough squares to the prepared baking sheets, spacing them about 1 inch apart. Because this dough toughens too much when rerolled, we save any cookie dough scraps and bake them as snacks for our café employees. They are best baked on their own baking sheet with the baking time reduced by 1 to 2 minutes.

Bake, rotating the baking sheets midway through baking, until the cookies are the slightest golden brown color, 12 to 14 minutes. Let cool on the baking sheets for 10 minutes, and then transfer the cookies to a wire rack. Let cool to room temperature.

Just before using the coulis, puree the solidified mass in a blender or food processor until it has the texture of pudding, about 3 minutes.

Invert the frozen parfait from the pan onto a cutting board, remove the plastic wrap and, using a large knife, cut the block into 2-inch squares. Use immediately or return to the freezer until ready to use.

To assemble, have ready small serving plates. Spoon 3 tablespoons of coulis onto each plate and smooth it with the back of the spoon into a 3-inch round.

Nestle a sablé into the coulis on each plate, and then top it with a parfait. Serve immediately.

© 2013 Succession H. Matisse / Artists Rights Society (ARS), New York

Henri Matisse
Allan Stein
ca. 1907
oil on canvas
21⅝ x 18⅛ in.
Collection of the Kaiserman
Family

———

In 1904, eight-year-old Allan Stein moved with his parents, Sarah and Michael Stein, from San Francisco to the Left Bank of Paris, near where relatives Leo and Gertrude Stein had recently settled. The eccentric American family quickly became central figures in the birth of modern art, befriending, collecting, and championing the most adventurous artists of the day, particularly Pablo Picasso and Henri Matisse (1869–1954), both of whom painted the young Allan.

This vivid, cartoonish portrait of the curly-haired boy in a fisherman's sweater is one of two paintings that Matisse made of Allan, who was a year younger than the artist's daughter, Marguerite, and a childhood playmate of hers. The artist and the boy shared a mutual affection. From one beachside summer vacation, Allan wrote to his Uncle Leo, "Matisse and his wife were here for a few days. We had walks and swims. . . . He taught me to dive again and how to swim underwater about 10 feet."

MATISSE PARFAIT

MAKES 16 INDIVIDUAL PARFAITS
HANDS-ON TIME: 1½ HOURS
FROM START TO FINISH: 6 HOURS

In the summer of 2011, SFMOMA presented a brilliant show co-organized by Janet Bishop called *The Steins Collect: Matisse, Picasso, and the Parisian Avante-Garde*, an exhibition of the art amassed by Gertrude Stein, her brothers Leo and Michael, and Michael's wife, Sarah. The family, all living in bohemian Paris in the 1920s, filled their homes with the artwork of their friends and contemporaries, including works by Henri Matisse and Pablo Picasso—paintings that were to become of dizzying importance to the art world.

The girly girls that we are, Leah, Tess, and I were immediately drawn to the Matisse piece *Allan Stein*, a sweet portrait of Sarah and Michael Stein's young son, Allan, with a bubblegum-pink background. Taking cues from color and texture elements in the painting, we decided to build a dessert with our interpretations of the various components. The pink background became strawberry coulis; Allan's hair was turned into chocolate curls; and his long, skinny neck became a slightly tart and tangy parfait made with yogurt. With my fondness for the woolen sweaters worn by French seamen, I became obsessed with Allan's sweater in the painting, especially the buttons at the shoulder and the detailing around the neck. Digging through my knitting supplies, I discovered I had some handspun yarn that was a very close color match to Allan's sweater, so I took out my large needles and knit small squares with the rough pattern of a fisherman's sweater. Set under the serving plates, the coasters were a lovely color and texture detail that brought the dessert together and kept me knitting all summer long.

NOTE: Agar (also called agar-agar) is made from seaweed and, like gelatin, it's used to solidify liquids. Agar flakes are available in Japanese markets and natural food stores, often near the seaweed. The key to smooth texture when working with agar flakes is to make sure they're completely dissolved. In this recipe, the final mixture is strained, so particles of agar aren't really an issue, but to get maximum gelling, it's crucial to cook the agar until a thick, clear gel forms. If agar flakes cannot be found, 1 teaspoon of agar powder can be substituted for 1 tablespoon of agar flakes.

DO AHEAD: This dessert has a few different components that require preparation before it can be assembled. The coulis must chill for at least 3 hours before processing, but can be made ahead and stored in an airtight container for up to 1 week. The parfaits need to chill for at least 4 hours before serving, but can be made ahead and stored in an airtight container in the freezer for up to 1 week. The chocolate curls can be made ahead of time and stored for 2 months in an airtight container at cool room temperature.

ABOVE AND BEYOND: Of course, you don't have to knit coasters for your Matisse dessert, but if you can't bear to see young Allan without his blue sweater, a knitting pattern can be found on page 144. Parfaits made in 2³/₄-inch diameter molds (see Resources, page 205) are the ideal serving size, and 4-inch square Heath plates (see Resources, page 205) are perfect under the parfaits and on top of the coasters.

STRAWBERRY COULIS

²/₃ cup (5.7 oz / 160 g) water

2 tablespoons sugar

Grated zest of 1 lemon

1 tablespoon agar flakes
(see Note, page 142)

¹/₂ cup (4.3 oz / 120 g) syrup from
Macerated Strawberries with Syrup
(page 41)

YOGURT PARFAIT

2¹/₂ gelatin sheets, or 1³/₄ teaspoons
powdered gelatin

¹/₄ cup (2.1 oz / 60 g) water,
if using powdered gelatin,
plus ¹/₂ cup (4.3 oz / 120 g) water

1 cup (8.3 oz / 232 g) plain
whole-milk yogurt

²/₃ cup (5.5 oz / 153 g) cold heavy cream

1 cup (7.1 oz / 200 g) sugar

¹/₂ teaspoon kosher salt

6 large egg yolks (4 oz / 114 g)

—

Chocolate Curls (see page 145)

To make the strawberry coulis, in a small saucepan over medium-low heat, bring the water, sugar, zest, and agar flakes to a boil, stirring constantly. Cook, still stirring, until the agar is completely dissolved and the mixture thickens into a clear gel with no visible agar pieces, about 8 minutes. Stir in the syrup from the strawberries and cook for 1 minute longer.

Strain the mixture through a fine-mesh sieve set over a small bowl. Cover with plastic wrap and refrigerate until firm, at least 4 hours or up to 1 week.

Meanwhile, make the parfait. Line an 8-inch square cake pan with plastic wrap.

If you're using gelatin sheets, fill a medium bowl with ice water and submerge the sheets in the water. If you're using powdered gelatin, pour the ¹/₄ cup (2.1 oz / 60 g) of water into a small bowl and sprinkle the gelatin evenly over the surface. Let either stand for 5 to 10 minutes.

In the bowl of a stand mixer fitted with the whisk attachment, whip the yogurt and cream on medium speed until the mixture holds soft peaks, about 2 minutes. Alternatively, whip the yogurt and the cream in a large bowl with a hand mixer or whisk. Transfer to a bowl, cover, and refrigerate until ready to use, up to 1 hour.

In a small saucepan over medium-low heat, warm the remaining ¹/₂ cup (4.3 oz / 120 g) of water, the sugar, and the salt and cook, swirling occasionally, until the sugar dissolves, and then continue simmering without stirring until the syrup registers 230°F on a digital thermometer. Meanwhile, wash and dry the mixer bowl and add the yolks. Using the whisk attachment, whip the yolks on medium speed until lightened in color, 3 to 4 minutes.

Immediately transfer the syrup to a heatproof liquid measuring cup. With the mixer running on medium-low speed, add the hot sugar syrup to the yolks in a thin, steady stream; aim to pour it into the small space between the mixer bowl and the whisk.

If using gelatin sheets, lift the softened sheets out of the bowl and squeeze out the excess water. While the yolk mixture is still hot, add the sheets or the bloomed powdered gelatin to the bowl and whip on low speed until the gelatin has dissolved and the mixture has cooled to room temperature, about 5 minutes.

Remove the bowl from the mixer. Using a flexible rubber spatula, gently but thoroughly fold in the whipped yogurt mixture until no streaks of color remain. Pour the mixture into the prepared baking pan and smooth with an offset spatula. Cover with plastic wrap and freeze until firm, about 2 hours.

To finish the coulis, puree the solidified mass in a blender or food processor until it has the texture of pudding, about 3 minutes.

Invert the frozen parfait from the pan onto a cutting board, remove the plastic wrap and, using a large knife, cut the block into 2-inch squares. Use immediately or return to the freezer until ready to use.

To assemble, have ready small serving plates. Spoon 3 tablespoons of strawberry coulis onto each plate and smooth it with the back of the spoon into a 3-inch round. Nestle a parfait into the coulis on each plate. Arrange chocolate curls on top of the parfaits and serve immediately.

KNITTING ALLAN STEIN'S SWEATER

To knit the 4-inch sweater square that completes the Allan Stein look, cast on 19 stitches worsted-weight yarn on size 10 needles.

PATTERN STITCH
Knit 4, purl 1, knit 4, purl 1, knit 4, purl 1, knit 4 (right side)*
Purl 4, knit 1, Purl 4, knit 1, Purl 4, Knit 1, purl 4 (wrong side)*
* Repeat these two rows 10 times

Cast off in pattern loosely. Cut yarn and weave in ends. Block flat, if needed.

MAKING CHOCOLATE CURLS

For the most impressive ringlets of chocolate, a large chunk of bulk chocolate (sold in stores such as Trader Joe's and Whole Foods) is key. A hefty block will allow you to curl dramatic sheets of chocolate that resemble Allan's curly locks. In a pinch, a retail bar of chocolate can be used, but the curls will be a bit thinner.

1 large block of bittersweet chocolate (about 8 ounces)

Warm the chocolate by holding it between your hands, or if the piece is very large, microwave it at full power for 5 seconds at a time. When it's ready for curling, the chocolate will be the barest bit warm and your fingernail can make an indentation without too much effort.

Hold the chocolate in a diagonal plane with one end on the work surface and the other angled toward your chest. Using a vegetable peeler and long, outward strokes, shave wide, thick ribbons of chocolate, pressing the blade firmly against the block. The heat of your hand should be enough to keep the chocolate at a good temperature for curling. If it starts to melt, wash your hands in cold water and then resume.

Ellsworth Kelly
Stele I
1973
weathering steel
216 in. x 120 in. x 1 in.
SFMOMA, the Doris and Donald Fisher Collection, and the Helen and Charles Schwab Collection, 99.354

Since the mid-twentieth century, American artist Ellsworth Kelly (born 1931) has engaged in a sustained investigation of shape, form, and light that has resulted in extraordinary paintings—often boldly colored—as well as works on paper, wall reliefs, and sculpture. In 1973, shortly after moving upstate from New York City, Kelly made the first of two steel pieces called *Stele*—a Greek word referring to an upright pillar or commemorative slab. With the eighteen-foot-high *Stele I*, Kelly realized an oblong form he'd begun exploring decades earlier in monumental proportions.

Wherever it is installed, the piece takes on a direct relationship with its surroundings, obliterating the view of whatever is behind it when seen frontally and, at just one inch thick, nearly completely disappearing when seen from the side. The experience of the piece not only changes as one moves around it but in relationship to the presence and shape of its shadow.

KELLY FUDGE POP

MAKES 8 TO 10 FUDGE POPS
HANDS-ON TIME: 15 MINUTES
FROM START TO FINISH: 4 TO 5 HOURS

Ellsworth Kelly's enormous sculpture, *Stele 1*, was the anchor in the Rooftop Garden when we opened our café in 2009. A 1-inch-thick oblong steel plate weighing seven tons and rising eighteen feet into the air perched on one narrow end, the sculpture seemed to defy gravity. The deep rust-colored patina of the Corten steel was an incredible contrast against gray volcanic stone walls of the Rooftop Garden and the stunning art deco Pacific Bell building that towers over the east side of the museum. Of course, I thought the piece looked like an enormous slab of chocolate. Trying to figure out a dessert based on the sculpture, I played with various truffle recipes and cakes baked in oblong pans, but nothing was giving me the rich matte color and texture of the weathered steel.

One day I was chatting with the museum's brilliant and witty social media guru, Ian Padgham, about *Stele 1*, and I asked him what the sculpture reminded him of. "A Fudgsicle, of course!" he said. And, so it was. I found some silicone ice-pop molds in the shape of the sculpture and developed a creamy, rich chocolatey base with a touch of natural cocoa powder to give the frozen fudge pops the reddish matte finish of Corten steel.

DO AHEAD: Stored in an airtight container, the fudge pops will keep for up to 2 weeks in the freezer.

ABOVE AND BEYOND: This recipe works well in any ice-pop mold, but if you want to create a miniature edible Ellsworth Kelly sculpture in your home, see Resources (page 205) to order the silicone ice-pop molds we use at the café.

8 ounces (227 g) high-quality bittersweet chocolate (62% to 70% cacao), coarsely chopped

1 tablespoon vanilla extract

1¹/₄ cups (10.4 oz / 290 g) heavy cream

1 cup (8.6 oz / 242 g) whole milk

¹/₄ cup (1.8 oz / 50 g) sugar

4 teaspoons natural (not Dutch-processed) unsweetened cocoa powder

1 teaspoon kosher salt

Have ready 10 ice-pop molds. If your molds are flexible like the ones we use at the museum, set them on a rimmed baking sheet.

Place the chocolate in a large heatproof bowl, add the vanilla extract, and set aside.

In a medium, heavy-bottomed saucepan, combine the cream, milk, sugar, cocoa powder, and salt. Cook over medium-low heat, whisking often to break up the lumps of cocoa powder, until bubbles start to form around the edges and the temperature of the mixture registers 180°F to 190°F on a digital thermometer.

Immediately pour the cream mixture over the chocolate and stir with a whisk or blend with an immersion blender until the chocolate is completely melted and the mixture is a smooth liquid (a thoroughly emulsified mixture will yield the most creamy fudge pop). Strain the mixture through a fine-mesh sieve set over a liquid measuring cup.

Pour the chocolate mixture into the ice-pop molds and freeze until solid, at least 4 hours or up to 2 weeks; follow the manufacturer's instructions for inserting the sticks. If you don't have ice-pop molds, pour the chocolate mixture into ice cube trays; freeze until partially frozen, about 30 minutes, and then insert a toothpick or short wooden skewer into each ice pop. Continue freezing until solid.

Unmold the fudge pops, dipping the molds into warm water to loosen, if needed, and serve.

John Zurier
Arabella
2005
oil on linen
84 in. x 58 in.
SFMOMA, gift of the artist
and Paule Anglim, 2007.42
——

Arabella is one of twelve abstract paintings that John Zurier (born 1956) first presented at San Francisco's Gallery Paule Anglim in 2005. Zurier had seen a Barnett Newman retrospective at the Philadelphia Museum of Art in 2002. As Zurier made this body of work, Newman's approach to structuring paintings was on his mind, as was his predecessor's embrace of imperfection, use of tape, and color choices.

Zurier has a very process-oriented practice. To create the lush surface of *Arabella*, he started with a support of coarse Russian linen, which he then covered with blue-green underpainting and a field of opaque red. He recalls later adding the red wash over the band at the right, but leaving the blue-green at the left exposed. In exploring compositions with vertical bands, the artist's interest was not only in "divisions of surface but as a way of bringing additional color harmony to monochrome painting."

ZURIER ICE POP

MAKES 10 ICE POPS
HANDS-ON TIME: 1 HOUR
FROM START TO FINISH: 5 HOURS

In addition to being a talented pastry chef, Leah is an accomplished painter who meditates on stripes and how the accumulation and layering of paint can create complex, color-saturated works. It's not surprising, then, that she was thrilled to find *Arabella*, a painting by John Zurier, one of her graduate school professors, on the fifth floor of the museum. A densely saturated red block of color over a minty green underpainting, *Arabella* depicts a semblance of a stripe and a pairing of contrasting colors. With Professor Zurier's words in her head, "The way color is out in the world and the way color operates in a painting—

they're very different things," Leah devised a striped ice pop, filling the molds most of the way with a strawberry base, and then adding a mint-cream ice base to top them off.

At the same time that the ice pops were ready for their debut at the café, John was having an art opening at a nearby gallery. Leah wanted to surprise him with the dessert she made in his honor, so with only three blocks between SFMOMA and the gallery, Leah got on her bike, ice pop in hand, and pedaled quickly to the opening. Despite her best efforts, she arrived with her arm covered in strawberry juice, so instead of an edible treat, she offered John a photo of the ice pop taken with her phone. In the following months, I swear that I saw John in the Rooftop Garden every time I was there, always with an ice pop in hand.

Although the strawberry base and the mint base were developed to be frozen together into a two-toned ice pop, each can be made into a delicious single-flavor treat.

NOTE: In the mint base, we expected to be able extract a pale green hue from the spearmint leaves, but they didn't release any color at all, so we added a tiny touch of turquoise food coloring to match the light green in the painting. The tip of a toothpick dipped in turquoise food coloring gel and swirled into the warm cream mixture added just the right amount of color we needed. The ice pops are delicious without the added coloring if you prefer to skip it.

DO AHEAD: Stored in an airtight container, the ice pops will keep for up to 2 weeks in the freezer.

ABOVE AND BEYOND: These ice pops are beautiful and delicious frozen in any ice-pop mold, but to get the vertical-stripe effect, it's necessary to use ones that lay flat when filled and frozen. Ice-pop molds made by Cold Molds (see Resources, page 205) are the perfect size and shape for both this recipe and the Kelly Fudge Pops (page 147).

STRAWBERRY ICE-POP BASE	MINT-CREAM ICE-POP BASE
1 pound (454 g) fresh strawberries	$^1/_3$ cup (2.7 oz / 77g) cold heavy cream
1 cup (8.6 oz / 240 g) water	2 teaspoons cornstarch
$^1/_2$ cup (3.5 oz / 100 g) sugar	$^2/_3$ cup (5.7 oz / 160 g) whole milk
3 tablespoons fresh lemon juice	$^1/_2$ cup (0.35 oz / 10 g) loosely packed fresh spearmint leaves
	$^1/_3$ cup (2.4 oz / 66 g) sugar
	Pinch of kosher salt
	Turquoise food coloring (see page 30; optional)

To make the strawberry base, wash, dry, and hull the strawberries. Cut the berries in half or quarter them if they are especially big.

Combine the strawberries, water, sugar, and lemon juice in a medium nonreactive saucepan and bring the mixture to a simmer over medium-low heat, stirring to help the sugar dissolve. Turn down the heat to the low, cover, and simmer until the berries are soft, 8 to 10 minutes. Remove from the heat and let the berries rest for 5 minutes.

Transfer the berry mixture to a fine-mesh sieve set over a 1-quart liquid measuring cup. Let stand for 5 minutes to allow the juice to drain from the berries; don't press on the fruit to extract additional liquid. You should have 4 cups (34 oz / 950 g) of strained strawberry juice.

Pour the strawberry base into the prepared molds, dividing it evenly; each one should be about two-thirds full. Freeze until firm, at least 2 hours; follow the manufacturer's instructions for inserting the sticks. If you don't have ice-pop molds, pour the base into ice cube trays, filling each cavity about half full.

To make the mint-cream base, whisk the cold cream and cornstarch in a medium saucepan until combined. Add the milk, spearmint leaves, sugar, salt, and food coloring (see Note, opposite). Set the pan over medium heat and cook, stirring frequently, until bubbles begin to form around the edges and the mixture registers 180°F to 190°F on a digital thermometer.

Remove the pan from the heat, cover, and let stand for 15 minutes. Strain the liquid through a fine-mesh sieve set over 2-cup liquid measuring cup. Discard the mint, then cover the measuring cup with plastic wrap and refrigerate until strawberry ice pops are frozen.

Remove the molds from the freezer and top them off with the mint-cream base. Continue freezing until solid. If using ice cube trays, top with the mint-cream base; freeze until partially frozen, about 30 minutes, and then insert a toothpick or short wooden skewer into each ice pop. Continue freezing until solid.

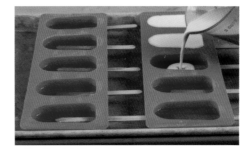

Unmold the ice pops, dipping the molds into warm water to loosen, if needed, and serve.

Tony Cragg
Guglie
1987
wood, rubber, concrete, metal, stone, and plastic
3 elements: 84 in. x 23 in. x 23 in., 101 in. x 21 in. x 21 in.,
    74 in. x 18 in. x 18 in.
The Doris and Donald Fisher Collection at the
    San Francisco Museum of Modern Art

Though he has lived in Germany since 1977, Tony Cragg (born Liverpool, 1949) is one of the principal artists associated with an especially vital period for British sculpture in the 1980s. The artist served as Great Britain's representative to the Venice Biennale in 1988, in which *Guglie* was shown, and won the prestigious Turner Prize the following year.

With interests in both the urban and the organic, Cragg has built a consistently inventive practice. For *Guglie*, which is Italian for spires, the artist worked in the spirit of Italian Arte Povera artists, who were known for their use of everyday materials and elemental forms. Cragg's three concentric stacks of scavenged material—rubber tires, wooden discs, rusty gears, pipe fittings, pink and green film canisters—mimic upward reaching shapes typically used symbolically. As Cragg notes, however, "I'm not a religious person—I'm an absolute materialist—and for me material is exciting and ultimately sublime."

CRAGG ICE CREAM CONE

MAKES 8 ICE CREAM CONES
HANDS-ON TIME: 1 1/2 HOURS
FROM START TO FINISH: 9 HOURS

In September 2009, SFMOMA announced that it had partnered with Donald Fisher, founder of Gap, Inc., to house the extensive collection of modern and contemporary art that Fisher had acquired with his wife, Doris. The entire collection would be on display after the completion of SFMOMA's massive three-year expansion, but to introduce a small portion, the museum planned a three-month exhibition shortly after the announcement. Thrilled to receive the list of the new artworks, I immediately sent off an email to Leah: "Tony Cragg! Stripes! In the Rooftop Garden!"

Guglie is a group of three conical towers assembled from wood, rubber, concrete, metal, stone, and plastic. With all of the varying rusted, painted, and textured materials, the layers look like stripes on an upside-down ice cream cone—a perfect item to serve during the summertime show. I designed a paper template for an ice cream cone sleeve and handed it off to Leah, who painted *Guglie*-like stripes that would wrap around the cone. With a production schedule already cramped with desserts, we asked the boys at Humphry

Slocombe, a San Francisco ice cream shop lauded for its wild flavors, to suggest a few ice creams for the Cragg cone. Inspired by the season and the pink and brown stripes of the sculpture, we went with two not-too-unusual—but totally delicious—flavors that were perfect together: strawberry sorbet and malted milk chocolate. Humphry Slocombe's malted milk chocolate ice cream is one of my all-time favorite flavors, and I couldn't be happier to have the recipe so that I can make it at home. Jake and Sean like their ice creams on the salty side, and I love them for that. This recipe is perfect for my taste, but if you are sensitive to saltiness, reduce the salt amount in the chocolate ice cream as you prefer.

NOTE: As much as I love these Humphry Slocombe ice creams, store-bought ice cream can also work in this dessert. Malted milk powder can be found in the ice cream cone and toppings section of most grocery stores. Carnation and Ovaltine brands are the most popular, but I especially love the British import brand Horlicks.

DO AHEAD: The ice cream base can be made up to 2 days before freezing. Both the ice cream and sorbet can be churned in advance; store the ice cream in an airtight container in the freezer to for up to 1 week and the sorbet for 2 weeks.

ABOVE AND BEYOND: An ice cream cone sleeve is definitely not necessary for this dessert, but it does add a special touch, turning the cone into a work of art. To download the template, visit www.modernartdesserts.com, then print in color, cut out each sleeve, wrap around a cone, and tape to secure it in place before you top the cone with ice cream.

HUMPHRY SLOCOMBE'S MALTED MILK CHOCOLATE ICE CREAM

2 cups (16.6 oz / 464 g) heavy cream

1 cup (8.6 oz / 242 g) whole milk

2 teaspoons kosher salt

3 ounces (84 g) milk chocolate, finely chopped

2 ounces (56 g) high-quality dark chocolate (70% cacao), finely chopped

3 large egg yolks (2 oz / 57 g)

1 cup (7.1 oz / 200 g) sugar

3 tablespoons malted milk powder (see Note)

HUMPHRY SLOCOMBE'S STRAWBERRY SORBET

1 pound (454 g) fresh strawberries, washed, dried, and hulled

1/2 cup (3.5 oz / 100 g) sugar

2 tablespoons red wine vinegar

Juice of 1/2 lime

1/2 teaspoon kosher salt

—

8 sugar cones

To make the ice cream, fill a large bowl halfway with ice water. Place a medium bowl in the ice-water bath and set a fine-mesh sieve across the top.

In a medium, heavy-bottomed saucepan over medium heat, warm the cream, milk, and salt, stirring often, until the mixture registers 180°F to 190°F on a digital thermometer and bubbles begin to form around the edges.

Meanwhile, combine the milk chocolate and dark chocolate in a second large bowl. In a second medium bowl, whisk together the egg yolks and sugar until well blended.

Remove the saucepan from the heat. Temper the egg yolks by gradually whisking about one-half of the warm cream mixture into the yolk mixture, and then whisk the tempered yolks into the cream mixture in the saucepan. Set the pan over medium heat and cook, stirring constantly with a rubber spatula and scraping along the bottom of the pan to prevent scorching, until the mixture begins to steam and is thick enough to coat the back of a spoon, 2 to 3 minutes.

Immediately pour the custard over the chocolates and whisk until the chocolate is melted and the custard is smooth. Whisk in the malt powder until dissolved. Pour the custard through the sieve into the chilled bowl. Let cool completely, stirring occasionally. Lay plastic wrap directly on the surface of the custard and refrigerate until cold, at least 3 hours, but preferably overnight. (Stored in an airtight container, the ice cream base will keep for up to 2 days in the refrigerator.)

Freeze the base in an ice cream machine according to the manufacturer's instructions.

Transfer the ice cream (it will be quite soft) to a 1-quart container, cover tightly, and freeze until firm, at least 4 hours.

To make the sorbet, puree the strawberries, sugar, vinegar, lime juice, and salt in a food processor until smooth. Strain the puree through a fine-mesh sieve set over a medium bowl and discard the seeds. Cover with plastic wrap and refrigerate until cold, at least 2 hours.

Freeze the sorbet base in an ice cream machine according to the manufacturer's instructions.

Transfer the sorbet (it will be quite soft) to a 1-quart container, cover tightly, and freeze until firm, at least 4 hours.

To serve, place a large scoop of the chocolate ice cream on a cone. Top with a scoop of sorbet.

Alejandro Cartagena
Fragmented Cities, Juarez #2, from the series
  Suburbia Mexicana
2007
inkjet print
15⁷/₈ in. x 20 in.
SFMOMA, accessions Committee Fund purchase, 2011.171

Fragmented Cities, Juarez #2 is part of *Suburbia Mexicana*, a series of photographs by Alejandro Cartagena (born 1977). The images document the rampant sprawl outside the city of Monterrey, Mexico, where he moved from the Dominican Republic as a young teenager. Shot on a cloudy summer evening in the city of Juarez, Cartagena's image features a row of uncomfortably small new houses—each rigged up to a water tank and exterior maze of utilities. The box-like structures are only slightly differentiated by their candy-colored facades. Through beautiful and carefully composed images of often poorly constructed and underplanned communities, the artist calls into question the dreams of home ownership versus the realities of people living far from city centers, saddled with mortgages, in densely built areas without sufficient attention to parks, community centers, public transportation, and other amenities that allow residents of suburban regions to thrive.

CARTAGENA ICE CREAM AND SORBET TRIO

MAKES TWELVE 3-INCH SQUARES
HANDS-ON TIME: 2 HOURS
FROM START TO FINISH: 1 ¹/₂ DAYS

When I heard that SFMOMA was curating a show called *Photography in Mexico* for spring 2012, my heart sank. A few years earlier, an exhibition called *Exposed: Voyeurism, Surveillance, and the Camera since 1870* taught me photography was a medium that didn't easily translate to dessert (see page 16). The upcoming show would present Mexico's photographic tradition, from the 1920s to today, and touch on a wide range of topics; it was massive in scope and I couldn't get a handle on any one theme. We spent weeks obsessing over another image, but eventually I went back to the strategy I used with *Exposed*: I just looked for an image I liked (see page 15).

A photo that I loved right away for its colors and graphic shapes was *Fragmented Cities, Juarez #2,* from the series *Suburbia Mexicana* by Alejandro Cartagena, a young contemporary artist. Leah, Tess, and I imagined the gray swath in the foreground as slate and the colored houses as different flavors of sorbet. We decided to make layered blocks of sorbet and vanilla ice cream: the yellow house would be lemon, obviously; the pink house would be rose (inspired by rose ice cream I had in Mexico); and the green one would be avocado. I filled three baking sheets each with a thin layer of vanilla ice cream to set up in the freezer overnight, and then I whirred up sorbets bases for churning and layering atop the ice cream the next day.

The next morning, I found out that SFMOMA was hosting a talk with two of the artists from the *Photography in Mexico* show, and that Cartagena was one of them. We managed to arrange a tasting with him, and he was thrilled that his work had inspired the dessert we presented to him—and we were beyond excited to meet the artist who inspired our dessert.

NOTE: Making 3 batches of ice cream and 3 batches of sorbet for a single dessert is just not doable for most home cooks. I've given instructions for each of the three combinations we made, and called for a portion size larger than we served at the café, so you need only make one flavor. You can choose to do whichever sounds best to you.

Rose water is sold in Middle Eastern markets and often in health-food stores. Meyer lemons are a lemon-orange hybrid that have the tanginess of a lemon and a slight sweetness from the orange; their flavor pairs delightfully with the vanilla ice cream. Eureka lemons can be substituted for a slightly more sour, but equally delicious, sorbet.

DO AHEAD: The ice cream and sorbet bases can be made up to 2 days in before freezing and stored in the refrigerator. Stored in an airtight container, the cut or uncut ice cream and sorbet pair will keep for up to 2 weeks in the freezer.

ABOVE AND BEYOND: To serve the dessert exactly as we did at the museum, you'll need to make 3 batches of vanilla ice cream and freeze them in 3 separate pans. Then, make one batch of each type of sorbet and layer one flavor over each batch of ice cream. Cut into $1^1/2$-inch squares and set one of each on a slate cheese board (see Resources, page 205).

Vanilla Ice Cream (page 166),
frozen in a 9 by 13-inch pan

AVOCADO SORBET

$3^1/3$ cups (28.6 oz / 800 g) water

$2^1/4$ cups (16 oz / 450 g) sugar

$1/3$ cup (2.9 oz / 80 g) fresh lime juice

$3/4$ teaspoon kosher salt

3 medium ripe avocados ($1^3/4$ cups / 18 oz / 506 g total), pitted and peeled

ROSE SORBET

4¹/₂ cups (38.6 oz / 1080 g) water

2 cups (14.3 oz / 400 g) sugar

³/₄ cup (6.4 oz / 180 g) rose water

1 drop pink food coloring
(see page 30; optional)

MEYER LEMON SORBET

2 cups (17 oz / 475 g) fresh
Meyer lemon juice

Grated zest of 1 Meyer lemon

3 cups (25.7 oz / 720 g) water

2 ¹/₂ cups (17.9 oz / 500 g) sugar

1 drop yellow food coloring
(see page 30; optional)

To make the avocado sorbet, in a medium nonreactive saucepan over medium heat, bring the water, sugar, lime juice, and salt to a boil. Cook, stirring to dissolve the sugar, for 1 minute. Transfer to a liquid measuring cup.

In a food processor, puree the avocados until smooth, about 3 minutes. With the machine running, add the liquid in a slow, steady stream. Strain the puree through a medium-mesh sieve set over a medium bowl, cover, and refrigerate until cold, at least 3 hours.

To make the rose sorbet, in a medium saucepan over medium heat, bring the water and sugar to a boil, stirring to dissolve the sugar. Transfer to a medium bowl and let cool to room temperature.

Stir the rose water and pink food coloring into the sugar syrup, cover, and refrigerate until cold, at least 2 hours.

To make the Meyer lemon sorbet, using a vegetable peeler, remove the zest of 1 lemon in wide ribbons. In a medium saucepan over medium heat, bring the zest, water, and sugar to a boil, stirring to dissolve the sugar. Remove from the heat and let cool to room temperature.

Add the lemon juice to a medium bowl, and then strain the sugar syrup through a fine-mesh sieve into the bowl. Stir in the yellow food coloring, cover, and refrigerate until cold, at least 2 hours.

Freeze your chosen sorbet in an ice cream machine according to the manufacturer's instructions (churn to the texture of soft-serve) and then pour over the prepared vanilla ice cream. Smooth with an offset spatula, cover tightly, and freeze until firm, at least 4 hours.

Remove the ice cream from the freezer and transfer to a cutting board. Remove the plastic wrap and, using a large knife, cut the block into 3-inch squares. Use immediately or return to the freezer until ready to use.

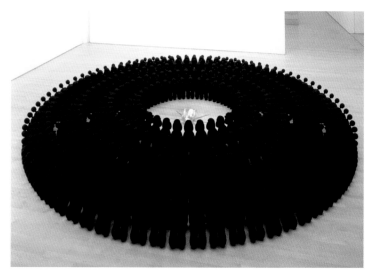

Katharina Fritsch
Kind mit Pudeln (Child with Poodles)
1995/1996
plaster, foil, polyurethane, and paint
15³/4 in. x 201¹/2 in. x 201¹/2 in.
SFMOMA, Accessions Committee Fund purchase, 96.490

With a vivid imagination and exacting sensibility, Dusseldorf artist Katharina Fritsch (born Essen, 1956) creates psychologically charged sculpture inspired by memories and dreams, fairy tales, literature, religion, and real life. A giant rat sits on a sleeping man's chest. Hundreds of brains form a tower. A chicken has turned bright blue.

In *Child with Poodles*, 224 miniature black poodles encircle a baby resting on a golden star who calls to mind the Christ child. It is not possible to know what has drawn so many dogs to the baby, who appears trapped and vulnerable, albeit blissfully oblivious, at the center of a curious and menacing or possibly protective group. In speaking of the piece, Fritsch recalled Goethe's story of Faust, in which the protagonist brings home a poodle and thus unwittingly opens himself up to the forces of the devil.

© Artists Rights Society (ARS), New York / VG Bild-Kunst Bonn, Germany

FRITSCH ICE CREAM SANDWICH

MAKES 10 TO 12 ICE CREAM SANDWICHES
HANDS-ON TIME: 1¹/2 HOURS
FROM START TO FINISH: 9 HOURS

In the three weeks that I had to create art-inspired desserts for the opening of the Blue Bottle Coffee Bar in the Rooftop Garden, I tried to come up with as many ideas as I could. I knew I wouldn't have time to test all of them, so for the opening, I chose to work on the ideas that were based on landmark pieces on exhibit. Katharina Fritsch's *Kind mit Pudeln* (Child with Poodles) was such a focal point in the museum—the 224 black poodles with a white baby figurine occupied the floor space of an entire gallery—that I knew right away a poodle-themed dessert would resonate with visitors. Salted chocolate sablé cookies made perfect edible poodles, and the white baby at the center of the sculpture inspired a vanilla ice cream filling: a poodle-shaped ice cream sandwich. Salty, sweet, creamy, and crunchy, this dessert is still talked about all these years later.

DO AHEAD: This ice cream sandwich has two different components that both require preparation before it can be assembled. The mixed, rolled, and cut chocolate sablé dough must cool for at least 45 minutes before baking and can be stored in the refrigerator for 2 days. Stored in an airtight container, the baked cookies will keep for up to 1 day at room temperature. The ice cream requires about 4 hours of chilling, churning, and freezing time before being cut. The churned ice cream can be poured into the designated pan, wrapped tightly, and stored in the freezer for up to 1 week.

Stored in an airtight container, the assembled ice cream sandwiches will keep in the freezer for up to 1 week.

ABOVE AND BEYOND: Shape isn't necessary for the deliciousness of this dessert, so this recipe calls for making square ice cream sandwiches to eliminate excess waste (though I doubt the scraps would actually go uneaten!). At the museum, we make poodle-shaped ice cream sandwiches by using a poodle cookie cutter to cut the dough, as well as to stamp out the ice cream filling. Poodle cutters are relatively easy to find, but if you can't locate one in your local cookware store, see Resources (page 205).

Chocolate Sablé Dough (page 168)
Vanilla Ice Cream (recipe follows), frozen in a 9 by 13-inch pan

Set the sablé dough on a large sheet of parchment paper and press it into a flat, even, rectangle measuring about 5 by 6 inches. Lay a second sheet of parchment paper on top and roll out the dough to an even $1/8$ to $1/4$-inch thickness. Remove the top sheet of parchment and, using a large knife or pizza wheel, cut the dough into 2-inch squares. The dough will be soft, so don't try to remove the squares until after chilling. Slide the parchment paper with the dough onto a baking sheet, cover with plastic wrap, and refrigerate until the dough is cold and firm, at least 45 minutes or up to 2 days. The longer the dough chills, the less it will spread during baking.

Position racks in the upper and lower thirds of the oven. Preheat the oven to 350°F. Line 2 baking sheets with parchment paper.

Use a small metal spatula to transfer the dough squares to the prepared baking sheets, spacing them about 1 inch apart. Because this dough toughens too much when rerolled, we save any cookie dough scraps and bake them as snacks for our café employees. They are best baked on their own baking sheet with the baking time reduced by 1 to 2 minutes.

Bake until crisp, about 7 minutes, rotating the baking sheets midway through baking. (Note: because the sablés don't change color during baking, it's wise to bake a test batch of one or two cookies to check baking time for your oven before committing your whole batch; see Baking Times, page 25.) Let cool on the baking sheets for 10 minutes, and then transfer the cookies to a wire rack. Let cool to room temperature.

Remove the ice cream from the freezer and invert it out of the pan onto a clean cutting board. Peel off the plastic wrap. Working quickly, use a hot knife to cut the ice cream into 2-inch squares. Place a square of ice cream on a cookie and top with another cookie. Set the ice cream sandwich on a large plate or rimmed baking sheet and place in the freezer. Repeat with the remaining ice cream squares and cookies, putting each sandwich in the freezer as you go. If your ice cream starts to melt, slide the cutting board into the freezer and let chill until the ice cream is firm enough to work with. Freeze the ice cream sandwiches for at least 1 hour to firm and meld the textures.

FRITSCH ICE CREAM SANDWICH

Vanilla Ice Cream

MAKES ABOUT 1 QUART

HANDS-ON TIME: 45 MINUTES

FROM START TO FINISH: 8 HOURS

Making custard-based ice cream can be a little intimidating the first few times you try it, but with a few batches under your belt, you'll find yourself dreaming of all of the varieties of ice cream you can make at home. This recipe is for classic vanilla, and the options for variations are infinite. Add some fresh fruit to the ice cream as it churns for a delicious summer treat, steep a few sprigs of spearmint in the cream along with the vanilla bean and throw in some chopped chocolate during churning for mind-blowing mint chip, or experiment with unusual flavors like black sesame, as we did for the Wong Ice Cream Sandwich (page 171).

NOTE: You can substitute $1/2$ teaspoon vanilla extract for the vanilla bean, warming it along with the cream and sugar mixture.

DO AHEAD: The ice cream base can be made up to 2 days before churning and stored in an airtight container in the refrigerator. Stored in an airtight container, the ice cream will keep for up to 2 weeks in the freezer.

---

2 cups (16.6 oz / 464 g) heavy cream

1 cup (8.6 oz / 242 g) half-and-half

$2/3$ cup (4.7 oz / 133 g) sugar

$1/2$ vanilla bean

6 large egg yolks (4 oz / 114 g), at room temperature

Fill a large bowl halfway with ice water. Place a medium bowl in the ice-water bath and set a fine-mesh sieve across the top.

In a medium, heavy-bottomed saucepan, combine the cream, half-and-half, and sugar. Scrape the vanilla bean seeds into the cream mixture, and drop in the hull. Set the pan over medium-low heat and warm the mixture, stirring occasionally, until it registers 180°F to 190°F on a digital thermometer and bubbles begin to form around the edges. Remove from the heat, cover, and let the vanilla bean steep for 10 minutes. Once steeped, remove and discard the vanilla bean.

Put the egg yolks in a second medium bowl and whisk to break up. Temper them by gradually whisking in $1/4$ cup (2 oz / 58 g) of the warm cream mixture. Repeat until you've added 1¹/₂ cups (12.4 oz / 348 g) of the cream mixture to the yolks and the yolk mixture is warm. Slowly whisk the tempered yolks into the cream in the saucepan. Set the pan over low heat and cook, stirring constantly, until the mixture is thick enough to coat the back of a spoon, about 10 minutes.

Immediately pour the custard through the sieve into the chilled bowl. Let cool completely, stirring occasionally. Lay plastic wrap directly on the surface of the custard and refrigerate until cold, at least 3 hours, but preferably overnight.

Freeze the base in an ice cream machine according to the manufacturer's instructions. Meanwhile, if you're making the Fritsch Ice Cream Sandwich (page 163) or Cartagena Ice Cream and Sorbet Trio (page 159), line a 13 by 9-inch baking pan with plastic wrap. Churn the ice cream just to the texture of soft-serve; the ice cream needs to be soft to pour it into the pan.

Transfer the ice cream (it will be quite soft) to a 1-quart container or the prepared baking pan. Smooth the surface with an offset spatula, cover tightly with plastic wrap, and freeze until firm, at least 4 hours.

Chocolate Sablé Dough

MAKES 20 TO 30 COOKIES, DEPENDING ON SIZE AND SHAPE
HANDS-ON TIME: 20 MINUTES
FROM START TO FINISH: 1 HOUR

This is my go-to recipe for just about any art-inspired dessert needing a rigid, dark-brown element. With a nice crisp crunch and a generous helping of large-grained sea salt, these shortbread-like cookies are the perfect combination of chocolatey, buttery, sweet, and salty.

DO AHEAD: Covered with plastic wrap, the rolled and cut sablé dough will keep for up to 2 days in the refrigerator.

---

1 2/3 cups (8.3 oz / 232 g) all-purpose flour
1/2 cup (1.4 oz / 40 g) natural (not Dutch-processed) unsweetened cocoa powder
1/2 teaspoon baking soda
15 tablespoons (7.5 oz / 210 g) unsalted butter, at room temperature
1 cup (7.1 oz / 200 g) sugar
1/2 teaspoon Maldon sea salt (see page 31)
1 teaspoon vanilla extract

Sift the flour, cocoa powder, and baking soda into a medium bowl.

In the bowl of a stand mixer fitted with the paddle attachment, beat the butter on low speed until smooth, 1 to 2 minutes. Add the sugar and salt and beat on low speed until well combined. Add the vanilla extract and mix just until incorporated. Scrape down the bowl with a rubber spatula, and then beat on medium speed until light and fluffy, 4 to 5 minutes.

Scrape down the bowl, and then add the flour mixture. Mix on low speed just until the dough is uniform, about 15 seconds, scrape down the sides of the bowl and mix for another minute. Refer to the recipe for the modern art dessert that you're making for directions on rolling, cutting, and baking the dough.

VARIATIONS

If you're making the Dijkstra Icebox Cake (page 99) or Wong Ice Cream Sandwich (page 171), replace 1/4 cup (0.8 oz / 23 g) of the natural cocoa powder with the same amount of black cocoa powder (see page 28).

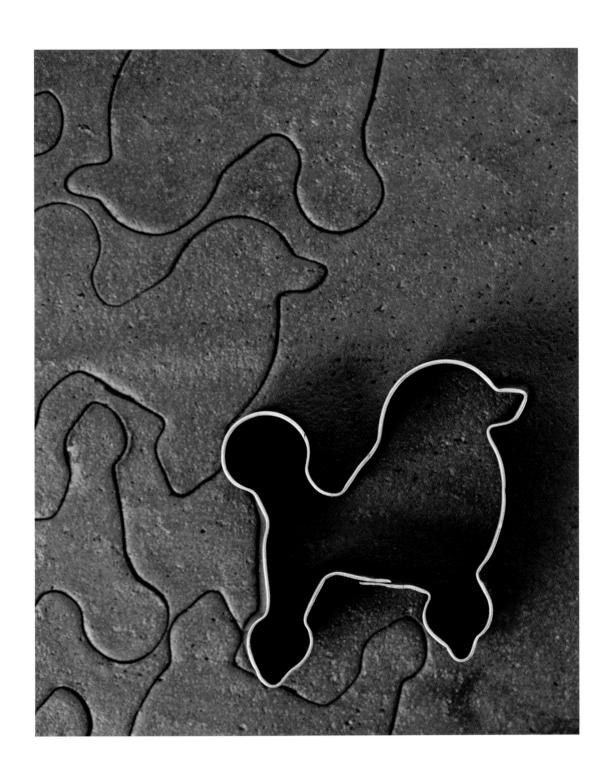

FRITSCH ICE CREAM SANDWICH

Tobias Wong
Bulletproof Quilted Duvet
2004
ballistic nylon and cotton
86 in. x 86 in.
SFMOMA, gift of Josée
    Lepage, 2011.5

———

Throughout his short career, Canadian-born Tobias Wong (1974–2010) made provocative objects that played to collective desires, obsessions, and fears. Straddling the worlds of art and design, he often riffed off existing products—dipping a Tiffany pearl earring into rubber to make a pair of black/white earrings, for instance, or flipping the position of the diamond in the classic solitaire engagement ring to turn it into a weapon. He and collaborator Ken Courtney received a cease and desist order after transforming plastic McDonald's drink stirrers, known to have doubled as drug paraphernalia in the 1980s, into gold-plated cocaine spoons.

Hand-quilted with a rose, vines, hearts, and diamonds, and backed with cozy gray flannel, Wong's queen-sized *Bulletproof Quilted Duvet* was meant to be used and was. By selecting industrial strength black nylon for the top, however, Wong, who suffered from regular night terrors, points to the absurdity of trying to protect ourselves in a post-9/11 world.

WONG ICE CREAM SANDWICH

MAKES 10 TO 12 ICE CREAM SANDWICHES
HANDS-ON TIME: 1 1/2 HOURS
FROM START TO FINISH: 9 HOURS

Henry Urbach, curator of architecture and design at SFMOMA from 2006 to 2011 was, coincidentally, my yoga partner for a while. He had just put together the first in-depth presentation of the work by Tobias Wong when he asked me after yoga one day if I would consider making a dessert based on one of Wong's pieces. I was stunned. Since when did the curators care about my silly little cake project? Would I consider it? Of course I would! With my ego barely able to squeeze through the door, I dashed over to the museum to see the just-opened exhibition.

A small gallery on the second floor was filled with personal pieces that, at first glance, looked like everyday objects: a McDonald's stir stick, mittens, and a quilt among them. Upon further inspection, I realized that Wong had recreated these mundane items through the lens of excess—the stir stick was a solid gold cocaine spoon, the mittens were customized with a hole for holding a cigarette, and the quilt was made of bulletproof fabric.

The show would be running through the summer, so ice cream sandwiches seemed like the perfect treat. I resurrected the popular Fritsch Ice Cream Sandwich (page 163), this time using black cocoa powder in the chocolate sablé to give it a deep, ebony color, and before baking, I scored the dough with a diamond pattern that recalled Wong's quilt. Leah bought some black sesame paste at our local hippie-food mart for flavoring the ice cream. It took some experimenting for her to get the proportions right, but when there was just enough sesame paste in the base, the ice cream took on a grayish color, the vanilla came through to nudge the savory sesame into sweet territory, and the flavor was delicious. The final detail was gold foil wrappers—our way of applying Wong's excess to our ice cream sandwiches.

NOTE: You can substitute $^1/_2$ teaspoon vanilla extract for the vanilla bean, warming it along with the cream and sugar mixture.

DO AHEAD: Covered with plastic wrap, the rolled and cut sablé dough will keep for up to 2 days in the refrigerator. Stored in an airtight container, the sablés will keep for 1 day at room temperature.

The ice cream can be made ahead and stored in an airtight container in the freezer for up to 2 weeks. The assembled sandwiches can be stored in an airtight container in the freezer for up to 1 week.

ABOVE AND BEYOND: The cookies, of course, don't need to be quilted in order for the sandwiches to be delicious, but it's an easy step that adds a little pizzazz to the dessert. Score the rolled-out dough with a diamond pattern before cutting it into squares; see the photo on page 175 for details (see Resources, page 205, for information on the Ateco adjustable dough divider that we use). Gold foil wrapping is an excessive but very Wong way to present these ice cream sandwiches (see Resources, page 205, for ordering information).

BLACK SESAME ICE CREAM

2 cups (16.6 oz / 464 g) heavy cream

1 cup (8.6 oz / 242 g) half-and-half

$^2/_3$ cup (4.7 oz / 133 g) sugar

$^1/_2$ vanilla bean

3 tablespoons black sesame paste

2 teaspoons hot water

6 large egg yolks (4 oz / 114 g), at room temperature

—

Chocolate Sablé Dough (page 168; see Variation)

To make the ice cream, fill a large bowl halfway with ice water. Place a medium bowl in the ice-water bath and set a fine-mesh sieve across the top.

In a medium, heavy-bottomed saucepan, combine the cream, half-and-half, and sugar. Scrape the vanilla bean seeds into the cream mixture, and drop in the hull. Set the pan over medium-low heat and warm the mixture, stirring occasionally, until it registers 180°F to 190°F on a digital thermometer and bubbles begin to form around the edges. Remove from the heat, cover, and let the vanilla bean steep for 10 minutes. Once steeped, remove and discard the vanilla bean.

In a small bowl, whisk together the black sesame paste and hot water until combined. Put the egg yolks in a second medium bowl and whisk in the sesame paste mixture. Temper the yolks by gradually whisking in $1/4$ cup (2 oz / 58 g) of the warm cream mixture. Repeat until you've added $1^1/2$ cups (12.4 oz / 348 g) of the cream mixture to the yolks and the yolk mixture is warm. Slowly whisk the tempered yolks into the cream in the saucepan. Set the pan over low heat and cook, stirring constantly, until the mixture is thick enough to coat the back of a spoon, about 10 minutes.

Immediately pour the custard through the sieve into the chilled bowl. Let cool completely, stirring occasionally. Lay plastic wrap directly on the surface of the custard and refrigerate until cold, at least 3 hours, but preferably overnight. (Stored in an airtight container, the ice cream base will keep for up to 2 days in the refrigerator.)

Meanwhile, set the sablé dough on a large sheet of parchment paper and press it into a flat, even, rectangle measuring about 5 by 6 inches. Lay a second sheet of parchment paper on top and roll out the dough to an even $1/8$ to $1/4$-inch thickness. Remove the top sheet of parchment and, using a large knife or pizza wheel, cut the dough into 2-inch squares; you will need 20 to 24 cookies. The dough will be soft, so don't try to remove the squares until after chilling. Slide the parchment paper with the dough onto a baking sheet, cover with plastic wrap, and refrigerate until the dough is cold and firm, at least 45 minutes or up to 2 days. The longer the dough chills, the less it will spread during baking.

While the dough chills, freeze the base in an ice cream machine according to the manufacturer's instructions. Line a 13 by 9-inch baking pan with plastic wrap while the ice cream churns.

Transfer the ice cream (it will be quite soft) to the prepared baking pan. Smooth the surface with an offset spatula, cover tightly with plastic wrap, and freeze until firm, at least 4 hours.

Position racks in the upper and lower thirds of the oven. Preheat the oven to 350°F. Line 2 baking sheets with parchment paper.

Use a small metal spatula to transfer the dough squares to the prepared baking sheets, spacing them about 1 inch apart. Because this dough toughens too much when rerolled, we save any cookie dough scraps and bake them as snacks for our café employees. They are best baked on their own baking sheet with the baking time reduced by 1 to 2 minutes.

Bake until crisp, about 7 minutes, rotating the baking sheets midway through baking. (Note: because the sablés don't change color during baking, it's wise to bake a test batch of one or two cookies to check baking time for your oven before committing your whole batch; see Baking Times, page 25.) Let cool on the baking sheets for 10 minutes, and then transfer the cookies to a wire rack. Let cool to room temperature.

Remove the ice cream from the freezer and invert it out of the pan onto a clean cutting board. Peel off the plastic wrap. Working quickly, use a large knife to cut the ice cream into 2-inch squares. Place a square of ice cream on a cookie and top with another cookie. Set the ice cream sandwich on a large plate or rimmed baking sheet and place in the freezer. Repeat with the remaining ice cream squares and cookies, putting each sandwich in the freezer as you go. If your ice cream starts to melt, slide the cutting board into the freezer and let chill until the ice cream is firm enough to work with. Freeze the ice cream sandwiches for at least 1 hour to firm and meld the textures.

WONG ICE CREAM SANDWICH

Cindy Sherman
Untitled #415
2004
chromogenic color print
68 x 44¹/₂ in.
Courtesy the artist and
Metro Pictures, New York
———
Cindy Sherman (born 1954) has made an unparalleled contribution to visual culture through her photographs. In nearly all of them she has served as the model, but they are not self-portraits per se. In her *Untitled Film Stills* from the late 1970s, the body of work for which she first garnered serious critical attention, Sherman assumed a whole host of characters associated with female roles in movies—from girl next door to pinup—taking on all the visual tropes of studio 8 x 10 glossies.

Sherman has turned up the volume in some of her most recent series, including the clowns. In *Untitled #415*, the photographer dons cake makeup, a skull cap, and prosthetic nose, as well as an exuberant floral topcoat with a triple-wrapped piano key belt. Embodying extremes within an emotional and performative spectrum, clowns make for particularly compelling subject matter for an artist long interested in dress-up and layers of personae.

SHERMAN ICE CREAM FLOAT

MAKES 8 FLOATS
HANDS-ON TIME: 45 MINUTES
FROM START TO FINISH: 8 HOURS

Before going through my Rineke Dijkstra phase in college (page 99), I went through an epic Cindy Sherman phase. I was a huge fan of her *Untitled Film Stills*, a series of beautiful black-and-white portraits inspired by midcentury glamour, so I was shocked and a little frightened by her later series of clown portraits. The disturbingly garish photos of the artist in clown face paint and prosthetics really tested my Sherman fandom. So when SFMOMA was planning a Sherman retrospective for the summer of 2012, I was pretty sure I knew which images I was *not* going to base a dessert on.

My inclination was to reference the artist's transformation into the characters in her photos. We had a few ideas for paint-by-number-style desserts: guests could transform an image of Sherman into one of her personae using lemon curd, chocolate ganache, and other edible "paints." However, when I ran the concept by Erin O'Toole, the curator who installed the exhibition at SFMOMA, she suggested that we find inspiration in a particular work in the show, rather than in Sherman's process. Fair enough.

As an alternative, Erin suggested that we consider *Untitled #415*, an image of a clown holding a bottle of pink soda. Vanilla ice cream would reference the white face paint and raspberry sorbet would match the color of the clown's mouth and the dot on its nose. Since we love the small details, Leah found soda bottles like the one in the photo, Tess suggested Disco Dust (edible glitter that shimmers like the clown's hat), and I made a coaster that incorporated the brocade pattern of the clown's coat. Once again, I was reminded that a piece that frightens or disturbs me can be just as inspirational as one that I love.

NOTE: As much as I love making my own ice creams and sorbets, store-bought ice cream and sorbet can also work in this dessert.

DO AHEAD: Both the ice cream and the sorbet can be made up to 2 weeks in advance and stored in an airtight container in the freezer. The soda concentrate can be made up to 1 week ahead and stored in an airtight container in the refrigerator.

ABOVE AND BEYOND: To make a dessert truly inspired by Cindy Sherman's photo, make coasters using the print on the clown's coat. Visit www.modernartdesserts.com to download a coaster template and see Resources (page 205) for ordering custom-made coasters. Serve the bubblegum soda concentrate from a bottle shaped just like the one the clown is holding and adorn the float with hologram of silver Disco Dust (see Resources, page 205, for ordering information for both the bottles and Disco Dust).

RASPBERRY SORBET
1 cup (7.1 oz / 200 g) sugar
3/4 cup (6.4 oz / 180 g) water
3 tablespoons fresh lemon juice
3/4 pound (10.1 oz / 284 g) fresh raspberries

BUBBLEGUM SODA CONCENTRATE
10 pieces bubble gum, preferably Bazooka Joe or Double Bubble
1/4 cup (1.8 oz / 50 g) sugar
1 1/2 cups (12.9 oz / 360 g) cold water

—

Vanilla Ice Cream (page 166)
4 cups (34.4 oz / 960 g) cold sparkling water

To make the sorbet, in a medium nonreactive saucepan over medium heat, bring the sugar, water, and lemon juice to a boil, stirring to help the sugar dissolve. Remove from the heat and let cool to room temperature.

Puree the raspberries in a food processor until smooth. Pour the cooled sugar syrup into the raspberry puree and stir well. Strain the puree through a fine-mesh sieve set over a medium bowl and discard the seeds. Cover with plastic wrap and refrigerate until cold, at least 2 hours or up to 2 days.

Freeze the sorbet base in an ice cream machine according to the manufacturer's instructions.

Transfer the sorbet (it will be quite soft) to a 1-quart container, cover tightly, and freeze until firm, at least 4 hours.

To make the bubblegum soda concentrate, combine the bubble gum and sugar in a mortar and crush with a pestle until the bubblegum is softened.

Transfer the mixture to a small pitcher or lidded container and pour in the water. Stir until the sugar dissolves. Cover and refrigerate, agitating the mixture from time to time, until cold and infused with bubblegum flavor, about 4 hours. Strain into a lidded container and refrigerate.

To serve, place one scoop of ice cream in the bottom of a pint glass and top with a scoop of raspberry sorbet. Pour in $1/4$ cup (2.1 oz / 60 g) of the soda concentrate and $1/2$ cup (4.3 oz / 120 g) of the sparkling water, and then insert a straw.

MAKING RASPBERRY GRANITA

If you're short on time or don't have an ice cream machine, the raspberry sorbet base can be frozen into granita instead.

Place an 8-inch square cake pan or similar 2-quart baking dish in the freezer for about 30 minutes.

Strain the raspberry sorbet base into the chilled baking dish.

Place in the freezer and freeze for 45 minutes. Using a fork, agitate the slushy mixture. Freeze for another 45 minutes, then agitate with a fork once again. Repeat this process once more, or until the granita is fully frozen and fluffy, about 3 hours total.

Ruth Laskey
Twill Series (Khaki/
Blackened Golden Brown/
Blackened Deep Yellow)
2011
hand-dyed and handwoven
    linen
27 x 22 in.
Courtesy the artist and
    Ratio 3, San Francisco,
    from the collection of
    Diana Nelson and John
    Atwater

———

Over the last several years, Ruth Laskey (born 1975), a 2010 SECA Art Award recipient, has gained increasing recognition for her elegant and sophisticated weavings. Laskey began her practice as a painter. Working in the legacy of minimalism and post-minimalism—artists for whom the form and structure of a work of art are one and the same—Laskey was drawn to the loom, as she's said, "to be involved in the creation of the entire structure of a painting, and to consider all elements of the work integral to its final physical form."

The six weavings crafted for the SECA exhibition, part of her larger *Twill Series*, were all made on the loom at the same time. For this body of work, the artist was interested in considering geometric forms in dialogue with one another, presenting and layering shapes like triangles, diamonds, and squares. Once she had the idea for the series, Laskey started by working out the compositions on paper. In *Twill Series (Khaki/ Blackened Golden Brown/ Blackened Deep Yellow)*, the right triangle appears to overlap the left, thereby implying a three-dimensionality. Each finished work bears the warmth and subtle imperfections of having been made by hand.

LASKEY LEMON SODA
WITH BAY ICE CUBES

MAKES 8 SODAS
HANDS-ON TIME: 30 MINUTES
FROM START TO FINISH: ABOUT 3 HOURS

In 2010, Ruth Laskey, a talented artist who weaves hand-dyed threads into graphic shapes, was one of the Bay Area artists chosen for the biennial SECA (Society for the Encouragement of Contemporary Art) award and whose work would be featured at SFMOMA. She also happened to be Leah's classmate from the California College of the Arts. Thrilled to collaborate with an artist as she produced her work, we arranged a studio visit to see the weavings Ruth was creating for the show. She had a series of six sketches, each with two intersecting shapes of different colors, and she had started weaving the pieces based on her sketches. I suggested assigning a flavor to each color, and where the colors overlapped, so would the flavors. We decided that a liquid of one flavor chilled with ice cubes of a second flavor would be an interesting approach: as the ice cubes melted, the flavors would slowly overlap.

My good friend Paul Einbund, an extraordinary sommelier and a genius at making seasonal sodas, taught us how to make a concentrated syrup by muddling an ingredient with sugar, adding cold water, and then chilling the mixture to allow the flavor to infuse. When sparkling water is added to the concentrate, the result is a lightly sweetened soda with pure flavor.

Leah discovered that just about anything could be given this treatment—from fresh fruit and herbs to licorice candy, and even bubblegum (see page 177)—giving us limitless options for homemade sodas. I like to use standard Eureka lemons in this recipe because I prefer their classic, extra-sour flavor, but Meyer lemons will also work.

We created a soda and ice cube combination for each of the six weavings created for the SECA exhibition, from her larger twill series, and rotated through them on a daily basis: peppermint soda with licorice ice cubes for the blue/black weaving, green pepper soda with orange blossom ice cubes for the orange/green, chokecherry soda with rose ice cubes for the two-toned pink weaving, bubblegum soda with violet ice cubes for the pink/purple, hibiscus soda with eucalyptus ice cubes for the magenta/green, and lemon soda with bay ice cubes for the yellow/green.

We served each drink on a custom wood tray made for us by the installation crew at the SFMOMA. Stained to match the frames around Ruth's weavings, the tray held the glass and two small vials containing threads used in the artwork that had been scented to correspond with the flavors in the drink. With visual, taste, and olfactory components, the Laskey sodas offered guests a multisensory experience and a direct connection to the art, and they were our most conceptual creations to date.

DO AHEAD: The ice cubes can be made in advance and stored in an airtight container in the freezer for up to 3 months. The soda concentrate can be made up to 1 week ahead and stored in an airtight container in the refrigerator.

ABOVE AND BEYOND: At the museum, we use small half-sphere silicone molds to make flavored ice cubes, but any ice cube tray will work. Keep in mind, though, the smaller the cubes, the quicker they'll melt, and the sooner the flavors will merge in the drink. A small piece of bay leaf can be added to the cube for additional flavor and a pretty pop of color. Scented textile threads might be impossible to make at home, but my friend Daniel Patterson, chef-owner of Coi restaurant in San Francisco, came up with a great way of incorporating aromas while eating or drinking. Just dab a drop of lemon and bay essential oil (see Resources, page 205) on your wrist, and when you bring the glass to your mouth, you'll take in the fragrance.

LEMON SODA CONCENTRATE	BAY ICE CUBES
Grated zest of 2 small lemons	$^3/_4$ cup (6.4 oz / 180 g) water
$^1/_4$ cup (1.8 oz / 50 g) sugar	1 tablespoon sugar
2 tablespoons fresh lemon juice	2 bay leaves
$1^1/_2$ cups (12.9 oz / 360 g) cold water	—
	4 cups (34.4 oz / 960 g) cold sparkling water

To make the lemon soda concentrate, combine the zest and sugar in a mortar and crush with a pestle until fragrant, moist, and tinted yellow.

Transfer the mixture to a small pitcher or lidded container and pour in the lemon juice and water. Stir until the sugar dissolves. Cover and refrigerate, agitating the mixture from time to time, until cold and infused with lemon flavor, about 2 hours.

To make the ice cubes, combine the water, sugar, and bay leaves in a small saucepan and bring to a boil, stirring to help the sugar dissolve. Boil for 1 minute, remove from the heat, and let stand for 20 to 30 minutes.

Strain the infused water through a fine-mesh sieve set over a liquid measuring cup. Pour into ice cube molds, and freeze until solid, about 2 hours.

To serve, place 3 to 5 ice cubes in each of eight 8-ounce drinking glasses, and then add 3 tablespoons (or more, to taste) of lemon concentrate per drink. Pour in $^1/_2$ cup (4.3 oz / 120 g) of the sparkling water per serving and stir gently. Serve immediately.

Jeff Koons
Michael Jackson and Bubbles
1988
ceramic, glaze, and paint
42 in. x 70$\frac{1}{2}$ in. x 32$\frac{1}{2}$ in.
SFMOMA, purchase through
the Marian and Bernard
Messenger Fund and
restricted funds, 91.1

——

At the time Jeff Koons
(born 1955) had this
oversized ceramic figurine
fabricated from a public-
ity photograph, Michael
Jackson was already one
of the most famous people
in the world. He'd visited
the White House, he'd won
eleven Grammy awards,
and *Thriller* was on its way
to becoming the best-
selling record album of all
time. Koons was fascinated
with Jackson, equating the
pop singer's celebrity with
the role he imagined Christ
having had in his lifetime.
With *Michael Jackson and
Bubbles*, the artist plays
homage to the singer,
calling his sculpture of
Jackson posed with his pet
chimp in his lap a "contemporary Pietà." In showing
Jackson—an African Ameri-
can male—looking more
like an idealized Caucasian
female, the piece also
points to issues of race,
gender, sexuality, and the
obsessive pursuit of physical beauty that became
even more troubling later
in Jackson's life.

KOONS WHITE HOT CHOCOLATE
WITH LILLET MARSHMALLOWS

MAKES 4 DRINKS
HANDS-ON TIME: 30 MINUTES
FROM START TO FINISH: 3 TO 4 HOURS

For *The Anniversary Show*, one of SFMOMA's seventy-fifth anniversary exhibitions in 2010, I knew that the Jeff Koons piece *Michael Jackson and Bubbles* would be one of the most important—and fun—works on which to base a dessert. Michael Jackson had died six months before the show was to open, and the world still seemed to be in a collective Michael Jackson remembrance phase with "Wanna Be Startin' Somethin'" blasting out of just about every car in San Francisco.

I wanted the Koons dessert to reflect the gold and white color palette of the piece, and my inclination was to work with bananas of course, because there's a chimpanzee in the sculpture. My intention was to freeze a banana, and then coat it in white chocolate before gilding the entire thing in edible gold leaf. I assumed that it would look phallic, but I wasn't prepared for the anatomically correct results of my first test.

I wasn't yet bold enough to serve what looked like a penis to our customers (see page 15), so my focus shifted from bananas to bubbles. I envisioned white and gold bubbles floating atop a pure white liquid. Upon discovering some Turkish teacups, all the pieces fell into place. Winter was approaching, and a hot beverage would be a great addition to our menu, so we created white hot chocolate lightly spiced with cardamom and lemon zest. Snowy in color, the drink showed off the cups' ornate gold swirls that resembled Michael Jackson's locks in the sculpture. We topped the hot chocolate with delicious bubble-shaped Lillet marshmallows and then adorned them with gold leaf. A perfect tribute to the Koons sculpture.

NOTE: Essential oils, sold in some herbal shops and natural foods markets, are highly concentrated distillations of herbs, flowers, or spices. As long as they are steam-distilled and labeled food grade, they're safe to use in cooking. If you can't find cardamom essential oil, add 3 whole green cardamom pods when heating the milk; let the mixture steep, covered, for 10 minutes; and then strain the milk over the white chocolate.

Once the marshmallows have set, they are still quite sticky. The best way to conquer the stickiness is to be generous with the cornstarch and confectioners' sugar mixture, dusting your hands, tools, and all marshmallow surfaces.

This recipe requires an accurate thermometer for taking the temperature of the sugar syrup. Instant-read thermometers are notoriously inaccurate (which is why I love my thermocouple; see page 25), so if you own an instant-read thermometer, it's good practice to check its calibration before beginning. Simply bring a small pot of water to a boil and verify that the thermometer registers 212°F (at sea level) when inserted into the water.

DO AHEAD: This recipe makes enough chocolate ganache for 4 servings of hot chocolate. The ganache can be stored in an airtight container in the refrigerator for up to 1 week, and can be made ahead, or saved for another round of hot chocolates another day. See Working with Chocolate Ganache, page 91, for reheating instructions. The marshmallows take 3 to 4 hours to set, but can be made up to a month in advance and, in fact, the curing time gives them an even better texture. Stored in an airtight container, the marshmallows will keep for 1 month at room temperature.

Note that this recipe makes more marshmallows than you need for the hot chocolate. Since the marshmallows are best made in this batch size and have a 1-month shelf life, consider using the leftovers for mini s'mores or as a boozy take on the Fuller Hot Chocolate (page 191).

ABOVE AND BEYOND: The Koons White Hot Chocolate really came together when I found over-the-top golden Turkish teacups, and then topped three small marshmallows with gold leaf (see Resources, page 205, for information on ordering both the cups and gold leaf). To make the marshmallows in the shape of small bubbles, generously sift cornstarch mixture into a flexible $1^2/_3$-inch half-sphere mold (see Resources, page 205). To fill the mold, fit a piping bag with a $^1/_2$-inch plain tip, fill the bag with marshmallow mixture, and pipe marshmallow into each indentation. Let stand at room temperature for 2 to 3 hours until set. Turkish teacups are much smaller than the cups I call for in this recipe, so if you're using them, a good rule of thumb is to use $1^1/_4$ teaspoons of ganache per ounce of milk.

LILLET MARSHMALLOWS

5 gelatin sheets, or $3^3/_4$ teaspoons powdered gelatin

$^1/_3$ cup (2.9 oz / 80 g) water, if using powdered gelatin

3 tablespoons Lillet Blanc

$^1/_4$ cup (1.1 oz / 31 g) cornstarch

$^1/_4$ cup (1 oz / 28 g) confectioners' sugar

$^3/_4$ cup (5.3 oz / 150 g) granulated sugar

$^1/_4$ cup plus 2 tablespoons (2.9 oz / 82 g) light agave syrup

Pinch of kosher salt

WHITE HOT CHOCOLATE WITH CARDAMOM

5 ounces (140 g) white chocolate, coarsely chopped

$^1/_4$ cup (2.1 oz / 60 g) whole milk

Grated zest of $^1/_2$ lemon

1 drop cardamom essential oil (see Note, opposite)

—

4 cups (34.4 oz / 960 g) whole milk, steamed or warmed

To make the marshmallows, if you're using gelatin sheets, fill a medium bowl with ice water and submerge the sheets in the water. If you're using powdered gelatin, pour the water into a small bowl and sprinkle the gelatin evenly over the surface. Let either stand for 5 to 10 minutes. Meanwhile, sift the cornstarch and confectioners' sugar into a small bowl.

Line an 8 by 8-inch baking pan with 2 sheets of parchment or waxed paper, laying the sheets perpendicular to each other so that the bottom and all sides of the pan are covered. Sift enough cornstarch mixture into the prepared pan to completely and generously cover the bottom. Reserve the remaining cornstarch mixture.

In a small saucepan over medium-high heat, stir together the granulated sugar, the agave, 1 tablespoon of the Lillet Blanc, and the salt. Bring the mixture to a boil without stirring and cook until the temperature registers 238°F to 240°F on a digital thermometer.

Meanwhile, if using gelatin sheets, lift the softened sheets out of the bowl, squeeze out the excess water, and put the gelatin and the remaining 2 tablespoons of Lillet Blanc in the bowl of a stand mixer fitted with the whisk attachment. If using powdered gelatin, add the bloomed gelatin to the mixer bowl along with 2 tablespoons of the Lillet Blanc.

With the mixer turned off, pour all of the hot sugar syrup over the gelatin. Whip on low speed for 30 seconds, increase the medium speed and beat for 30 seconds, and then increase the speed to high and whip for 10 to 11 minutes until the mixture is smooth, glossy, and holds medium-firm peaks. It won't begin to resemble marshmallow until around the 5-minute mark.

Working quickly, transfer the mixture to the prepared pan and smooth the surface with a greased offset spatula. Let stand at room temperature for 3 to 4 hours until set.

Sift a generous amount of the reserved cornstarch mixture over the surface of the marshmallow. Remove from the pan by running a knife along any stuck edges, and then carefully peel away the parchment paper. Cover all edges with cornstarch mixture. Using a clean, hot knife or clean, hot scissors, cut the marshmallow into $1^1/_2$-inch squares. Generously dust all cut edges with cornstarch mixture to prevent sticking.

To make the ganache for the hot chocolate, put the chocolate in a medium heatproof bowl.

In a small, heavy-bottomed saucepan over medium-low heat, warm the milk, stirring often, until it registers 180°F to 190°F on a digital thermometer and bubbles start to form around the edges. (Alternatively, put the cream into a microwavable liquid measuring cup or bowl and microwave at full power for about 60 seconds.)

Pour the hot milk over the chocolate, and add the lemon zest and cardamom oil. Stir or blend with an immersion blender until the chocolate is melted and the ganache is smooth.

To make the hot chocolate, rewarm the ganache to pourable consistency (see Working with Chocolate Ganache, page 91), if needed, and place 3 tablespoons of warm ganache into each 10-ounce ceramic cup. Pour 1 cup (8.6 oz / 242 g) of the steamed milk into each cup. If you pour holding the vessel containing the milk 12 inches above the cup, gravity will provide all the agitation that's required to blend the ganache with the milk. No stirring needed.

Top each cup with two marshmallows and serve.

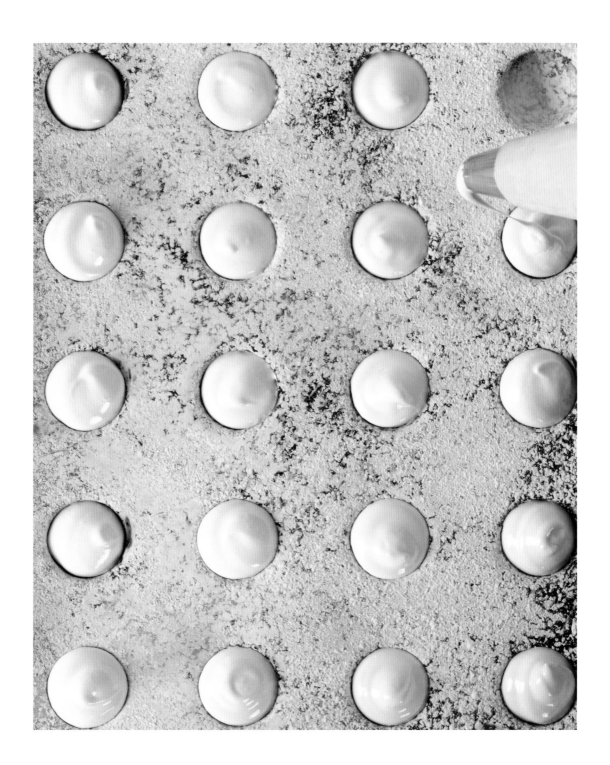

KOONS WHITE HOT CHOCOLATE WITH LILLET MARSHMALLOWS

189

Buckminster Fuller
Proposed Tetrahedral City
1965
collage on gelatin silver print
15⁵/₁₆ in. x 19 in.
Department of Special Collections, Stanford University Libraries
Courtesy the Estate of Buckminster Fuller

Buckminster Fuller (1895–1983) was in a category all his own. Radical and visionary as a thinker, writer, and inventor, Fuller worked tirelessly in the service of a more livable and sustainable planet. He is best known for patent drawings for geodesic domes, which have been built many thousands of times across the globe. In the 1960s, Fuller came up with the idea of a tetrahedral city: a massive, triangular-shaped, floating structure that could efficiently accommodate hundreds of thousands of people, while solving the problem of the high cost of land in major metropolitan areas. The tetrahedron could float in Tokyo Bay, San Francisco Bay, or any-where in the world. The San Francisco design was part of a 1967 exhibition titled *Projects for Macrostructures* at Richard Feigen's New York gallery and was featured on the cover of the March 1967 issue of *Arts Magazine*. Fuller's ideas for movable neighborhoods were even supported by Lyndon John-son and the Department of Housing and Urban Development.

FULLER HOT CHOCOLATE
WITH MARSHMALLOW AND SEA SALT

MAKES 8 DRINKS
HANDS-ON TIME: 30 MINUTES
FROM START TO FINISH: 3 TO 4 HOURS

Buckminster Fuller was an influential figure in California architecture and theory and, grow-ing up here the 1970s and 1980s, I was fascinated by the off-the-grid hippies who built geodesic dome houses in the mountains above my hometown. Not knowing much more about Fuller, I was curious when I heard that the SFMOMA would be curating a presenta-tion of his work and its influence on Bay Area design.

Before we actually saw the show, Leah, Tess, and I noticed an item on the exhibition checklist labeled "Telegram Re: Alcatraz Island Tetrahedral City," which started our minds racing with ideas. We had no clue what the telegram was about—or what shape a tetrahedron is—but we envisioned geodesic domes floating around in the San Francisco Bay, which, of course, made us think of little geodesic marshmallows floating in hot chocolate. I was thrilled when I finally saw the piece: a sketch of a city in the form of an enormous pyramid floating in the middle of the bay. An oversized, pyramid-shaped marshmallow would be even cooler floating in hot chocolate!

What wasn't so easy was our plan to harvest seawater from the exact location of Fuller's proposed city so that we could make our own sea salt to flavor the marshmallows (see page 195). It took a little work to find a boat captain who would ferry us to the spot, but we finally found an enthusiastic collaborator in Captain Charlie Jennings. Captain Charlie was unphased by our crazy plan and spent hours with us as we squealed over the sea lions and plotted the exact location. With our buckets full, we headed back to the museum where we slowly boiled down the seawater until all that was left were flaky crystals of salt. The tetrahedral marshmallows, lightly sprinkled with the sea salt and then floated in the hot chocolate, were delicious little models of the city that Fuller proposed.

NOTE: Once the marshmallows have set, they are still quite sticky. The best way to conquer the stickiness is to be generous with the cornstarch and confectioners' sugar mixture, dusting your hands, tools, and all marshmallow surfaces.

This recipe requires an accurate thermometer for taking the temperature of the sugar syrup. Instant-read thermometers are notoriously inaccurate (which is why I love my thermocouple; see page 25), so if you own an instant-read thermometer, it's good practice to check its calibration before beginning. Simply bring a small pot of water to a boil and verify that the thermometer registers 212°F (at sea level) when inserted into the water.

DO AHEAD: This recipe makes enough chocolate ganache for 8 servings of hot chocolate. The ganache can be stored in an airtight container in the refrigerator for up to 1 week, and can be made ahead, or saved for another round of hot chocolate another day. See Working with Chocolate Ganache, page 91, for reheating instructions. The marshmallows take 3 to 4 hours to set, but can be made up to a month in advance and, in fact, the curing time gives them an even better texture. Stored in an airtight container, the marshmallows will keep for 1 month at room temperature.

Note that this recipe makes more marshmallows than you need for the hot chocolate. Since the marshmallows are best made in this batch size and have a 1-month shelf life, consider using the leftovers for mini s'mores (page 111) or as a less boozy take on the Koons Hot Chocolate (page 185).

ABOVE AND BEYOND: When making marshmallows for this hot chocolate, I call for Maldon sea salt in case gathering seawater and then boiling it until it evaporates isn't on your list of things to do. But if you're up for the challenge, making sea salt is really easy (see Making Your Own Sea Salt, page 195). Just be sure to collect water that's clean and pristine. To make the tetrahedral marshmallows, generously sift the cornstarch mixture into a flexible $2^3/4$ by $1^1/2$-inch flexible pyramid mold (see Resources, page 205). To fill the mold, fit a piping bag with a $^1/2$-inch plain tip, fill the bag with marshmallow mixture, and pipe marshmallow into each indentation. Sprinkle a pinch of sea salt over the bottom of each marshmallow and let stand at room temperature for 2 to 3 hours until set.

MARSHMALLOWS
5 gelatin sheets, or $3^3/4$ teaspoons powdered gelatin

$^1/3$ cup (2.9 oz / 80 g) water, if using powdered gelatin, plus 3 tablespoons

$^1/4$ cup (1.1 oz / 31 g) cornstarch

$^1/4$ cup (1 oz / 28 g) confectioners' sugar

$1^1/2$ teaspoons vanilla extract

$^3/4$ cup (5.3 oz / 150 g) granulated sugar

$^1/4$ cup plus 2 tablespoons (2.9 oz / 82 g) light agave syrup

Pinch of kosher salt

Maldon sea salt, for garnish (see page 31)

CHOCOLATE GANACHE
8 ounces (224 g) high-quality bittersweet chocolate (62% to 70% cacao), finely chopped

1 cup (8.3 oz / 232 g) heavy cream

—

8 cups (69.1 oz / 1936 g) whole milk, steamed or warmed

To make the marshmallows, if you're using gelatin sheets, fill a medium bowl with ice water and submerge the sheets in the water. If you're using powdered gelatin, pour the $^1/3$ cup (2.9 oz / 80 g) of water into a small bowl and sprinkle the gelatin evenly over the surface. Let either stand for 5 to 10 minutes. Meanwhile, sift the cornstarch and confectioners' sugar into a small bowl.

Line an 8 by 8-inch baking pan with 2 sheets of parchment or waxed paper, laying the sheets perpendicular to each other so that the bottom and all sides of the pan are covered. Sift enough cornstarch mixture into the prepared pan to completely and generously cover the bottom. Reserve the remaining cornstarch mixture.

In a small saucepan over medium-high heat, stir together the remaining 3 tablespoons of water, granulated sugar, agave, and kosher salt. Bring the mixture to a boil without stirring and cook until the temperature registers 238°F to 240°F on a digital thermometer.

Meanwhile, if using gelatin sheets, lift the softened sheets out of the bowl, squeeze out the excess water, and put the gelatin in the bowl of a stand mixer fitted with the whisk attachment. If using powdered gelatin, put the bloomed gelatin directly into the mixer bowl. Add the vanilla extract to the mixer bowl.

With the mixer turned off, pour all of the hot sugar syrup over the gelatin. Whip on low speed for 30 seconds, increase to medium speed and beat for 30 seconds, and then increase the speed to high and whip for 10 to 11 minutes until the mixture is smooth, glossy, and holds medium-firm peaks. It won't begin to resemble marshmallow until around the 5-minute mark.

Working quickly, transfer the mixture to the prepared pan and smooth the surface with a greased offset spatula. Lightly sprinkle the top with Maldon sea salt and let stand at room temperature for 3 to 4 hours until set.

Sift a generous amount of the reserved cornstarch mixture over the surface of the marshmallow. Remove from the pan by running a knife along any stuck edges, and then carefully peel away the parchment paper. Cover all edges with cornstarch mixture. Using a clean, hot knife or clean, hot scissors, cut the marshmallow into 1 1/2-inch squares. Generously dust all cut edges with cornstarch mixture to prevent sticking.

Meanwhile, to make the chocolate ganache, put the chocolate in a medium heatproof bowl.

In a small, heavy-bottomed saucepan over medium-low heat, warm the cream, stirring occasionally, until it registers 180°F to 190°F on a digital thermometer and bubbles start to form around the edges. (Alternatively, put the cream into a microwavable liquid measuring cup or bowl and microwave at full power for about 60 seconds.)

Pour the hot cream over the chocolate and, using rubber spatula, stir until the chocolate is mostly melted. Blend with an immersion blender or transfer to a food processor and process until the chocolate is completely melted and the mixture is smooth and shiny. (Alternatively, set the bowl over a saucepan of just simmered water and whisk until the chocolate is melted and the mixture is smooth.)

To make the hot chocolate, rewarm the ganache to pourable consistency (see Working with Chocolate Ganache, page 91), if needed, and place 1/4 cup (2.3 oz / 64 g) of ganache into each 10-ounce ceramic cup. Pour 1 cup (8.6 oz / 242 g) of the steamed milk into each cup. If you pour holding the vessel containing the milk 12 inches above the cup, gravity will provide all the agitation that's required to blend the ganache with the milk. No stirring needed.

Top with two marshmallows and serve.

MAKING YOUR OWN SEA SALT

In 2011, I collaborated with my friend, photographer Zoe Crosher, to make seven desserts inspired by a series of her photographs of beautiful beach scenes around the Los Angeles area that were linked to the untimely demise of various celebrities. I had the idea to harvest seawater from these exact locations, turn the water into salt, and then create a dessert inspired by each of her photographs, using the site-specific salt in each. The desserts were only made for one exhibition of her photographs, and I hoped for a way to include this intimate site specificity into one of my SFMOMA desserts.

When we had the idea to make a dessert inspired by Buckminster Fuller's Tetrahedral City, I found my chance. We hired a boat captain, donned the necessary rain gear and life vests, and charted a course to Buckminster Fuller's precise location. Back at the kitchen, Leah slowly simmered the seawater until only flakes of salt remained. When I tasted the salt, I was surprised by how much it reminded me of San Francisco—somehow it captured the foggy, briny essence of our city. The mild saltiness was a perfect complement to our sweet marshmallows and bittersweet hot chocolate.

To make your own sea salt, gently simmer about 1 gallon of clean, pure seawater until all of the water has evaporated and you're left with beautiful flakes of sea salt.

FULLER HOT CHOCOLATE WITH MARSHMALLOW AND SEA SALT

Francesca Woodman
Untitled, Providence,
  Rhode Island
1975–76
gelatin silver print
5⁹/₁₆ in. x 5⁹/₁₆ in.
Courtesy George and Betty
  Woodman

——

Though her entire output dates from her adolescence or very young adulthood, Francesca Woodman (1958–81) made a uniquely compelling body of photographs—mostly consisting of nude self-portraits. Woodman grew up in Boulder, Colorado in a family that encouraged her creative life and she started photographing around the age of thirteen. Soon after enrolling at the Rhode Island School of Design in 1975, she abandoned her dorm room to live and work in the old Pilgrim Mills dry goods building in Providence.

Woodman preferred working indoors, particularly in spaces crumbling with age and neglect. As in this photograph, she was attentive to architectural detail and geometry and the placement of her body within it. Her gesturing arms and blurred floral dress suggest they were in motion at the moment of the shutter's release.

WOODMAN CHEESE AND CRACKERS

MAKES ABOUT 28 CRACKERS WITH CHEESE
HANDS-ON TIME: 40 MINUTES
FROM START TO FINISH: 2 HOURS

When SFMOMA presented the first Francesca Woodman retrospective in the United States in over two decades, I was excited to immerse myself in the work of another influential female photographer whom I studied in college. I love Woodman's juxtaposition of textures, her way of placing soft and vulnerable human forms in withered, deteriorating environments. My plan was to base a dessert on a photograph with this type of contrast. Of all of the images in the show, the one of the artist wearing a Victorian-style floral coat and flowing dress while posing in a crumbling room was my favorite.

At the time the Woodman retrospective opened, I had just returned from a vacation in Scandinavia where I would have been happy to live on only Norwegian hardtack, rye bread, soft cheeses, and smoked salmon. The combination of hearty rusticity and soft refinement of these foods were like elements in the Woodman photo: I saw the crumbling room as a cracker made with whole wheat and rye; her flowing skirt as soft cheese; and the pattern on her coat as beautiful, delicate edible flowers.

To create a tender cracker with the heartiness of my Norwegian inspiration, I used two types of rustic flour and incorporated the butter using the same technique that's used to make flaky pie dough. A little bit of yogurt added tang and tenderness to the cracker. To slather onto the crackers, I wanted a soft-textured fresh cheese that was simple to make in our tiny kitchen. Ricotta cheese was just the type. A sprinkling of colorful edible flowers from Leah's garden and a touch of black Hawaiian sea salt perfected the rustic-elegant presentation of the Woodman Cheese and Crackers.

NOTE: To create rough edges reminiscent of Francesca Woodman's photograph, we split our cracker dough into thirds, rolled it out, and then cut pieces incorporating the rough edge for a more rustic-looking cracker.

DO AHEAD: The ricotta cheese can be made in advance and stored in an airtight container in the refrigerator for up to 1 week. The cracker dough can be rolled out, wrapped tightly in plastic, and stored in the refrigerator for up to 1 week. Stored in an airtight container, the baked crackers will keep for 1 day at room temperature.

ABOVE AND BEYOND: Any large-grained sea salt will work in this recipe, but to add a final touch of color as well as unique flavor, use beautiful black sea salt from Hawaii (see Resources, page 205).

RICOTTA CHEESE
$1^1/2$ cups (13 oz / 363 g) whole milk
$1/2$ cup (4.1 oz / 116 g) heavy cream
$1/2$ teaspoon Maldon sea salt (see page 31)
$1^1/2$ tablespoons fresh lemon juice

RYE CRACKERS
$1/2$ cup (2.5 oz / 70 g) whole wheat
pastry flour
$1/2$ cup (2.1 oz / 60 g) rye flour
1 tablespoon sugar
1 teaspoon Maldon sea salt (see page 31)
1 teaspoon baking powder

1 teaspoon caraway seeds
4 tablespoons (2 oz / 56 g) cold unsalted
butter, cut into small chunks
$1/4$ cup (2.1 oz / 60 g) whole-milk
plain yogurt

—

Colorful edible flower petals, for garnish
Maldon sea salt (see page 31), for garnish

To make the ricotta cheese, line a colander with a double layer of cheesecloth and set the colander over a bowl.

Combine the milk, cream, and salt in a small saucepan and cook over medium-low heat, stirring often to prevent scorching, until the mixture registers 190°F on a digital thermometer.

Remove the pan from the heat and gently stir in the lemon juice. Let stand for 5 minutes, and then pour the curds and whey through the cheesecloth-lined colander. Let drain at room temperature until the cheese is thick and spreadable, about 1 hour.

Transfer the cheese to a container, cover tightly, and refrigerate.

Combine the whole wheat flour, rye flour, sugar, salt, baking powder, and caraway seeds in the bowl of a stand mixer fitted with the paddle attachment. Mix briefly on low speed to blend. Add the butter and mix on low speed until the mixture resembles coarse meal, 1 to 2 minutes. Add the yogurt and continue mixing just until the dough comes together into a ball, 10 to 20 seconds.

Turn out the dough onto a large sheet of parchment paper and press it into a flat, even rectangle measuring about 5 by 6 inches. Lay a second sheet of parchment paper on top and roll out the dough to an even $1/8$-inch thickness. Remove the top sheet of parchment and, using a chef's knife, cut the dough into rough 2 by 4-inch rectangles. The dough will be sticky, so don't try to remove the rectangles until after chilling. Slide the parchment with the dough onto a baking sheet and refrigerate until the dough is firm, at least 30 minutes or up to 1 week.

To make the crackers, position racks in upper and lower thirds of the oven. Preheat the oven to 400°F and line two baking sheets with parchment paper.

Using a small spatula, carefully remove the crackers and place them on the prepared baking sheets, spacing them 1 inch apart.

Bake, rotating the baking sheets midway through baking, until the crackers are golden brown and crisp, 10 to 12 minutes. Let cool for 10 minutes on the baking sheets, and then use a spatula to transfer the crackers to a wire rack to finish cooling.

To serve, spread a layer of ricotta cheese about $1/8$ inch thick onto each cracker. Scatter a few edible flowers over the ricotta and sprinkle with sea salt.

Mark Bradford
Strawberry
2002
photomechanical reproductions, acrylic gel medium, permanent-wave end papers, and other media on canvas
72 in. x 84 in.
Collection of Barbara and Bruce Berger

———

Since the year 2000, Mark Bradford (born 1961) has distinguished himself for his stunning large-scale collages. Though they resemble abstract painting, and draw upon its history, the work is distinct for both its physical form and commitment to content, particularly issues or events of social consequence.

Of primary interest has been the gritty culture of South Central Los Angeles where Bradford lived as a child, worked alongside his mother at the family beauty salon, and still maintains a studio. *Strawberry* is one of many pieces to incorporate scavenged paper, in this case cut-up advertising posters and permanent-wave end papers, both deftly layered into a loose glowing grid. While the title of the work and its red-colored elements call to mind the sweet summer fruit, Bradford notes that the reference is actually to a derogatory nickname given to addicts who sell their bodies for crack.

BRADFORD CHEESE PLATE

MAKES 4 CHEESE PLATES
HANDS-ON TIME: 1 1/2 HOURS
FROM START TO FINISH: 2 DAYS

Because the Woodman Cheese and Crackers (page 197) were such a hit at the café, for the next big show, a retrospective of Mark Bradford's abstract collages, we hoped to find inspiration for other types of savory snacks. Bradford's work is richly layered in repeating patterns, so we started brainstorming an edible made of layered pieces. After a failed and soggy attempt at making Japanese-style rice balls covered in sheets of seaweed (based on Bradford's *Kobe I Got Your Back)*, we looked for new ideas in his large-scale pieces. *Strawberry*, with its orange and yellow hues, immediately made me think of slices of Velveeta cheese, so we formed a plan based on slices of cheese (not Velveeta) and housemade crackers.

Nikki Rosato, an adorable cheesemonger with a love of art, brought us samples of semi-firm cheeses in varying shades of white, yellow, and orange. We tasted, analyzed colors, and chose a delicious group of four cheeses that would look and taste great together on the plate. A touch of house-made apricot butter and a slice of *membrillo* (sticky Spanish quince paste that pairs perfectly with cheese) added the deep red-orange hues to the assemblage.

For the crackers, I had a perfect recipe, swiped from a great friend. Before opening their own restaurant, State Bird Provisions, my good friends Nicole Krasinski and Stuart Brioza worked as private caterers, turning run-of-the-mill parties into incredible culinary affairs. For larger events, they would occasionally borrow our commissary kitchen to do their prep work, and when preparing for a big event called Outstanding in the Field, where the duo cooked on the beach for a group of 100, Nicole used our kitchen to prepare some lovely buttermilk crackers for an appetizer. I took a serious liking to the wafer-thin and salty crackers, leaving her barely enough for her to serve at the dinner. Nicole graciously shared her recipe before kicking me out of my kitchen—and away from her crackers.

NOTE: These crackers are best when they're super-thin and golden in color. In order to achieve maximum thinness—near translucency—make sure the dough is well chilled before rolling. Bake the rectangles until golden brown and you will be rewarded with some of the most sublime crackers you've ever tasted.

In order to reproduce the bright orange hue in Bradford's original, we use apricots treated with sulfer dioxide, the most commonly available type of dried apricots. Apricots dried without sulfer dioxide will yield delicious results, they just won't lend the same bright color.

DO AHEAD: This cheese plate has a number of different components that should be prepared ahead of time and then assembled just before serving. Consider making the apricot butter ahead of time, as the dried apricots need to soak overnight before cooking; the finished product can be stored in an airtight container in the refrigerator for up to 2 weeks. The cracker dough needs at least 2 hours and 30 minutes to chill before baking, but the rolled and cut dough will keep for up to 1 week in the refrigerator in an airtight container and should be baked and cooled just before assembling the cheese plate. Stored in an airtight container, the baked crackers will keep for 1 day at room temperature.

ABOVE AND BEYOND: In order to create perfectly symmetrical shapes for our cheese and crackers, Leah surreptitiously snuck into the galleries with a ruler to measure the shapes of our muse. She scaled the measurement proportionally to fit our plates, and had a cookie cutter crafted with rounded edges (see Resources, page 205) to use as our die.

APRICOT BUTTER

4 ounces (112 g) dried apricots

1^1/$_4$ cups (10.7 oz / 300 g) water, plus more as needed

^{1}/$_4$ cup (1.8 oz / 50 g) sugar

BUTTERMILK CRACKERS

1 cup (4.3 oz / 121 g) pastry flour, plus more for rolling

1^1/$_2$ teaspoons sugar

^{1}/$_2$ teaspoon kosher salt

^{1}/$_4$ teaspoon baking powder

3 tablespoons (1.5 oz / 42 g) cold unsalted butter, cut into cubes

^{1}/$_3$ cup (2.9 oz / 80 g) buttermilk

Olive oil or melted butter, for brushing

Maldon sea salt (see page 31), for sprinkling

—

3 or 4 different types of semifirm cheeses (we use Beemster Classic, Vella Daisy Cheddar, Lamb Chopper, and Drunken Goat)

1-inch square of *membrillo*, sliced ^{1}/$_2$ inch thick

To make the apricot butter, place the apricots and water in a small saucepan. Cover the pan and let soak overnight at room temperature.

Add the sugar to the pan and bring to a boil over medium heat, stirring to help the sugar dissolve. Turn down the heat to maintain a simmer and cook, uncovered, until the fruit is soft, about 20 minutes. Add a bit more water if the apricots begin to look dry.

Transfer the apricots and liquid to a food processor and puree until smooth, about 4 minutes. Strain the puree through a medium-mesh strainer into a container, using a rubber spatula to help push it through. Cover and refrigerate until needed.

To make the crackers, combine the flour, sugar, kosher salt, and baking powder in the bowl of a food processor. Pulse to blend. Gradually add the chilled butter cubes and pulse until the mixture has the consistency of a fine meal.

Transfer the flour mixture to a large bowl and make a well in the center. Add the buttermilk to the well and use your hands to incorporate the liquid into the dry ingredients until the mixture forms a dough. Lightly flour a work surface and knead the dough a few times, wrap tightly in plastic wrap, and refrigerate until cold, at least 2 hours or up to 1 week.

Dust a large sheet of parchment paper with flour and set the chilled dough on top. Cover with a second sheet of parchment paper and roll out the dough as thinly as possible—no thicker than ^{1}/$_8$ inch thick, and preferably so thin that the dough is almost translucent (see Note, opposite). Refrigerate for 10 to 15 minutes, until chilled, then remove the top piece of parchment and, using a large knife or pizza wheel, cut the dough into 2^1/$_2$ by 3-inch rectangles. With a fork, poke holes into the dough at regular intervals to allow steam to escape while baking (a process known as *docking*). Slide the parchment paper with the dough onto a rimmed baking sheet and freeze until firm, about 30 minutes.

Position racks in the upper and lower thirds of the oven. Preheat the oven to 350°F and line two baking sheets with parchment paper.

Using a small spatula, carefully remove the crackers and place them on the prepared baking sheets, spacing them 1 inch apart. Brush the dough with the olive oil and sprinkle with the Maldon salt. Bake, rotating the baking sheets midway through baking, until the crackers are golden brown, 10 to 12 minutes. It's better to err on the side of too brown than not brown enough, because an undercooked cracker will be soft and unsatisfying. Let cool on the baking sheets for 10 minutes, and then remove the crackers.

To assemble the cheese plate, slice the cheeses $1/8$-inch thick, and then cut the slices into $2^1/2$ by 3-inch rectangles.

Using an offset spatula, spread a thin smear of apricot butter along the bottom half of the serving plate. Arrange the cheese slices, 2 or 3 crackers, and the *membrillo* on the plate in a slightly overlapping design that resembles the painting.

RESOURCES

BLACK COCOA POWDER
• kingarthurflour.com, amazon.com

GELATIN
• *Silver (160 bloom) gelatin:* amazon.com

MALDON SEA SALT
• kingarthurflour.com, amazon.com

THERMOCOUPLE
• *Extech Thermocouple:* Type K mini-type thermocouple from grainger.com

RECIPE SUPPLIES

AVEDON PARFAIT (PAGE 127)
• *2-inch cube silicone molds:* jbprince.com
• *El Rey white chocolate chips (also called pastilles or feves):* worldwidechocolate.com
• *Chocolate transfer sheets:* chocotransfersheets.com

BRADFORD CHEESE PLATE (PAGE 201)

- *Custom 2½ by 3-inch (6.4 by 8-cm) cookie cutter:* frankencutters.com
- *Cheeses and membrillo:* your local gourmet grocery

CARTAGENA ICE CREAM AND SORBET TRIO (PAGE 159)

- *12 by 5½-inch slate board:* crateandbarrel.com

CASTRILLO DÍAZ PANNA COTTA (PAGE 123)

- *4-ounce, 2½-inch diameter cup, Beaker glass candleholder:* cb2.com
- *Luster Dust, Nu Silver:* amazon.com, sugarcraft.com

DIEBENKORN TRIFLE (PAGE 93)

- *13-ounce cup, Marta double old-fashioned:* cb2.com

DIJKSTRA ICEBOX CAKE (PAGE 99)

- *Photo plate, 3-inch coaster:* shutterfly.com

FRITSCH ICE CREAM SANDWICH (PAGE 163)

- *Poodle cookie cutter:* surlatable.com

FULLER HOT CHOCOLATE WITH MARSHMALLOW AND SEA SALT (PAGE 191)

- *Pyramid marshmallow molds 2¾ by 2¾ by 1½-inch, 2.5 ounce:* jbprince.com

KAHLO WEDDING COOKIES (PAGE 103)

- *Speedball block printing starter kit:* utrechtart.com, amazon.com
- *Speedball Speedycut Block 4 x 5.5:* utrechtart.com, amazon.com
- *Speedball printing ink, red, white, brown, and copper:* utrechtart.com, amazon.com
- *3½ by 3½ by 1½-inch kraft boxes:* nashvillewraps.com
- *4 by 2 by 9-inch cellophane bags:* nashvillewraps.com
- *Printed ribbon:* finerribbon.com

KELLY FUDGE POP (PAGE 147)

- *Medium ice-pop molds (4-ounce capacity):* coldmolds.com

KOONS WHITE HOT CHOCOLATE WITH LILLET MARSHMALLOWS (PAGE 185)

- *Gold wrap turkish tea set:* shopturkey.com
- *Half sphere 0.7 ounce, 1⅔-inch diameter flexipan:* jbprince.com

KUDLESS S'MORES (PAGE 111)

• *Marshmallow mold, faceted break-up bar candy mold:* sugarcraft.com

LASKY LEMON SODA WITH BAY ICE CUBES (PAGE 181)

• *Essential oils:* libertynatural.com
• *Half sphere 0.7 ounce, $1^2/_3$-inch diameter flexipan:* jbprince.com

LICHTENSTEIN CAKE (PAGE 69)

• *Polka dot decorating stencil/grill:* jbprince.com, amazon.com

MATISSE PARFAIT (PAGE 141)

• *4-inch square condiment tray, linen color, Plaza line:* heathceramics.com
• *Navy teal worsted weight yarn:* catskill-merino.com
• *Silicone $2^3/_4$-inch diameter molds $1^1/_3$-inch high, 3 ounce:* jbprince.com

MONDRIAN CAKE (PAGE 79)

• *16 by 4 by 4-inch Pullman loaf pan:* bigtray.com, amazon.com, or wilton.com
• *Ateco adjustable dough divider, 6 wheels:* bigtray.com, amazon.com
• *Gel paste food coloring, AmeriColor brand Super Red, Lemon Yellow, and Royal Blue:* wilton.com, sugarcraft.com

RYMAN CAKE (PAGE 63)

• *8 x 2-inch square pan:* bigtray.com, amazon.com or wilton.com
• *12-inch square wood art board, $1^1/_2$-inch deep:* utrecht.com or a thick piece of wood cut to 12 inches square
• *Unprimed Belgian linen:* utrechtart.com
• *Cake turntable:* I prefer the Ateco brand, but a less expensive Wilton cake turntable will work just fine for the home: bigtray.com, amazon.com, or wilton.com
• *Lemon Verbena Essential oil:* libertynatural.com

SHERMAN ICE CREAM FLOAT (PAGE 177)

• *2-ounce mini cola style glass bottle:* jbprince.com
• *Hologram Silver Disco Dust:* layercakeshop.com
• *Photo plate, 3-inch coaster:* shutterfly.com

THIEBAUD CHOCOLATE CAKE (PAGE 55)

• *Heath $8^1/_4$-inch Salad Plate in Opaque White:* Coupe line from heathceramics.com

A TRIO OF THIEBAUD CAKES (PAGE 33)

• *6 by 2-inch cake pan and 8 by 3-inch cake pan:* bigtray.com, amazon.com, or wilton.com

• *Cake turntable:* I prefer the Ateco brand, but a less expensive Wilton cake turntable will work just fine for the home: bigtray.com, amazon.com, or wilton.com

TUYMANS PARFAIT (PAGE 135)

• *Wilton silicone heart mold, 12 cavities, each $1^1/_2$ by $1^1/_2$ by 1-inch deep:* wilton.com

WARHOL GELÉE (PAGE 117)

• *4-inch square condiment tray, onyx color, Plaza line:* heathceramics.com

WONG ICE CREAM SANDWICH (PAGE 171)

• *Black sesame paste:* livingtreecommunity.com

• *5 by 7-inch gold foil papers:* sugarcraft.com

WOODMAN CHEESE AND CRACKERS (PAGE 197)

• *Black Hawaiian sea salt:* saltworks.us, amazon.com

ZURIER ICE POP (PAGE 151)

• *Medium ice-pop molds (4-ounce capacity):* coldmolds.com

ACKNOWLEDGMENTS

Oh, James Freeman. How could I have known that the uptight coffee guy in the Peugeot station wagon would become my husband, my boss, and my favorite person in the whole world? You are my everything. Thank you for letting me make my art in your cafés, for building a perfect life with me, and for being a fantastic father. I love you and Dashiell so much.

Leah Rosenberg, I literally couldn't have done all of this without you. You are an exemplar of hard work and an incredible talent. You are fierce in your generosity and the very soul of what we do at the SFMOMA. I'm so proud to call you one of my dearest friends and one of the people who I admire the most. Thank you for every moment you've devoted to our project and for being a stupendous person. This book is ours.

Tess Wilson, how did I get so lucky to find you? Thank you for your sweet tooth that brought you into my life, for not punching me in the face when I asked you to work for me, and for becoming a baker just because I asked. What a team you and Rosenberg are! I am truly lucky to have you. And to the rest of our staff at the SFMOMA, past and present (Emiliano Arguello, Rigo Ramireztorres, Belzazar Chim, Argelio Arguello, Sanja Wetzel, Sarah Moore, Alyssa Meijer Drees, Joseph Zohn, Chris Buerkle, and John Watts, to name a few), thank you for cutting slice after slice of Thiebaud cake and for making the most delicious coffee drinks in any museum ever.

Clay McLachlan, you are truly my partner in crime. I wasn't sure that this was your style of book, but you proved me so completely wrong. You are such a talent and, again, your name deserves to be on the cover in exactly the same size lettering as mine. Look at what we did! It's incredible!

To my Dad, of course, thank you. Thank you for paying for me to go to art school even after I broke your one rule during the first quarter ("If you get a tattoo or anything pierced, I'm not paying for school anymore." Which I did—both—and you didn't.) Thank you for investing in Miette—even though I'm pretty sure you would rather I had been a dentist. Thank you for being my example of hard work and determination; knowing that you're proud of me is exactly why I work like I do. I love you.

For everyone in my family, thanks for putting up with the bratty little sister who decided to move far away from home. My family is by birth, by marriage, and chosen, and I adore you all: Bob, Mom, Tom, Rachel, Aaron, Josephine, Sydney, Morgan, Jeff, Blythe, Rémy, and Vanessa. To my sister, Jenna, who is the glue that holds this Chitty-Chitty Bang-Bang of a family together, I am so thankful for everything you do. Truly.

To all of the customers who have paid $18 and ventured up five floors to visit us at our café in the Rooftop Garden: thank you. Thank you for being enthusiastic about what we do and for filling the Internet with pictures of the Mondrian cake.

Thank you to everyone at Ten Speed Press, especially my steadfast editor Melissa Moore and the incredibly talented Betsy Stromberg for designing such a beautiful book. This one was a doozy, but it is so beautiful and streamlined because of you two. To Aaron Wehner, Kelly Snowden, Patricia Kelly and everyone else in the Ten Speed / Random House team, thank you for believing in this book and making it fantastic. And to my agent, Laura Nolan, thanks for looking out for me.

Tara Duggan, you are my secret weapon. Thank you so much for digging into this book, helping me find organization and a better way with my own words. I can't thank you enough for all of the hours you spent trying to tame this beast with me.

Janet Bishop, I am so honored that you took on this book project, and your words have elevated this book to an incredible level. Your insight, expertise, and approachable tone are the perfect compliments to my visceral and (often) ridiculous approach to these artworks. Thank you so much.

Anne Bast Davis, I really don't know if I could have started this book (or finished it) without you. The artwork permissions were such a scary part of the project that, for years, stopped me from starting the book. You made one of the most challenging parts of the book process so much easier; your knowledge, patience with me, and organizational skills are an inspiration.

To the three ladies who convinced me that I could write this book and have been my biggest fans in this adventure. Libby Garrison: From the beginning you have been our biggest cheerleader and my go-to person at the SFMOMA for executing all kinds of crazy schemes. Thank you for finding an audience for these desserts, for pushing me to make this book happen, and for being one of the sweetest-natured people I've ever met. Leilani Labong: You were the spark! I am so thankful for your enthusiasm and honesty about this project. Charlotte Druckman: Thank you for making the first organizational steps for getting this book off the ground. I'm sad that we didn't get to spend months toiling over this together, but you were right; I could do it on my own! I treasure our friendship.

To Rose Levy Beranbaum, my hero. Thank you for teaching me to bake, for sharing your recipes in this book, for your words of advice about the red velvet cake, for your keen eyes in proofreading this book, and for your generous words in the foreword. How did I get so lucky to know you? Thank you to Nicole Krasinski, Jake Godby, and Sean Vahey for your recipes. You all have been such an inspiration to me. To Harold McGee, Jan Harold Brunvand, Rose Levy Beranbaum, and Celia Sack, thank you so much for your help in unraveling the red velvet cake mysteries.

Thank you to so many of the employees (past and present) at the SFMOMA who have made us not only feel welcome, but also like a part of your museum. Your enthusiasm and support has meant more than you can imagine: Neal Benezra, Gary Garrels, Sandra Farish-Sloan, Susan Backman, Peter Denny, Rick Peterson, Joe Brennan, Jim Weber, Sharon Shepherd, Kent Roberts, Jenny Gheith, Sandra Phillips, Corey Keller, Erin O'Toole, Jessica Brier, Simon Blint, Patricia Stapley, Ian Padgham, Anne-Marie Conde, John Holland, Stella Lochman, Frank Smiegel, Matt Lopez, Willa Koerner, Kate Mendillo, Joseph Becker, Jennifer Dunlop Fletcher, Lanlian Szeto, all of the security guards (even the grumpy ones), the engineering team—who change our lightbulbs, oblige us with trips to the roof for photo shoots, and turn a blind eye to our secret herb gardens—and the info desk for making our guests feel welcome. And thank you Charlie Villyard for your outstanding pictures over the years. I'm glad to be able to include a few in this book.

Veronica Becerra Hayden, Raul Hurtado, Katie McMahon Rathbun, Coach McClain, Jessica Lankenau, and Walt Bell all collaborated to help keep me, my home, and my family healthy and happy while I spent years in the kitchen making these desserts. And then months sitting at the desk in my home office writing this book. Thank you all.

Janet Bishop is very much indebted to her SFMOMA curatorial colleagues, mentioned above, in the departments of painting and sculpture, photography, and architecture and design for their collective expertise on the art that inspired these desserts. Janet offers further thanks to curatorial interns Camille Canon and Lili Elsesser (both avid bakers), and administrative assistant Nadiah Fellah, for their additional research.

Finally, thank you so much to my team of 110 volunteer recipe testers, all of whom provided feedback and guidance to make these (sometimes intimidating) recipes so much better and easier for the home baker. I wish I could write a paragraph to each of you, but a list will have to suffice: Alex Whitehurst, Alicia Penzel, Amanda Smith, Amy Cleary, Anna Gui, Annalea Reegan, Betty Sun, Carolyn Fleg, Cindy Choi, Emily Whitehurst, Erik Klepper, Imelda Punsalan, Jenne Patrick, Jennifer Ivanovich, Joanne Sy, John and Lee Joh, Julie Wagne, Kathleen Emma, Kathy Ems, Kimberlee Tsai, Kirk and Ei-Lun Yokomizo, Krissy Poole, Laurie Pauker, Lois Mead, Luisa Barron, Maria Saguisag-Sid, Meryl Hillerson, Michele Garcia, Monique Rodriguez, Moya Magilligan, Rose Fera, Sayuri Parks, Seton Mangine, Tami Strang, Aki Shibuya, Alicia Peterson, Aliza J. Sokolow, Amanda Moore, Amber Wipfler, Amy Gregg, Andrea De Jear, Anya Bergman, Beatrice Hsu, Beth Caissie, Bianca Barela, Bobby Young, Candy (Wing-yiu) Ko, Cecilia Hoosen, Christina Ng, Christine Nichols, Emily Kehrberg, Erin Sanders, Esther Johanna Kraß, Esther Sung, Gia Pascarelli, Gregory Soltys, Gretchen Yagielski, Hami Kim, Hayley Evans, Heidi Poulin, Henrique Berlinck dUtra Vaz, Jaina Selawski, Jasmine Guillory, Jenna Brotman, Jennifer L. Flasko, Jenny Jennings, Jessica Chien, Jessica Gorman, John Herzig, Joyce Jeng, Katie Gunter, Katie Worden, Kei Yamaguchi, Kevin Durkin, Kiyoko Ikeuchi, Lindsay Wheelock, Lisa Pereira, Lulu Zheng, Lynn Chang, Maggie Spicer, Marie Angel, Marlies Helene Dachler, Mary Catherine Cooney, Mary Ray, Melissa Mansur, Meredith Narrowe, Michelle Effron, Michelle Polzine, Molly Greden, Nathalie Cheng, Nicole Hefner, Pat Dailey, Pearl Rogers, Rachel Hofer, Ramona Pedersen, Randi Perry, Robbie Welling, Sabrina Sanchez, Samantha White, Sandy Mullin, Sashi McEntee, Shannon Mulcahy, Sharon Lim Ortiz, Shizuka Wakashita, Stéphane Gadbois, Stephanie Pratt, Susan Gibbs, Susan Tahir, Tate Brazas, and Tobias Eisenmann.

INDEX

A

Adams, Fred, 75–76
Allan Stein (Matisse), 141
*An all white painting measuring
    9¹/₂" x 10" and signed twice
    on the left side in white umber*
    (Ryman), 63
Apricot Butter, 203
Arabella (Zurier), 151
Avedon, Richard, 127
Avedon Parfait, 127–31
Avocado Sorbet, 160–61

B

Backman, Susan, 33
Baking pans, 21
Baking sheets, 21
Baking times, 25
Beard, James, 76
Bender, Albert M., 103
Beranbaum, Rose Levy, 1–3, 39,
    77, 88
Bishop, Janet, 18, 141
Black Sesame Ice Cream, 172–73
Blenders, immersion, 23

Blue Bottle Café, 5–6, 10, 11
Bobisuthi, Holly, 104
Bourgeois, Louise, 5
Bradford, Mark, 201
Bradford Cheese Plate, 201–4
Brioza, Stuart, 202
Brunvand, Jan Harold, 75
Build Your Own Newman, 107–9
Bulletproof Quilted Duvet (Wong), 171
Butter, 27
Buttercream
    Vanilla Buttercream, 42–43
    working with, 43
Buttermilk Crackers, 203

C

Cakes
    Dijkstra Icebox Cake, 99–101
    Génoise, 94–95
    Lichtenstein Cake, 69–74
    Mondrian Cake, 79–87
    Old-Fashioned Chocolate Cake,
        60–61
    Red Velvet Cake, 71–72, 75–77
    Rose's Downy Yellow Butter
        Cake, 39–40

Rose's White Velvet Cake, 88–89
    Ryman Cake, 63–66
    Thiebaud Chocolate Cake, 55–59
    Thiebaud Pink Cake, 45–48
    Thiebaud White Cake, 36–38
    Thiebaud Yellow Cake, 51–53
Cake turntables, 22
Calder, Alexander, 5
Cartagena, Alejandro, 159–60
Cartagena Ice Cream and Sorbet
    Trio, 159–61
Castrillo Díaz, Rosana, 5, 123
Castrillo Díaz Panna Cotta, 123–25
Cheese
    Bradford Cheese Plate, 201–4
    Cream Cheese Frosting, 71, 72–73
    Ricotta Cheese, 198–99
    Woodman Cheese and
        Crackers, 197–99
Child with Poodles (Fritsch), 163
Chocolate, 27–28
    Build Your Own Newman, 107–9
    Chocolate-Coffee Ganache,
        56, 57
    Chocolate Ganache, 90–91, 108,
        109, 113, 114, 193, 194
    Chocolate Sablé Dough, 168
    Cragg Ice Cream Cone, 155–57

curls, 145

Dijkstra Icebox Cake, 99–101

Fritsch Ice Cream Sandwich, 163–65

Fuller Hot Chocolate with Marshmallow and Sea Salt, 191–94

Humphry Slocombe's Malted Milk Chocolate Ice Cream, 156–57

Kelly Fudge Pop, 147–48

Kudless S'Mores, 111–15

Old-Fashioned Chocolate Cake, 60–61

Red Velvet Cake, 71–72, 75–77

Thiebaud Chocolate Cake, 55–59

Wong Ice Cream Sandwich, 171–74

Chocolate Cake (Thiebaud), 55

Cocoa powder, 28

Coffee
Chocolate-Coffee Ganache, 56, 57

Coffee Panna Cotta, 124–25

Composition (No. III) Blanc-Jaune/ Composition with Red, Yellow, and Blue (Mondrian), 79

Convento (Meyer), 16

Cookies
Build Your Own Newman, 107–9

Chocolate Sablé Dough, 168

Earl Grey Sablés, 137–38, 139

Kahlo Wedding Cookies, 103–5

Courtney, Ken, 171

Crackers
Bradford Cheese Plate, 201–4

Buttermilk Crackers, 203

Rye Crackers, 198, 199

Woodman Cheese and Crackers, 197–99

Cragg, Tony, 155

Cragg Ice Cream Cone, 155–57

Cream Cheese Frosting, 71, 72–73

Crème Fraîche, 131
Crème Fraîche Parfait, 137, 138

Crosher, Zoe, 195

D

De Panne, Belgium, August 7, 1992 (Dijkstra), 99, 100

Diebenkorn, Richard, 93

Diebenkorn Trifle, 93–97

Dijkstra, Rineke, 99

Dijkstra Icebox Cake, 99–101

Display Cakes (Thiebaud), 7, 33–34, 36, 42, 51

Drinks
Fuller Hot Chocolate with Marshmallow and Sea Salt, 191–94

Koons White Hot Chocolate with Lillet Marshmallows, 185–88

Laskey Lemon Soda with Bay Ice Cubes, 181–83

Sherman Ice Cream Float, 177–79

Dunn, Liz, 9, 10

E

Earl Grey Sablés, 137–38, 139

Eggs, 28

Einbund, Paul, 182

Equipment, 21–25

F

Falkner, Elizabeth, 64

Feigen, Richard, 191

Fisher, Donald, 155

Float, Sherman Ice Cream, 177–79

Flour, 30

Food coloring, 30–31

Fragmented Cities, Juarez #2 (Cartagena), 159

Freeman, James, 5, 10, 11

Frieda and Diego Rivera (Kahlo), 103

Fritsch, Katharina, 163

Fritsch Ice Cream Sandwich, 163–65

Frostings
Cream Cheese Frosting, 71, 72–73

Vanilla Buttercream, 42–43

See also Ganache

Fudge Pop, Kelly, 147–48

Fuller, Buckminster, 191–92, 195

Fuller Hot Chocolate with Marshmallow and Sea Salt, 191–94

G

Ganache
Chocolate-Coffee Ganache, 56, 57

Chocolate Ganache, 90–91, 108, 109, 113, 114, 193, 194

White Chocolate Ganache with Cardamom, 129, 130

working with, 91

Garrels, Gary, 17

Gates, Vanessa, 11

Gelatin, 31

Gelée
Mint Milk Gelée, 118, 119

Nocino Gelée, 124, 125

Pomegranate Gelée, 95, 96

Rose Milk Gelée, 118, 119

Strawberry Gelée, 118, 119

Warhol Gelée, 117–20

Génoise, 94–95

Graham Crackers, 113, 114–15
Kudless S'Mores, 111–15

Granita, Raspberry, 179

Grynsztejn, Madeleine, 135

Guglie (Cragg), 155

H

Honey-Pistachio Parfait, 129–30
Humphry Slocombe's Malted Milk
   Chocolate Ice Cream, 156–57
Humphry Slocombe's Strawberry
   Sorbet, 156, 157

I

Ice cream
   Black Sesame Ice Cream,
      172–73
   Cartagena Ice Cream and
      Sorbet Trio, 159–61
   Cragg Ice Cream Cone, 155–57
   Fritsch Ice Cream Sandwich,
      163–65
   Humphry Slocombe's Malted
      Milk Chocolate Ice Cream,
      156–57
   Sherman Ice Cream Float,
      177–79
   Vanilla Ice Cream, 166–67
   Wong Ice Cream Sandwich,
      171–74
Ice Pop, Zurier, 151–53

J

Jackson, Michael, 185
Jennings, Charlie, 192

K

Kahlo, Frida, 103
Kahlo Wedding Cookies, 103–5
Kelly, Ellsworth, 147
Kelly Fudge Pop, 147–48
Kennedy, Jackie, 117
Kind mit Pudeln (Fritsch), 163

Koons, Jeff, 185
Koons White Hot Chocolate with
   Lillet Marshmallows, 185–88
Krasinski, Nicole, 60, 202
Kudless, Andrew, 111
Kudless S'Mores, 111–15

L

Laskey, Ruth, 181–82
Laskey Lemon Soda with Bay Ice
   Cubes, 181–83
Lemons
   Cartagena Ice Cream and
      Sorbet Trio, 159–61
   Diebenkorn Trifle, 93–97
   Laskey Lemon Soda with Bay
      Ice Cubes, 181–83
   Lemon Curd, 49–50
   Lemon Mousse, 95, 96
   Meyer Lemon Sorbet, 161
   Thiebaud Yellow Cake, 51–53
Lemon Verbena Swiss Meringue,
   65–66
Lichtenstein, Roy, 69
Lichtenstein Cake, 69–74
Lillet Marshmallows, 187–88

M

Macerated Strawberries with
   Syrup, 41
Man in Polyester Suit
   (Mapplethorpe), 15
Maple-Yogurt Panna Cotta, 124, 125
Mapplethorpe, Robert, 15
Marshmallows, 113, 114, 193–94
   Fuller Hot Chocolate with
      Marshmallow and Sea Salt,
      191–94
   Kudless S'Mores, 111–15
   Lillet Marshmallows, 187–88

Matisse, Henri, 141
Matisse Parfait, 141–44
McGee, Harold, 76–77
Measurements, 22, 30
Meringue, Lemon Verbena Swiss,
   65–66
Meyer, Pedro, 16
Meyer Lemon Sorbet, 161
Michael Jackson and Bubbles
   (Koons), 185
Microplane graters, 23
Microwave ovens, 23
Miette, 8–10
Mint
   Mint Milk Gelée, 118, 119
   Warhol Gelée, 117–20
   Zurier Ice Pop, 151–53
Mixers, stand, 24
Mondrian, Piet, 79
Mondrian Cake, 12, 13, 79–87
Monet, Claude, 69
Monroe, Marilyn, 117
Mousse, Lemon, 95, 96

N

The Nest (Bourgeois), 5
Newman, Barnett, 107, 151
Nocino Gelée, 124, 125

O

Ocean Park #122 (Diebenkorn), 93
Old-Fashioned Chocolate Cake,
   60–61
O'Toole, Erin, 178
Ovens
   baking times and, 25
   microwave, 23

P

Padgham, Ian, 147
Panna cotta
    Castrillo Díaz Panna Cotta,
        123–25
    Coffee Panna Cotta, 124–25
    Maple-Yogurt Panna Cotta,
        124, 125
Parfaits
    Avedon Parfait, 127–31
    Crème Fraîche Parfait, 137, 138
    Honey-Pistachio Parfait, 129–30
    Matisse Parfait, 141–44
    Tuymans Parfait, 135–39
    Yogurt Parfait, 143
Picasso, Pablo, 141
Piping bags and tips, 24
Pomegranates
    Diebenkorn Trifle, 93–97
    Pomegranate Gelée, 95, 96
Pops
    Kelly Fudge Pop, 147–48
    Zurier Ice Pop, 151–53
Portnoy, Boris, 128
Proposed Tetrahedral City (Fuller), 191
P_Wall (Kudless), 111–12

R

Raspberries
    Raspberry Granita, 179
    Raspberry Sorbet, 178–79
Ray, Meg, 9–10
Red Liz (Warhol), 117, 118
Red Velvet Cake, 71–72, 75–77
Ricotta Cheese, 198–99
Right Angle Plus One (Serra), 16
Rivera, Diego, 103
Ronald Fischer, Beekeeper, Davis,
    California, May 9, 1981
    (Avedon), 127–28

Rosato, Nikki, 201–4
Rosenberg, Leah, 11–14
Roses
    Rose Milk Gelée, 118, 119
    Rose Sorbet, 161
Rose's Downy Yellow Butter Cake,
    39–40
Rose's White Velvet Cake, 88–89
Rouen Cathedral Set V
    (Lichtenstein), 69
Rye Crackers, 198, 199
Ryman, Robert, 63
Ryman Cake, 63–66

S

Sack, Celia, 76
St. Valentine (Tuymans), 135–36
Salt
    making sea, 195
    types of, 31
San Francisco Museum of Modern
    Art (SFMOMA), 7, 11–18
Scales, digital, 22
Self-Portrait (Warhol), 117
Serra, Richard, 16–17, 107
Seven Still Lifes and a Rabbit
    (Thiebaud), 55
Sherman, Cindy, 177–78
Sherman Ice Cream Float, 177–79
Simple Syrup, 44
    Simple Syrup with Raspberry
        Eau-de-Vie, 44
S'Mores, Kudless, 111–15
Soda, Laskey Lemon, with Bay Ice
    Cubes, 181–83
Sorbet
    Avocado Sorbet, 160–61
    Cartagena Ice Cream and
        Sorbet Trio, 159–61
    Humphry Slocombe's
        Strawberry Sorbet, 156, 157

Meyer Lemon Sorbet, 161
    Raspberry Sorbet, 178–79
    Rose Sorbet, 161
    Sherman Ice Cream Float, 177–79
Spatulas, offset, 23–24
Stein, Allan, 141–42, 144
Stein, Gertrude, 141
Stein, Leo, 141
Stein, Michael, 141
Stele 1 (Kelly), 147
Strawberries
    Cragg Ice Cream Cone, 155–57
    Humphry Slocombe's
        Strawberry Sorbet, 156, 157
    Macerated Strawberries with
        Syrup, 41
    Matisse Parfait, 141–44
    Ryman Cake, 63–66
    Strawberry Gelée, 118, 119
    Thiebaud Pink Cake, 45–48
    Thiebaud White Cake, 36–38
    Warhol Gelée, 117–20
    Zurier Ice Pop, 151–53
Strawberry (Bradford), 201
Suburbia Mexicana (Cartagena), 159
Syrups
    Simple Syrup, 44
    Simple Syrup with Raspberry
        Eau-de-Vie, 44

T

Taylor, Elizabeth, 117, 118
Tea
    Earl Grey Sablés, 137–38, 139
Thermocouples, 25
Thiebaud, Wayne, 7, 33, 55
Thiebaud Chocolate Cake, 55–59
Thiebaud Pink Cake, 45–48
Thiebaud White Cake, 36–38
Thiebaud Yellow Cake, 51–53
Trifle, Diebenkorn, 93–97

A Trio of Thiebaud Cakes, 13, 33–53
Tuymans, Luc, 135–36
Tuymans Parfait, 135–39
Twill Series (Laskey), 181

U

Untitled (Castrillo Díaz), 5, 123
Untitled, Providence, Rhode Island
  (Woodman), 197
Untitled #415 (Sherman), 177–78

V

Vanilla
  Vanilla Buttercream, 42–43
  Vanilla Ice Cream, 166–67
Violet Coulis, 137

W

Walnuts
  Kahlo Wedding Cookies, 103–5
Warhol, Andy, 117
Warhol Gelée, 117–20
Wedding Cookies, Kahlo, 103–5
White chocolate
  Avedon Parfait, 127–31
  Koons White Hot Chocolate
    with Lillet Marshmallows,
    185–88
  tempering, 132–33
  White Chocolate Ganache with
    Cardamom, 129, 130
Wilson, Tess, 13–14
Wong, Tobias, 171
Wong Ice Cream Sandwich, 171–74
Woodman, Francesca, 197
Woodman Cheese and Crackers,
  197–99

Y

Yogurt Parfait, 143

Z

Zim Zum I (Newman), 107
Zurier, John, 151–52
Zurier Ice Pop, 151–53